Drawing on Difference

Having a learning difficulty may render people more susceptible to mental ill health for a variety of reasons, including limited ways of coping with stress; lack of informal support networks; vulnerability to physical, sexual and financial abuse and enforced dependency on others. Despite recent widespread belief to the contrary, psychotherapy and counselling can have great benefits for such people, and art therapy has become one of the few psychotherapeutic services to which people with learning difficulties have access.

The contributors to this book discuss the practicalities of providing art therapy in variety of settings (hospital, community centre, school, therapist's home), and illustrate through case studies their experience of working with people who have differing degrees of learning difficulty or who have experienced traumas such as bereavement or rape. They concentrate on exploring the skills and limitations of both client and therapist, and on the key issues of clinical effectiveness and clinical supervision. The book also encourages reflection on the similarities and differences between art therapy and related professions of counselling and other arts therapies.

Drawing on Difference contributes to our understanding of this too often neglected branch of art therapy and is a valuable resource for art therapists, counsellors, psychotherapists and for professionals in the allied disciplines of music, dance and movement and dramatherapy.

Mair Rees manages an arts therapies service within Cardiff Community Healthcare NHS Trust.

Contributors: Lillie Fennell; Lesley Fox; Chris Gale; Penny Hallas; Rose Hughes; Enfys Jones; Edward Kuczaj; Hilary Lomas; Richard Manners; Rachel Matthews; Joanna Pearce; Sigrid Räbiger; Mair Rees; Margaret Stack; Sandie Taylor; Simon Willoughby-Booth.

Drawing on Difference

Art therapy with people who have learning difficulties

Edited by Mair Rees

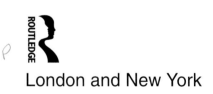

London and New York

First published 1998 by Routledge
11 New Fetter Lane, London EC4P 4EE

Simultaneously published in the USA and Canada
by Routledge
29 West 35th Street, New York, NY 10001

© 1998 Mair Rees the collection as a whole;
individual chapters © the authors

Chapter 6 was previously published as 'Humpty Dumpty Had a Great
Fall' in *Inscape* vol. 1 (1) 1996, and is reprinted here by permission of
the editors of *Inscape*. The extract in Chapter 6 from 'The Stolen Child'
is from *The Collected Poems of W.B. Yeats* and is reprinted here by
permission of Scribner and of A.P. Watt Ltd on behalf of Michael Yeats.

Typeset in Times by Keystroke, Jacaranda Lodge, Wolverhampton
Printed and bound in Great Britain by Biddles Ltd, Guildford and King's Lynn

British Library Cataloguing in Publication Data
A catalogue record for this book is available from the British Library

Library of Congress Cataloging in Publication Data
Drawing on difference : art therapy with people who have learning
    difficulties / edited by Mair Rees.
        Includes bibliographical references and index.
        1. Mentally handicapped—Rehabilitation. 2. Art therapy.
    3. Mentally handicapped—Mental health. I. Rees. Mair
    RC451.4.M47D7   1998
    616.85'889065156—dc21   97–38891

ISBN 0–415–15479–0 (hbk)
ISBN 0–415–15480–4 (pbk)

Contents

Illustrations

FIGURES

TABLES

Contributors

Lillie Fennell holds a Diploma in Counselling and works as a counsellor both independently and at an evening leisure facility for people with learning difficulties. She is researching how counselling can assist towards self-advocacy and has a special interest in Citizen Advocacy. She is currently studying for an MA.

Lesley Fox is a registered art therapist who was awarded the Diploma in Art Therapy from Goldsmith's College in 1981 and an MA in Art Therapy by the University of Hertfordshire in 1993. Her main experience is with people who have learning difficulties, and has been predominantly with clients living in the community rather than the hospital institution. She has been employed as an art therapist since 1983 by what has become an NHS Trust, initially as a member of a community mental handicap team and currently as a member of a therapeutic core team. She is particularly interested in working with clients with autism, and contributed a paper on the subject to the 'Theoretical Advances in Art Therapy' Conference in 1995.

Chris Gale qualified as a music therapist at the Nordoff-Robbins Music Therapy Centre in 1983. Since then he has worked in a wide variety of settings with both adults and children who have learning difficulties. He has also worked in the field of child and adolescent psychiatry. He moved to Wales in 1987, and has worked in three different areas of the country, using either Welsh or English languages in sessions as appropriate. He has been actively involved in promoting the development of the arts therapies professions in Wales.

Penny Hallas trained as an art therapist in Birmingham in 1984. She subsequently worked in a variety of settings with people who have learning difficulties. For five years, she worked as part of a community support team in North Yorkshire. In 1993, Penny joined the Arts Therapies Service in Cardiff Community Healthcare NHS Trust. She is especially interested in the application of group psychotherapy with people who have learning difficulties.

Rose Hughes studied fine arts before training as an art therapist at Birmingham in 1982/3. She subsequently obtained her MA in Art Therapy from St Albans College of Art and Design (now the University of Hertfordshire).She has had articles published in *Inscape*, the journal of the British Association of Art Therapists. She has worked in various clinical settings and currently is employed as Senior Art Therapist for the East Surrey Priority Care NHS Trust psycho-therapy service as well as for Jewish care and other non-statutory agencies. She lives in South London.

Enfys Jones works as a counsellor for a health authority and in a private setting. Her freelance work includes individual and group work with people who have learning difficulties. She also works for adult education services where she is particularly involved in supporting self-advocacy groups. Both Enfys Jones and Lillie Fennell are founder members of the Counselling Interest Group for South-East Wales, which seeks to encourage and support community counselling agencies to offer their services to people with learning difficulties.

Edward J. Kuczaj is Head of Art Therapy Services for people with learning difficulties within the Phoenix NHS Trust in Bristol. He has particular expertise in the areas of challenging behaviour, sexual abuse and loss in relation to people with learning difficulties. He is an experienced trainer and has designed and delivered a range of in-service training programmes on topics such as relationship awareness, communication skills and loss and bereavement. He is particularly interested in the development of training programmes for art therapy students on clinical placements. Edward is currently the regional co-ordinator for the British Association of Art Therapists.

Hilary Lomas trained as an art therapist at Goldsmith's College, London in 1983. Since qualifying, she has worked in the field of mental health and with both adults and children who have learning difficulties. She has developed a special interest in groupwork, initially through her work in therapeutic communities, then through developing a network of supportive psychotherapy groups in South Wales. This interest has continued in her current work as an art therapist for Cardiff Community Healthcare NHS Trust. She also works as a freelance art therapist and supervisor and has recently completed a qualification in family therapy.

Richard Manners gained a degree in fine art in 1978 and qualified as an art therapist in 1981. He has devoted his working career to the development of arts therapies for people with learning difficulties in Wales. He has particular interest in the clinical aspects of self-advocacy and art therapy, which has led him in the early years of his practice, to be involved in community arts and education. In the latter years, he has managed learning difficulties services and held several general management positions as a senior manager in community health. He has lectured and run art therapy workshops nationally and internationally. He is currently Head of Arts Therapies for Gwent Community NHS Trust.

Rachel Matthews is a dramatherapist and joined TAITH Arts Therapies Service, part of Cardiff Community Healthcare NHS Trust in 1994. Her remit involves both individual and groupwork with people who a wide range of learning difficulties. She conducts sessions in both hospital and community bases. She has also worked as a therapist and trainer on a freelance basis and has collaborated with other arts therapists and psychotherapists.

Joanna Pearce is Senior Art Therapist in the Learning Difficulties Service of Edinburgh Healthcare NHS Trust. She trained as an art therapist at the University of Sheffield and has worked in the NHS Learning Difficulties Service in Edinburgh since 1988. She has a particular interest in working with people who have personality disorders and forensic problems and also those individuals with a dual diagnosis of mental illness in addition to a learning difficulty. She has given workshops at summer schools and training events in Scotland and is currently completing a research study of a groupwork project for residents who are facing the closure of the long-stay institutions where they live.

Sigrid Räbiger trained as an art teacher and first taught in grammar schools. She gravitated towards special needs while raising her family, working as a home tutor to school-phobic children and also working with the elderly and disabled. In 1980, she joined Family Tree, a small private school for autistic children of good prognosis, who were gradually integrated into mainstream primary schools. During this time, she took her Art Therapy Diploma at St Albans and on qualifying, became an art therapist at a school for children with severe learning difficulties. She is also a dyslexia therapist and support teacher and is at present studying for an MA in psychoanalysis.

Mair Rees manages TAITH, the Arts Therapies Service for people with learning difficulties which is part of Cardiff Community Healthcare NHS Trust. She is a psychology graduate who qualified as an art therapist in 1983, from what is now the University of Hertfordshire. Since then, she has worked in a variety of settings including the NHS and the non-statutory sector. She has contributed to the training of art therapists and recently completed an MSc in Supervision and Training at the University of Bristol. She has undertaken research exploring spatial elements in the pre-representational art work of women with severe learning difficulties. She has a particular interest in promoting access to a full range of psychotherapy and counselling services for people with learning difficulties. At the time of writing she was expecting the birth of her first child after several years of fertility investigations and treatment.

Margaret Stack is a registered general nurse and trained as a textile designer in

Ireland in the early 1980s. Having taught design for a year, she spent a further four years working with adults who have learning difficulties as an arts and crafts instructor. In 1992, she completed her art therapy training in St Albans and has continued to work with this client group as an art therapist within an NHS Trust. Margaret is currently studying part-time for an MA in Art Psychotherapy at Goldsmiths' College, London.

Sandie Taylor has worked for many years as a researcher and is currently employed as a clinical support worker for an arts therapies service in Cardiff. She obtained her honours degree from North-East London Polytechnic in 1985 and her D.Phil. at Sussex University in 1990. Having an interest in legal psychology, she went on to study for her MSc in Criminology at the University of Wales, Cardiff in 1991. Since then she has been involved with research on drugs and crime. She has also taught psychology and criminology at 'A' level and Masters Degree respectively, and is currently involved in teaching criminology by distance learning.

Simon Willoughby-Booth is Head of the Art Therapy Service and professional advisor for art therapy at Edinburgh Healthcare NHS Trust. He has been working in the NHS Learning Difficulties Service in Edinburgh as an art therapist since 1978, and has been involved in hospital, education and community settings. For ten years he acted as advisor to a self-advocacy group for people with learning difficulties in Lothian and has been active in several advocacy initiatives in the health service. He has lectured and given workshops throughout the UK and Europe and has developed several training initiatives, including the first Scottish Art Therapy Summer School and several courses in conjunction with the University of Hertfordshire. He has published a number of articles on art therapy and learning difficulties and on the arts in healthcare.

Acknowledgements

To my sister-in-law Margaret Alison with hope for a future full of possibilities.
To Neil, my rock and anchor for all your love and support.
To my precious unborn child and constant companion in compiling this book.

A NOTE ON THE ILLUSTRATIONS

Every effort has been made to obtain permission to reproduce the artwork in this book, although this has not been possible in every case. The publisher would be pleased to hear from anyone who could help trace the copyright holders of these works.

Introduction

Mair Rees

People with learning difficulties are people first and foremost. The fact that they may have intellectual/physical/sensory disabilities should never obscure their humanity. 'They' are most certainly not an homogeneous group of people.

Disability is often categorised as mild, moderate, severe or profound. In reality, people with mild and sometimes moderate levels of learning difficulty may hold down jobs, may marry and have children or form long-term partnerships. This is far less likely for people with severe or profound levels of disability, partly because of their reliance on others to fulfil their needs and partly because of social prejudices and taboos. The more severe the degree of learning difficulty, the more likely it is to be accompanied by additional difficulties such as communication problems, sensory impairment and physical handicaps.

The term learning difficulties and its historical antecedents, for example, learning disabilities, mental handicap, mental retardation, imbecility, feeble-mindedness, etc. arouse powerful and ambivalent emotions in most people. Some of this discomfort has been directed towards the label itself, resulting in a regular updating of the nomenclature. Some professionals such as Sinason (1992) advocate the need to sweep aside the trappings of euphemism, so that our real feelings, attitudes and prejudices can be exposed and acknowledged. Whilst I have considerable sympathy with this view, I am also mindful of the fact that user groups such as the People First movement feel that if they must have a label at all, then learning difficulty is the preferred option. It is in order to respect these wishes that the term learning difficulty is used throughout the course of this book.

In the government's 'Health of the Nation' document (Department of Health 1995), learning difficulty (or learning disability) is described as:

> Reduced ability to understand new or complex information, to learn new skills (impaired intelligence) . . . reduced ability to cope independently (impaired social functioning) . . . which started before adulthood, with a long term effect on development.
>
> (Department of Health 1995: 3)

Some authors have highlighted the problems associated with definitions of learning difficulty, implying their susceptibility to tautological thinking and self-fulfilment.

> The definition of learning disability is difficult and in practice 'learning disability' often appears to be a functional and circular definition which includes anyone who has been assessed as needing services provided for people with learning disabilities.
>
> (ARC/NAPSAC 1993: 1)

It is estimated (Department of Health 1995) that one person in every thousand has a mild learning difficulty and will need support at some time in their life, whilst between three and four people in every thousand have a severe learning difficulty and will require frequent and ongoing support throughout their lives.

Despite the seemingly dominant spectre of Victorian institutions, the vast majority of people with learning difficulties have always been cared for at home within their families. The rights of people with learning difficulties to live their lives as an integral part of the community and to access local resources was enshrined in the Community Care Act 1992.

It is difficult to estimate the proportion of qualified art therapists who work with people who have learning difficulties. The British Association of art therapists Register does not provide this level of detail. However, in a recent unpublished survey of 120 qualified art therapists in Britain (Rees 1996), 33% of respondents stated that at least part of their caseload comprised people who have learning difficulties.

The majority of publically funded art therapy services for people with learning difficulties developed within the confines of traditional Victorian and Edwardian institutions. It is probably only in the 1960s and early 1970s that the term 'art therapy' was being employed in these contexts for the first time, although artists and educationalists had been interested in the therapeutic use of art with such people for a long time prior to this.

As the old hospitals close, art therapists are increasingly finding themselves being resettled along with their clients. For some services this has meant a bitter struggle for survival. However, for others, it has provided opportunities to extend their services to the many people with learning difficulties who have never stepped over the threshold of an institution. Inevitably such sweeping political and contextual changes will require art therapists to reflect on their practice to date and perhaps to develop new ways of responding to the changing needs of their clients.

Over the past 10–15 years there has been a mushrooming of titles available on the topic of art therapy in Britain. Whilst a few of these volumes have included chapters on the practice of art therapy with people who have learning difficulties (Stott and Males 1984; Kuczaj 1990; Tipple 1992; Rees 1995), there has not been an entire book dedicated to the subject. Perhaps this is rather surprising when we consider that it is possible that up to a third of practising art therapists work with people who have this label.

I wonder whether as a profession and as human beings we continue to carry some deep-seated prejudices about the nature of disability. My sense is that despite a recent revolution in the field of advocacy and human rights there is still an intangible belief that therapeutic work with people who have learning difficulties is neither as academically rigorous or as worthwhile as with other groups of people. A cloak of devaluation and despair can shroud not only those receiving services but extends equally to those providing services. I recall a promising young art therapy trainee whose delight at having secured his first post in a service for people with learning difficulties was tarnished by a consultant psychiatrist who told him he would be 'wasted' in such a field.

It seems clear that we can all be prone to displacing some of the feelings we have about people with learning difficulties onto other colleagues and even services themselves. The pain of wasted lives becomes wasted effort, wasted services. The feelings of being second-best, not up to scratch, taking crumbs from the rich man's table are as common within services for people with learning difficulties as they are amongst people with learning difficulties themselves. This leakage of responses and emotions can collude with and reinforce the *status quo* making change, movement and development difficult in both provision and people.

On the positive side, art therapists may take some comfort in the fact that art therapy is one of the psychotherapeutic professions which people with learning difficulties have been able to access. Apart from notable exceptions like the Tavistock Clinic, there has been a stubborn resistance to offering psychotherapy or counselling services to people with learning difficulties. This seems to be based on an unsubstantiated prejudice that such people are too damaged to benefit from these services (Bender 1993). Consequently, people with learning difficulties who were experiencing distress in their lives were either treated with drugs, or with behaviour-modification techniques (Waitman 1992).

Ironically, it is now widely acknowledged (Department of Health 1995) that certain factors associated with having a learning difficulty may render people more susceptible to mental ill health. These factors include:

- Limited ways of coping with stress
- Multiple life events (for example, death of a parent compounded by removal from family home to live amongst strangers)
- Side effects of neurological problems sometimes associated with learning difficulty, such as brain damage and epilepsy
- Lack of informal support networks
- Vulnerability to physical, sexual and financial abuse
- Systematic disempowerment, that is, lack of opportunity to exercise full rights as a citizen to partake in socially valued roles.

Enforced dependency and lack of autonomy may have a profound effect on the life of a person with learning difficulties. They may have very little real choice over the course of their life and their support networks usually consist primarily of people who are paid to be with them. Often people are infantilised and this tendency may be reinforced by the fact that their experiences of love and intimacy are all in the past of their childhood, with little opportunity for creating a family or home of their own in adulthood. Identifying with such agonising loss can be almost unbearable for people who support those with learning difficulties. Consequently, there is a tendency to turn a blind eye to the possible emotional experiences of people with learning difficulties and to believe that intellectual disability is some sort of balm for intensely painful feelings.

It is these sorts of issues that many art therapists have grappled with in their work with people who have learning difficulties. However, whilst it is true to say that art therapists have provided continued support to people with learning difficulties over several decades, attitudes and practices within the profession appear to have evolved in tandem with changing public and political perceptions.

In Britain, the earliest published account of art therapy with people who have learning difficulties was by Stott and Males in 1984. However, it should be noted that, all along, what appears in print seems to lag behind what was actually happening in practice. In their chapter in Dalley 1984, which serves as an introduction to their work, Stott and Males advocate a developmental approach to the application of art therapy in this field. The basis for this philosophy was that by encouraging clients through the sequential stages of drawing development, the benefits would generalise to other areas of the person's functioning. The value of such a philosophy must surely have been that it instilled a sense of hope and purposeful change, bringing a breath of fresh air to institutions where stagnation and decay were the order of the day. However, such ways of working seem only to tie in very generally with models of psychotherapeutic practice.

Slowly, it seems a broader psychotherapeutic basis for art therapy with people who have learning difficulties was being established. Also in 1984, a conference entitled 'Art Therapy as Psychotherapy in Relation to the Mentally Handicapped?' was hosted by one of the post-graduate art therapy training establishments in St Albans. The question mark after the title seemed to epitomise the insecurity that the profession still experienced with regard to its skills base in this area. Interestingly, whenever I see the conference quoted these days, the question mark is conspicuous by its absence: evidence of our growing professional confidence?

A further conference 'Art Therapy for People with Severe to Marginal Learning Difficulties' was held at the University of Leicester in 1989. By this time, contributors seemed more assured of their ability to tailor art therapy to meet the needs of people with learning difficulties and to apply a range of psychotherapeutic models and techniques.

In the study quoted earlier (Rees 1996), the majority of art therapists favoured a psychodynamic perspective. It seems that this preference is also reflected in the work of art therapists who serve clients with a learning difficulty (Hughes 1988; Tipple, 1992). Although it is difficult to find documentary evidence, my impression is that more humanistic styles of engaging are also beginning to impact on the work of art therapists in this field. Certainly in my own work, I have found the underlying values of person-centred psychology and its presumption of self-determination very useful in exploring issues around power and autonomy with my clients.

The intention in compiling this book has not been to produce a 'How to' manual, but rather to give an introduction to the diversity of art therapy which is being conducted with people who have learning difficulties. This diversity extends from the settings in which therapy takes place (hospital, community centre, school, therapist's home and community art therapy resource), the basis on which therapy is established, the skills and limitations of both therapist and client, the prerequisites of the host organisation and the theoretical bias of the therapist.

You may notice that some contributors working with similar issues have a very different outlook and approach. Undoubtedly, this stems partly from their different experiences within contrasting contexts, but also from the fact that we can only be our own type of therapist. Whilst we may be inspired by the work of others, many art therapists enter the profession at least partly because of their personal understanding of the power and intimacy of the art process. It is this belief in the healing power of creativity and the resilience of individuality which has sustained me in my work over the years. Starting work with every new client evokes first-night nerves, accompanied by a knowledge that I shall be a witness to an exquisite uniqueness which is specific to each individual's personal and art processes. Valuing differentness is a starting point for many art therapists. This position seems particularly compelling in the field of learning difficulties. Hopefully, it extends not only to our clients but also to respecting the diversity of outlooks which forms the kaleidoscope of art therapy with people who have learning difficulties.

It was the intention to aim for a good geographical spread of contributors for this book. To some extent this has been achieved, with examples from Scotland, the South-west and East England and Wales. I'm aware that there are places from which contributions have not been received (for example, Ireland and the North of England). The arts therapies service (a collective term referring to the professions of art therapy, music therapy, dramatherapy and dance and movement therapy) I currently manage is well represented in this book as is the work of other practitioners in the South Wales area. For this I make no apology but point out that local and cultural influences may impact on the work and the way it is executed and this is equally true for any other part of Britain.

I had the idea for this book a few years ago, but felt sure that 'someone else' must be on the brink of bringing such a concept to fruition. To my disappointment, no-one did. So, grasping the nettle, I made contact with other art therapists in this line of work. The response was encouraging and enthusiastic. I hope that the result will be both informative and a springboard for other budding authors to contribute further to our understanding of this fascinating, but all too often neglected branch of art therapy.

HOW THE BOOK IS ORGANISED

The book is divided into four sections:

Part 1 Background

This section provides an historical overview of one art therapist's professional journey and it also looks at some of the practical nuts-and-bolts of providing an art therapy service.

Richard Manners (Chapter 1) gives a personal account of his experiences as an art therapist in a number of different settings over the past seventeen years. He talks frankly about how changes in legislation and attitudes have impacted on his practice and on his view of himself as an art therapist. In Chapter 2, I (Mair Rees) present a profile of a current art therapy service and discuss some of the pre-requisites which I feel are necessary in providing an appropriate framework for supporting the practice of art therapy with people who have learning difficulties.

Part 2 Art therapy at work

This is the main body of the book, which is devoted to examples of art therapy practice from around the country within different contexts and explores a variety of themes and client needs.

In Chapter 3, Hilary Lomas and Penny Hallas describe their co-facilitation of an art therapy group for people with learning difficulties who have problems in their relationship with others.

Some of the key issues of control, autonomy and identity were enacted through a bitter argument which survived for the life of the group. Given the key themes of the group, it is interesting that the authors have chosen to review the work by carrying out retrospective interviews with group members, enabling participants to take an active role in the evaluation process. The chapter concludes with insightful observations on the therapists' own responses, including a consideration of some of the reoccurring counter-transference phenomena.

Simon Willoughby-Booth and Joanna Pearce (Chapter 4) reflect on their experiences with clients who appear to display a range of similar characteristics, that is, moderate learning difficulties, no specific mental health problems but occasional serious anti-social outbursts. In their chapter they explore their thoughts in the light of existing literature on the subject of borderline personality disorders. They conclude that art therapy may be particularly useful for people in this situation as it offers the possibility of a safe and concrete containment in a context where pre-verbal work can begin. Ultimately, it has been found that such clients can establish a profound relationship with themselves through the art work.

The next two chapters consider the subject of autism and autistic defence mechanisms in some clients who have learning difficulties. In Chapter 5 Lesley

Fox reviews current thinking around the concept of autism and its relationship with both art and therapy. She explores the therapeutic needs of such clients, with particular reference to the loss of symbolic function. Through examples of her work with individual clients she illustrates how it is possible for such individuals to begin exploring a potential space in which the roots of play and symbolisation are based. Margaret Stack (Chapter 6) gives a detailed account of individual art therapy with one client over a 2-year period. Whilst the individual in question has not been diagnosed as autistic, Stack employs Tustin's concept of 'autistic encapsulation' to understand how he organised his intra-psychic world and emotional experiences. She stresses the important role that art therapy can fulfil as a holding mechanism whilst some of the shell-like defences are tested and relinquished or revised.

In Chapter 7 Rose Hughes describes time-limited individual art therapy with a woman with learning difficulties who had been raped. Rose Hughes explores the concepts of will and violation and how integrity and the right to protection is not always valued highly on behalf of such individuals. The themes of disempowerment and deception are central, as is the manner in which the art process can be a way of reclaiming self-determination and control. The supportive function of the therapeutic alliance is also emphasised, as is the manner in which the art therapist became a witness and co-traveller on the personal journey of pain and injustice.

Sigrid Räbiger (Chapter 8) shares some of her experiences as an art therapist within educational settings. For her, there is a clear distinction between learning difficulties and severe learning difficulties. For some children with severe learning difficulties, she argues that art, far from being a therapy, may be an intrusion, threat or at best meaningless. She stresses the importance of correct assessment and the professional confidence to know when other approaches, for example, music therapy, may in fact be more beneficial. It is important to gauge the developmental level of the child before introducing art therapy. On the other hand, it is argued that art therapy *can* be introduced successfully, but may need to be changed to a structured, containing provision to meet the needs of children who are unclear about their boundaries.

In Chapter 9, Ed Kuczaj considers the issues of loss and bereavement in relation to the experiences of people with learning difficulties and their families. He highlights how the experience of grief can often be denied because of an individual's cognitive disability. He describes how loss can be all-pervasive in the lives of people with learning difficulties, beginning with their birth and the parents' feelings that they have lost a 'normal child'. Through art therapy, clients can explore their subjective experience of having a learning difficulty. He describes how the dichotomies of dependence/independence and similarity/difference are recurring themes in clients' work. He concludes by stressing that one of the most difficult lessons for a therapist to learn is how to be with the client and that this can only really be achieved by understanding our own needs and experiences of loss.

Part 3 Allied approaches

This section looks at the allied disciplines of music therapy, dramatherapy and counselling. The intention is to encourage reflection on the similarities and differences between art therapy and our cousin professions.

Chris Gale and Rachel Matthews (Chapter 10) describe their experiences of establishing and running a short-term project, namely a combined arts therapies assessment group for people with learning difficulties living within a hospital setting. The foundation of the project demanded high levels of co-operation between an art therapist, music therapist and dramatherapist, on both organisa-tional and clinical bases. The project encapsulated some key questions about the nature and purpose of assessment. In particular, how do we deduce whether therapy may be useful for clients who are unable to make their needs and views known overtly? The project also offered the opportunity for some direct comparisons between the methods of working of the three professionals involved and their relative merits of these methods in meeting specific client needs.

In Chapter 11, Lillie Fennell outlines some of the issues which she has found to be important in counselling people with learning difficulties on an individual basis, whilst Enfys Jones draws from her experience of groupwork with these people.

Part 4 Professional issues

This section explores two key issues which are in fact at the forefront of many art therapists' professional and clinical agendas, namely clinical effectiveness and clinical supervision.

Sandie Taylor (Chapter 12) looks at the issue of clinical effectiveness and how as art therapists we can begin to answer the increasingly asked question 'Does it work?' The chapter includes a review of research methodology which may be of interest to art therapists in any clinical field. We are also given a specific example of service evaluation and, in particular, current efforts towards clinical effectiveness research within an arts therapies service for people with learning difficulties.

In the final chapter (Chapter 13), I (Mair Rees) look at the issue of clinical supervision and its importance to the practice of art therapy. I review some of the literature on the topic and explore various models of supervision which have been proposed over the years. In the course of the chapter I also look specifically at the state of play *vis à vis* a supervision within art therapy and attempt to challenge some of our preconceptions and assumption. Finally I conclude with some of my observations of recurring or common themes which arise in the supervision of art therapists working with people who have learning difficulties.

THREADS OF EXPERIENCE

In compiling this introduction, I have become increasingly aware of common themes which have arisen from the work of contributors who at first glance appear to have submitted quite different offerings.

The power of the art process as a concrete holding mechanism is echoed again and again in the work of Lesley Fox, Margaret Stack, Simon Willoughby-Booth/Joanna Pearce and Sigrid Räbiger.

The subjective experiences of learning difficulty are acknowledged in the themes of disempowerment (Rose Hughes and Hilary Lomas/Penny Hallas) and the denial of personal experience and emotional response (Ed Kuczaj and Rose Hughes).

The powerful counter-transference feelings of art therapists working with people who have learning difficulties are described, in particular the therapists' sense of being totally deskilled or 'made stupid' (Hilary Lomas/Penny Hallas, Mair Rees, Ed Kuczaj and Margaret Stack).

Opportunities for assessing and more clearly defining our specific skills by co-operative and comparative work with other colleagues is evident in the chapters by Chris Gale/Rachel Matthews and Sigrid Räbiger.

Finally, hope for further empowerment of clients with learning difficulties is to be found in the principles and practice of user involvement in service evaluation set out in chapters by Sandie Taylor and Hilary Lomas/Penny Hallas.

In conclusion, it is my hope that as well as acknowledging respectfully the pain and privation that the label of learning difficulties may bring, this book will also celebrate the creative resourcefulness of the human spirit and the wisdom which comes from experiencing difference.

BIBLIOGRAPHY

ARC/NAPSAC (1993) *It Could Never Happen Here*, ARC/NAPSAC U.K.

Bender, M. P. (1993) 'The Unoffered Chair', *Clinical Psychology Forum*, 54: 7–12.

Department of Health (1995) *Health of the Nation: Learning Disabilities*, HMSO: London.

Hertfordshire College of Art and Design (1984) Proceedings of Conference *Art Therapy as Psychotherapy in Relation to the Mentally Handicapped?* (Not published.)

Hughes, R. (1988) 'Transitional Phenomena and the Potential Space in Art Therapy with Mentally Handicapped People', *Inscape*, Summer: 4–8

Kuczaj, E. (1990) 'Art Therapy with People with Learning Disabilities', in Liebman, M. (ed.) *Art Therapy in Practice*, Jessica Kingsley Publications: London.

Rees, M. (1995) 'Making Sense of Marking Space: Researching Art Therapy with People who Have Severe Learning Difficulties', In Gilroy, A. and Lee, C. (eds) *Art and Music, Therapy and Research*, Routledge: London.

Rees, M. (1996) *The Supervision of Art Therapists*, unpublished MSc dissertation, University of Bristol.

Sinason, V. (1992) *Mental Handicap and the Human Condition. New Approaches from the Tavistock*. Free Association: London.

Stott, J. and Males, B. (1984) 'Art Therapy for People who are Mentally Handicapped', in Dalley, T. (ed.) *Art as Therapy*, Tavistock Publications: London.

Tipple, R. (1992) 'Art Therapy with People who Have Severe Learning Difficulties', in Walleer, D. and Gilroy, A. (eds) *Art Therapy: A Handbook*, Open University Publications: Buckingham.

University of Leicester (1989) Proceedings of Conference *Art Therapy for people with Severe to Marginal learning Difficulties*. (Not published.)

Waitman, A. (1992) 'Demistifyfing Traditional Approaches to counselling and Psychotherapy' in Waitman, A. and Conboy-Hill, S. (eds) *Psychotherapy and Mental Handicap*, Sage Publications: London.

Part 1

Background

Chapter 1

A personal journey

Richard Manners

Central theme
- A subjective account of a 17-year career as an art therapist working with people who have learning difficulties.

Key points
- How historical changes in legislation and the philosophy of care have impacted on my work as an art therapist.
- My evolving perception of the role of an art therapist.
- Areas of conflict, challenge and success in the ongoing development of art therapy provision.

'What is most personal is most general'

(Carl R. Rogers 1961)

THE BEGINNING – FIRST EXPERIENCES OF ART THERAPY

It was 1976, one of Britain's hottest summers ever. I was in the second year of my Fine Art Degree at Newport College of Art and Design. I did not like art college much. I got really fed up with the way that the lecturers seemed to want to categorise everybody into an 'ism'. In their infinite wisdom they decided to call me an Abstract Expressionist Impressionist, whatever that means! I just wanted to shout back at them: 'No. I am not an Abstract Expressionist Impressionist-ism. I am really Richard Manners. What about looking at the real me?' However, for whatever reason, I found that I had become trapped in a system that left me feeling essentially inarticulate. So, rightly or wrongly, I remained silent. It seemed to me that if one did not easily fit into a category, or an 'ism', which was contemporary or easily slotted into a historical context, one was invalidated.

One day Edward Adamson, a pioneer of art therapy in this country, came to Newport and presented a lecture intriguingly titled: 'An introduction to art therapy'. It was a breath of fresh air to me. I was reminded of the time when, as a boy, I had visited a local artist to get some advice on a career as an artist. We talked about art being part of the community, the artist having a function just like a bricklayer, a plumber, a teacher, an electrician or a whatever and we talked about artists having as much value as those professions, rather than the romantic perception of artists being individuals who live and work in ivory towers, separate from communities. Through Edward Adamson I saw, for the first time, the possibility of art functioning in the community in a way that I felt empathetic towards. It was this revelation that really intrigued me. The images that Edward Adamson presented fascinated me. Each was unique to the individual. He did not attempt to understand the images in an art-historical context. Rather, he viewed them as a sensitive exploration of the relationship between two people, the therapist and the patient, and made it a journey of discovery based on an individual's life.

SETTING OUT – THE FIRST JOB

After college, and after a few false starts on various Youth Opportunities Programmes (remember YOPs?), in 1979 I got a job in Llanfrechfra Grange, Cwmbran, Gwent, a hospital for people with learning difficulties (as an occupational therapy assistant). This was an opportunity for me to explore the idea of a career in art therapy.

At this time I had very romantic idea about art therapy. The hospital was in a beautiful rural setting cut off from the rest of the community. It had 403 residents including twenty children, the wards were split into male and female, people were categorised as high-dependency, low-dependency, male-one, male-two, female-one, female-two, etc. Each lived in wards according to their category. At this time an art therapy department did not exist at the hospital.

For a year I worked with seventeen very severely handicapped men with learning difficulties and challenging behaviour. I set up art activities for all those who used the occupational therapy department. People were interested in what I was doing, although I was not really doing art therapy at all because I had no idea what it really was but, at this time, the powers that were had sufficient interest in art therapy to employ the first art therapist in learning difficulties in Wales at Llanfrechfra Grange, who built on my naive beginnings to establish an art therapy department.

GATHERING INFORMATION – TRAINING

In 1980 I left to undertake a Postgraduate Diploma at what was Hertfordshire College of Art and Design, St Albans (now the University of Hertfordshire). I was one of the youngest on the course at just twenty-two. The average age of the other art therapy students was about thirty-five. It was the fastest growing up that I have ever done. It was a very intense postgraduate course, but also most enjoyable. Everything that I previously could not have articulated, I could begin to articulate here.

At St Albans I was fortunate to meet Patsy Nowell-Hall, my personal tutor. She had ideas firmly rooted in Jungian, Gestalt and holistic therapy, using art, music and drama – whichever medium was appropriate to the needs of the client group. Hers was an eclectic approach that was flexible to meet whatever needs and demands we were to meet in the client group. Her guidance gave me a good foundation for my future development as an art therapist.

ESTABLISHING AN ART THERAPY PRACTICE IN A LARGE HOSPITAL

Following St Albans, I gained my first post as a Basic Grade art therapist in 1981, at Ely Hospital in Cardiff, a hospital dedicated to people with learning difficulties. I launched into this job with all the ideals that had enthused me at college. I had a burning desire to change the injustices I perceived were affecting people with a learning difficulties in the system, but I was brought up very short. Then only two, maybe three art therapists were working in Wales, and there had been an art therapist at Ely working for a short time just before I joined. The art therapy 'section' was in an open-plan warehouse set-up, where 120 people would come in every day to participate in industrial therapy and various other diversional activities. The room was not private and everybody could see inside. The hospital management classed me as part of the occupational therapy department, and I was subject to the financial and clinical priorities of that department. Art therapy was perceived then as a natural extension of the role of occupational therapy – to be a provider of diversionary and interesting day activities. It was expected that I would take in groups of clients, like taking classes at school. Another expectation was that I should teach arts and crafts, as a part of an activity-based curriculum that got the clients off the ward on a daily basis.

Community activity was limited to the occasional bus trip to the seaside, or wherever. The predominant 'therapy' was one of containment, behaviour modification and drug regimes. It was a profoundly controlling environment. Again, the patients (we call them residents now) were categorised and labelled, which defined which ward they lived on and which part of the Rehabilitation Unit they sat in (we called the warehouse the Rehabilitation Unit or Rehab for short). The Rehab did not help personal growth or educate the residents for rehousing in the community. Although many staff had this aim in their hearts, they were as frustrated as I was by the prevalent institutional culture. Industrial therapy was not a therapy at all. Companies who packaged and distributed items, such as wood screws, sent along the packaging and the loose screws to the Rehab to be packaged in sets of ten or twenty, and so on, before distribution to shop outlets. The residents were paid extremely low wages for this so that it would not affect their welfare entitlements. Wages were regularly stopped, or enhanced, as punishments, rewards or incentives, for appropriate behaviour.

ACCEPTANCE AND UNDERSTANDING

It was a long, long battle to influence the culture at Ely Hospital to accept art therapy as a psychotherapeutic model, and it took many workshops, talks and working alongside other professions (doing many things that I had never had to do before, and didn't know I had within me). I began to gain appropriate referrals, I started to regulate my own caseload, and my interventions were taken seriously alongside other treatment programmes.

About the same time as these developments were happening I put some walls around the art therapy section in the Rehab unit, and a door that could be opened and shut, to afford some privacy. However, the walls were flimsy and fell short of the ceiling and constant noise still surrounded us from the rest of the unit. Nevertheless, the walls were a step forward. I was getting good referrals from the other professions in the multi-disciplinary team. The fact that they were for dual diagnosis, challenging behaviour, communication difficulties and any combination of these, and for other clinical reasons and not because the resident was 'good at art' showed that there was some understanding about what it was all about.

SCEPTICISM

Yet the scepticism persisted. Why does he want to be secret behind those walls? Why isn't he telling us about what is going on in the therapy? Why has he got these strange ideas that put the patient first, asking them what they want, and what they feel? Those who came from a medical model, and those who had a behavioural background, found a person-centred, client-led approach hard to accept in a culture where their models of care were control or cure. Some had a vested interest in keeping art therapy under their control in order to achieve larger budgets and staff. Each year departments were encouraged to bid for the same pot of money to maintain or expand their establishment, which caused intense competition – usually the services with the most powerful voices won. Service development was therefore based on power, and not on residents' expressed or identified needs.

Perhaps there was basic human threat, a feeling of inadequacy when faced with the residents' often seemingly untenable aetiology and prognosis. Art therapy offers a tenable way in to communicate on a level with residents, often non-verbal, often playful and 'childlike', requiring the therapist to drop the more usual social graces. Many staff had long ceased to use these modes of expression or, indeed, kept them suppressed in a coat of socially acceptable armour, and therefore found art therapy embarrassing or 'childish'.

SPEAKING FOR OURSELVES

It was an uphill battle still. Inherent to the basic values of art therapy, the sessions provided an environment where residents could speak for themselves and take choices for themselves (this later became a semi-sanctioned movement called self-advocacy that I will elaborate on later). There was an agreement between myself and the client about the nature of what would go on. But the resident then returned to a ward situation where the culture was one of a controlled environment, of a misused behaviour-modification regime where there was little choice, and often in single-sex wards. Often the client was acutely aware of his or her differentness and had the simplest wish to be treated as normal. (I find 'normal' a difficult word in this context as I do not believe normality exists in the first place as a concept; it also serves to alienate the person with learning difficulties even further into their perceived differentness. I have played around with terms such as 'more usual', but this does not quite work either, so I will continue to use 'normal' as a term, with these reservations.) Statements like these often punctuated sessions: 'You do it, Richard; you are the teacher. I can't do it; you are the boss. You tell me!'. The residents perceived me as the controller, and themselves as passive participants, yet yearned for independence and ownership of their own lives. This is a debate that continues throughout my clinical work today. The loss of normality is a persistent theme of bereavement, which the institutional culture I have described here tends to perpetuate. I felt that my clinical practice was in jeopardy. Every day I was trying to work in a psychodynamic way in a culture that seemed unable to accommodate it. Very often I felt in despair; I felt anger and frustration; I realised that the culture in the hospital needed to change in order for the therapy to be effective. Looking back on things now, I feel that the nurses and the doctors were also in a very difficult situation. The community at large had an expectation that the residents and any difficulties they presented should be contained and controlled. I suppose what I was suggesting was perceived as anarchical and a threat to the *status quo*, given those expectations.

SUCCESS – DEVELOPMENT OF AN ARTS THERAPIES DEPARTMENT

I did have some success. After some time I was able to employ another art therapist and a music therapist, the waiting lists and the demand proving that there was a need. I was eventually able to gain a voice through the annual bidding system for finance. I had a growing support from sympathetic professionals, who could see the clinical benefit through the improvements to the residents. We began to develop alongside other services like Special Needs. Eventually, I gained promotion for myself and this led to separation from occupational therapy and clarification of the role and function of Arts Therapies as a distinct department in its own right with a dedicated budget. The biggest boost was in 1984 when the special school left the hospital to be integrated into mainstream education. They vacated a dedicated building, and I had an opportunity to move out of Rehab to develop an Arts Therapies service. We called the building the Greenfields Therapy Centre.

At Greenfields Therapy Centre we now had a private space of our own – and our own door that we had control over. We could carry confidential sessions out in privacy – we did not have to shout to make ourselves understood! The department had some status, internally, and after a while began to attract national and international interest through student placements and connections with the International Youth Service. Ironically, the hospital management used to wheel us out as a service to show how good and innovatory they were when local and international dignitaries were being shown around. However, the dignitaries actually found us really interesting and invited us to teach! We began to do lectures and workshops throughout Great Britain and abroad. Yet, despite this growing reputation for excellence and innovation, we still faced, for example, bizarre situations such as the residents, because of alleged misdemeanours, being routinely prevented from attending sessions, in order to deny them what was perceived to be a pleasant hour or two having fun with paints.

INTEGRATION

The Welsh Office published a ten-year strategy in 1983 in a document called 'The All-Wales Strategy for the Development of Services for Mentally Handicapped People' (mental handicap was the preferred label at that time). This paper was prepared as a result of extensive consultation with people with learning difficulties, parents, relatives, carers, service providers and the voluntary sector. Its core values were:

- people with a mental handicap have a right to ordinary patterns of life within the community;
- people with a mental handicap have a right to be treated as individuals ; and
- people with a mental handicap can expect, and have a right to ask for, additional help from the communities in which they live and from professional services to allow them the opportunity to develop their maximum potential as individuals.

(Welsh Office 1983:1–2)

At the strategy's heart was the philosophy that people with learning difficulties should be encouraged and supported to advocate (self-advocacy as opposed to legal advocacy or citizen advocacy) for themselves and that the community be supported to facilitate this. Where the person with learning difficulties was not able to self-advocate, an independent advocate was asked to support the individual where there was such a service available.

This was the philosophy that underpinned much of the change for learning difficulties services in the past fifteen years although, in recent years, even among those of its most ardent supporters it has been recognised as a document written from idealism rather than realism. However, it was something that, for the first time, provided a supportive context for art therapy and demanded immense cultural and practical changes in how and where services were currently provided.

I believe that for people with learning difficulties, the learning difficulty is not a problem in itself. The real obstacle is other people's often negative perception of that person and, in turn, the person with the learning difficulty's perception of the way they are being negatively viewed. I feel that communication, for example, can be as much a challenge to us as it might be to those people with learning difficulties. Some people with learning difficulties exhibit behaviour which we may find strange, but it is actually our inability to recognise these behaviours as valid and acceptable which further alienates the individual with learning difficulties from the community.

This ideology, coupled with the All-Wales Strategy and the challenges of an institutional culture I have described above, led me to become involved in Community Arts and Arts Education in an attempt to support the community in turn to support the client group as individuals were resettled to the community.

ART THERAPY? COMMUNITY ARTS? ARTS EDUCATION?

This was a very exciting time for me. I had a high public profile in local art colleges, and I felt validated for the first time after many years of struggle. However, these projects drew me away from the core function of providing therapeutic support for the residents of Ely Hospital. With hindsight, I might have chosen to bridge the gap between the community and the institution where I was working in a different way. Going for the more personally rewarding projects where immediate, positive feedback was forthcoming was all too easy. However, much good was achieved. Artists came into the hospital. The residents went out into integrated settings, such as art classes at Cardiff's Llanover Hall and Chapter Arts Centre. Many students went on to do art therapy. Educationalists and educational establishments became more aware of the needs of people with learning difficulties, and many new and innovatory projects were set up. I felt that the work provided some foundations for a community arts infrastructure that could accommodate resettled residents.

But my stepping out to be involved in these projects meant that there was some confusion about the role of art therapy. Was it education? Was it community art? Or was it a therapy? Criticism came my way stating that I was watering down the role of art therapy. I felt that, while occasionally such criticism had a point, our widening involvement between art therapy, the community and the hospital also provided an opportunity to articulate the differences between these areas and to heighten public as well as other institutions' awareness of Arts Therapies.

SUPERVISION

However, the work was taking its toll on me personally. I was working very long hours, I was becoming burnt-out and, worst of all, I began to resent the very giving that had always been such a motivation for me. It felt like people were taking from me and leaving me with no way of replenishing myself.

In all my years as an art therapist I had never had any clinical supervision and, in retrospect it seems to me that it is so important to secure this in any Arts Therapies department. Yet, for me at Ely, it simply wasn't provided. When I asked for it, it wasn't deemed necessary by the management structures to which art therapy was answerable. I feel that supervision adds objectivity to our practice. It is all too easy to fall prey to our own personal needs in environments such as I have described here. Strong beliefs can often cloud judgement. Supervision provides a channel to express frustrations and anger and thus it will help to prevent burn-out.

MOVING ON – ESTABLISHING COMMUNITY ARTS THERAPIES

I left Ely Hospital in 1991, leaving an established Arts Therapies department, which has since been further developed. I moved to what is now Gwent Community NHS Trust, back at Llanfrechfa Grange, to an established department that had a community-wide brief. This was the product of that first art therapist whom the powers-that-be had seen fit to employ back in 1979, just as I had been going off to study art therapy at college.

This was a great opportunity for me as a Head of Service to re-establish my practice, with the benefit of ten years' experience at Ely. Supervision was established, which has since given depth and development to my clinical work. I still had to battle to separate art therapy from occupational therapy, but the split happened fairly quickly. I spent some money on the actual department, which at that time consisted solely of two toilets and a shower-room, a provision for the staff which was never used! In ten years I'd gone from a warehouse to a toilet!

Two other art therapists were employed there, and a music therapist, which we quite quickly established as an Arts Therapies team. This soon expanded to include another music therapist and, recently, a drama therapist. At the time of writing our department is advertising for another senior music therapist and art therapist, which make it a truly established Community Arts Therapies team.

CHANGE

During my transition from Ely Hospital to Llanfrechfa I had undertaken management training, culminating in an MBA. I got the idea through all the battles and challenges I had faced that if you can't beat 'em, join 'em! Learn the language! Put on a suit! Cut off the ponytail! (The last was the most difficult.)

This transformation coincided with the Conservative government's major reforms of the NHS in the late 1980s and early 1990s. The advent of the internal market, the purchaser/provider split GP fundholding, contracting for services – all this was packaged in a new business culture which is epitomised in the NHS Trust. A key, but often unspoken, objective of the Conservative New Right was to undermine the professional hierarchies which they perceived to be powerful self-serving entities blocking the possibilities of any progress. The rhetoric the Conservative Government used to validate their attack was that of providing value for money (VFM), client-identified, needs-led services and enhancement of quality to the service-user.

The learning difficulties Directorate responded to these imperatives by reorganising. We lost all our heads of services and all the budget-holding responsibilities. We were placed in three geographical locations and, working to a general manager in each, we became clinical advisers rather than managers of services (and all this after achieving so much independence and identity for art therapy). I happened to be one of the general managers with a dual function to advise on Arts Therapies. We were called Care Provider Managers. In the next three years I changed my job as many times – I implemented an IT system, led a quality audit, a national pilot sponsored by the King's Fund, and project-managed the building of a new health centre (including the management of change required by all the services to achieve the strategic objective of providing collaborative care in a primary care team-setting around GPs – a 'one stop service'). Through-out all this I remained as clinical adviser for Arts Therapies. Often, my clinical ideals were in conflict with the more global managerial perspectives. We have now turned full circle, in that the department has won back its budgets and has me as Head of Service.

MORE CHANGE! – THE NEW BUSINESS CULTURE

As I write, a new Labour government has recently been elected. It is hoped, by many, that this will mean the end of the worst of the internal market and GP fundholding. It certainly means more change – for example, GP fundholding may be replaced by GP commissioning. However, I feel it would be wrong to think that the legacy of the Conservative government will be entirely overturned, as any government's goal must be to establish VFM when the public purse is limited. The imperatives embodied in projects such as Clinical Effectiveness, Clinical Audit (Welsh Office 1995) and outcome-based practice will continue. An air of panic prevails amongst some art therapists when these terms are used. How can a psychotherapy-based practice measure outcomes? Are we invalidated if we cannot prove our effectiveness? These fears are deepened when we hear of Trusts cutting or 'deleting' departments for not producing an effective service. Arts Therapies are seen as an easy target because of the continuing misperception in general of what we are about. It is very easy for the therapist, in the climate of the internal market and the new business culture, to perceive these tools as a burden imposed by management. And it is very easy to perceive the evidence gathered to be regarded as tools to persecute and reveal the existing services as ineffective.

But I believe we can measure our outcomes. We can prove we are effective. We can audit ourselves to prove it. We already do it! We have had years of experience in research, gathering information and communicating with others, born of the necessity of personal and professional journeys like mine. It is inherent in our practice that we are continually reflective, always examining our relationship with our clients and the external world, and making effective change accordingly. I believe we need to take steps to make our processes more formal and express our results in a easily consumable form. Audit (as well as many other management tools) can be integrated into our clinical practice. We, the clinicians, have opportunities to control our processes, and to determine for ourselves the most appropriate ways to respond to improve our clinical work with our patients.

CLINICAL FOCUS

My practice over the seventeen years has definitely changed. I am now much more focused on the psychodynamic relationship between client and therapist, instead of trying to be everything to everyone. I feel, however, that the community has grown to accommodate people with learning difficulties as they have been resettled into the community, so there is less need to be evangelical on their behalf. Nonetheless, there is still room for carefully articulated work in the interface, which can be clinically effective and beneficial to the client.

THE FUTURE

The current Arts Therapies Service focus is on the clinical issues of how can we work more collaboratively with other professions. Often professions work in isolation from each other yet are all working towards the same health gain, thus there is much duplication of administrative and managerial work, plus some clinical overlap. How can all the professions work together to achieve maximum health gain? This involves all the professions planning the care of an individual towards independent living, or maintenance of the present level of health or well-being. Some of the issues for us centre around maintaining confidentiality. How do we maintain the integrity of our practice whilst working alongside possibly conflicting models of care such as behaviour modification? When does an intense episode of Arts Therapy end and the maintenance work begin? Who carries out the maintenance work? Are our services going to be diluted in supervising or teaching others to do the maintenance work?

The same debate is being echoed around Primary Care teams and GPs. It is part of the clinical effectiveness debate. At present, GPs have not been concerned with the effectiveness of our services, having very little knowledge of what they comprise, preferring the learning difficulties service to take the responsibility. The present ideology of Primary Care and resettlement into the community of our clients is asking GPs to take more account of these services. It is imperative that we as arts therapists communicate and integrate our services into the Primary Care forum.

In addition, the clients and their carers have become more aware of the availability of the Arts Therapies – or the lack of availability. Increasingly, more children are being statemented for our services. There is a greater awareness amongst parents and carers of the potential of Arts Therapies to help those they care for, as well as themselves.

We must congratulate ourselves that we are being asked these questions and that these demands are being made of our services. It is an indication of how seriously the Arts Therapies are being taken – we have all come a long way from negotiating ourselves out of warehouses and converted toilets!

BIBLIOGRAPHY

Rogers, C. (1961) *A Therapist's View of Psychotherapy – On Becoming a Person*, Constable and Company.

Welsh Office (1983) *All-Wales Strategy for the Development of Services for Mentally Handicapped People*, HMSO.

Welsh Office (1995) *Towards Evidence-Based Practice*, HMSO.

Chapter 2

Frames of reference

Some operational and contextual issues influencing the practice of art therapy with people who have learning difficulties

Mair Rees

Central theme
- A discussion of some of the practical nuts-and-bolts issues involved in providing an effective and respectful art therapy service for people with learning difficulties.

Key points
- How the manner in which art therapy is provided may influence the way in which such a service is accessed, perceived and valued by users and carers.
- The importance and relevance of safeguards and standards.
- Promoting a sense of ownership amongst service users.

PREAMBLE

A great many changes have taken place within the service sectors over the past few years. The thrust to close large traditional hospitals for people with learning difficulties has meant that new models of care are being developed and tested throughout Britain. Largely, resources for residential provision are being transferred from Health to Social Services. Correspondingly, the Community Care Act has revolutionised the role of the latter, with greater emphasis on the management and purchasing rather than the direct provision of care. This has afforded the opportunity for non-statutory agencies to become providers of care or to extend the service they already offer. Consequently, in general there is now a greater number of players in the provision-of-services game.

Anecdotal evidence would suggest that patterns of work for art therapists may be evolving in line with the shift in services. Those who previously worked for Social Services may find themselves negotiating a contract for employment directly with a care manager, or may find their work divided between a number of different non-statutory agencies such as Mencap, NCH, Barnado's etc. It should also be noted that only a proportion of people with learning difficulties use residential services and that many live at home with their families or, in some cases, independently or with a partner.

Despite such radical changes and the transfer of resources from health to social care, the majority of art therapists still appear to be employed within the Health Service for at least part of their time (Rees 1996). In the same study, 27 per cent of a sample of 120 qualified art therapists worked with more than one client group. It is possible that diversity is the key to the continued and further development of art therapy services. People with learning difficulties may also benefit from accessing generic art therapy services, in that such provision is less stigmatising and less obviously reinforces the label of learning difficulty.

Whether or not an art therapy provision falls under the auspices of a social care or health-related service may have major implications for the way it is perceived by others. Many art therapy services have their historical roots in traditional learning difficulties hospitals where resources were centralised. I am sometimes of the opinion that many such services have survived by stealth, subterfuge and misapprehension! If we consider that few counselling or psychotherapeutic services for people with learning difficulties have ever developed or endured, then it is a cause for celebration that art therapy is still alive and kicking in this arena.

Art therapists have often battled with ignorance and misunderstanding of their role and profession. Colleagues will be familiar with the frustration that yet another referral for recreational art can bring. In the field of learning difficulties, the message that art therapy is essentially a psychotherapeutic tool seems particularly difficult to communicate. Interestingly, I have felt that at times colleagues in other professions (who often should know better) have not wished to hear the true nature of our work. Despite training and education initiatives, misconceptions are clung to with steadfast tenacity, for example, art therapy is for relaxation, for amusement, for people who are good at drawing.

Underlying all this is a kernel of folk wisdom that states art is inherently good for 'them' (this notion is challenged in Chapter 8).The concept of art as psychotherapy with people with learning difficulties seems to arouse uncomfortable feelings for some people . I have known those who, with alarming ease, have simultaneously held two dissonant views of art therapy with people who have learning difficulties: that is, first, that it is a powerful and potentially dangerous tool capable of unleashing wild and uncensored emotions, and second that it is impotent and facile.

In the past, this general muddle has sometimes worked to the advantage of art therapy; it is unlikely to continue to do so in the future. Within the Health Service there is increasing emphasis on demonstrable health gain and clinical effectiveness. In order for the outcomes of art therapy to be evaluated, purchasers must be clear about what they are buying and why. In some services, there seems to be confusion amongst managers about whether art therapy should be the responsibility of Health or Social Services. Again, we are back to the old chestnut of whether it is art or therapy.

Of course, not all art therapists work within the structure of an organisation – some work freelance or privately. I would be happy to be proved wrong, but informal knowledge suggests that in reality few people with learning difficulties access a service in this way.

Moreover, even if an art therapist is employed on a private sessional basis to work with a person who has learning difficulties, it is extremely unlikely that the contract will have been established initially with the client themselves. The hiring/firing will most likely be effected by a third party, a paid worker, family member or possibly advocate. Inevitably, that key person will feel that they have a stake in the therapy and will be eager to ensure that the client is benefiting from their involvement.

However, such concern, no matter how well intended may not always support the process of therapy. Even seemingly innocuous questions at the end of a session, such as 'What did you do today?' when a client has been incapacitated by despair, or 'Did you enjoy yourself?' when the session has been spent grieving over lost opportunities, can skew the therapeutic process. Sometimes, I feel that so many people have a vested interest in the lives of those with a learning difficulty that it is difficult for them to reclaim any autonomy or control.

In terms of the effects of art therapy, I have found that some of those who support clients with learning difficulties are ever fearful of their charges backsliding or becoming less able in unspecified ways. Regression, it seems, is intolerable if you have a learning difficulty, as so often are demonstrations of 'negative' emotions – anger, sadness, despair, frustration. I have frequently encountered spoken and unspoken fears that art therapy will open a Pandora's box of uncontrolled and uncontrollable emotion and (to mix metaphors) that it will be impossible to return the genie into the bottle.

Services for people with learning difficulties are often based on models of care which have behavioural underpinning, are goal-oriented and seek tangible evidence of clients' progress on a range of measures such as social and self-help skills. Very few of these models consider people's emotional well-being in any systematic fashion. Usually, such a focus is deliberately avoided as it is difficult to observe and is by its very nature highly subjective. Consideration of emotional well-being is therefore ignored or considered in indirect or oblique ways. All too often, in my experience, it is only when the client becomes a 'management problem' and likely to cause harm to self or others that attempts to consider feelings and motivation may be made. On the other hand, it can equally seem as if every aspect of the life of a person with learning difficulties is open to public scrutiny.

REFERRING TO ART THERAPY

Different art therapy services have very diverse policies with regard to referral. The service I currently work for, TAITH (see also Chapters 3, 10 and 12) has an open referrals policy whereby any professional or person close to an individual with learning difficulties within our specific catchment area may refer to the service. Self-referrals are also very much welcomed. We are currently exploring the issue of improving direct access to the service by projects such as a 'road-show' where members of the team visit day services and clubs to set up a stall and discuss art therapy with service-users there.

As a service, we have also identified a number of general areas of need which we feel would constitute appropriate referrals to the service. These are very broad categories, but give potential clients and carers an opportunity to consider whether their needs are likely to be met by what is on offer. An especially designed referral form can be useful, not just for the purpose of expediency but, by including the categories under which referrals may be accepted, the form can also give valuable basic information about the nature and purpose of the service being offered. In the service referred to, we have made efforts not to employ standard psychiatric labels, but to attempt to express possible needs in non-stigmatising and everyday language. Examples of such referral categories include:

- Problems in your relationships with others
- Difficulty in expressing and/or naming your feelings
- Needing an opportunity to explore difficult feelings/experiences from the past
- Life events causing stress (for example, bereavement or a change in living arrangements)
- Previously identified mental health problems
- Organising yourself in ways which make it difficult to take advantage of available life opportunities.

Reasons for referral may be complex and multi-faceted. At first sight, a referral for a client who 'does nothing all day' may seem inappropriate. However, closer scrutiny may reveal that the way this individual relates to other people makes it impossible for her or him to access available opportunities, thus greatly reducing the quality of life.

There may be a number of other people's agendas lurking under the guise of an art therapy referral. For example, a person may be referred by a key worker for difficulties in relationships with others when in fact the client in question may have newly acquired assertiveness skills (perhaps from attending a self-advocacy group), which are disrupting the *status quo* within her network of care. Some diligent detective work is often merited on receipt of a new referral. It may be useful to compile a checklist of the information required, ranging from the support needs of the client, family background and current living situation through to specific reasons for the referral – why has this particular person referred the client, for what purpose and why now?

In my current service, as part of a broader evaluation process, the decision was taken to investigate why potential service-users themselves felt that people with learning difficulties experience difficulties in their lives and consequently may require the services of an art therapist.

One hundred questionnaires were sent out and forty-five returned. People willing to participate were contacted through user and carer organisations, and also adult literacy groups. Users who took part were often supported in filling in questionnaires by their advocates or tutors. In response to the question 'What sort of things do you think cause people [with learning difficulties] to feel upset for a long time ?' the following categories of issues were highlighted:

Bereavement and loss

Over 40 per cent of respondents referred to bereavement or loss. This is very striking considering the inconsistent way in which people with learning difficulties are supported in coming to terms with death and grieving. I have worked with a number of clients who have been prevented from attending a loved one's funeral, or who have experienced other disruptions in their grieving process. (This issue is explored more fully in Chapter 9.)

Loneliness and the ability to express feelings frankly

Again a substantial number of people cited loneliness, insecurity and an inability to express feelings or to be listened to. This gives a sad insight into what it can be like to be a person with learning difficulties in our society and the shortcomings of services and communities to offer people a sense of worth and belonging. This seems particularly true of people who have lost or been separated from their families.

Bullying/being shouted at

Over a quarter of respondents were concerned with issues which seem to reflect feelings of powerlessness and other people's denial of their adult status.

Separation and relationship breakdown

A number of people referred to relationship breakdowns and separation from family as a cause of distress.

Major life changes

A number of respondents felt that moving house or having a change in routine could be stressful. One obvious group of people being affected were those being resettled from a large traditional hospital.

Whatever the source of the referral, its suitability will need careful consideration and prioritisation. (Some of the key issues around assessment of client need are discussed in Chapter 10.)

CONTRACTS AND BOUNDARIES

Partly because of the above issues, people with learning difficulties are rarely encouraged to be truly self-determining. As in all other aspects of their life, the choice as to whether or not art therapy will be an option may not initially be theirs. They will have little or no say in how therapy is funded or the service delivered. Even if the therapist is able to be flexible about where, when and how the therapy comes about, the client is unlikely to have the final say in this. Most likely, the therapist will rely on those who support the client to make the therapy possible. In reality, without this often very practical support and goodwill, clients would not physically arrive for sessions, so the work would never leave the starting-blocks.

It is essential for therapists to both forge good relationships with carers whilst also protecting the boundaries of the work with the client. This is rarely easy but almost always essential. In my experience, it is important to establish a clear contract with both client and carer from the outset. Contracts can be very practical in nature, outlining the how, where and when of therapy, but can also make explicit each participant's individual role in the proceedings. The contract can in some cases carry the key aims of therapy, but the client must feel comfortable about sharing this level of information with the carer. More specific aims may be agreed between client and therapist and remain within the domain of the art therapy session.

The method and mechanism for giving and receiving feedback should be addressed in the contract. How the carer might greet the client after an art therapy session or how they might respond if a client chooses to share some of what happened in a session may be referred to. Obviously, every eventuality cannot be addressed, and different issues will be more pertinent to different clients. However, a written contract can provide a useful backdrop to therapy and allow each participant to be clear about the extent of their role and responsibility. Information to include in a contract may be as shown in Figure 2.1.

I have found it useful to establish a preliminary meeting with client and carer (separate and/or together depending on circumstances) to agree the terms of a new contract prior to the commencement of therapy. Clearly, some clients are more able to take an active and overt role in such discussions than others. Involving clients who are non-verbal in such decision-making processes is always a challenge.

However, even contracting can be creative (honestly!).The use of images, particularly clear photographs, can kindle interest in many potential clients who are daunted by structured meetings and pages of text they are unable to understand. The use of symbols to convey information always seems inviting but, in reality, the more tangible, concrete and specific an image is, the less likely it is to be misleading. Whilst running the risk of over-generalising .I think it is fair to say that some people who have learning difficulties find it difficult to generalise and extrapolate, so it is important that any images used relate directly to the issue at hand.

Client's name

Therapist's name

Key aims of therapy

Where?

When?

How often?

For how long?

Transport arrangements

Who will support the client to attend?

How will support be offered?

Cancellation arrangements

What all parties need to know on an ongoing basis

How any important information will be communicated between sessions

Date for review of sessions

Format of review
    Who will be there?
    How will information be exchanged?
    What will not be shared

Who will receive copies of the contract?

Will information be kept in any other format?

Supervision arrangements

Limits of confidentiality

Figure 2.1 Example of a written contract

The use of photographs, say of alternative venues or modes of transport, can communicate to the client that they are an active part of the contracting process . However, choices offered must be real ones; if anything is non-negotiable then this should be stated honestly. People are rarely duped by false choices.

The contract itself can be made more user-friendly by the inclusion of photographs, for example, of the client, therapist, venue, mode of transport, methods of communication (telephone, letter, face-to-face). This sort of system can be very time-consuming to establish. However, access to good IT resources can permit a bank of photographs to be scanned into a PC and appropriate images selected and reproduced on each new contract. Clearly, there are data protection issues if photographs of clients are being stored. If computer resources are not available, photocopying can achieve acceptable results.

Whilst some clients may not feel comfortable or even interested in keeping a copy of a contract for themselves, a small pocket-sized card with some of the key information/images may seem more manageable and attractive. Other clients may prefer to have access to the information on an audio cassette; this shouldn't be too difficult, expensive or time-consuming to arrange.

The key to all this is flexibility and diversity. People with learning difficulties are an extremely diverse group with astonishingly different skills and needs. Art therapists must be mindful of this fact when exploring means of communication and negotiation.

A contract also has the effect of validating the work. The sessions matter, the venue matters, it matters whether someone turns up or not, the therapist matters, the carer matters and above all the client matters. This may seem obvious and fundamental, but apathy and disregard can be a cancer in services for people with learning difficulties, reducing everything to the lowest common denominator. I do not feel it is too dramatic to stress that there are powerful unconscious forces afoot which can undermine respect, confidence, hope and vitality. The best way I know of guarding against these is to establish regular and frequent checking mechanism such as contracts, reviews and supervision (nice holidays also help!).

Contracts also undoubtedly raise expectations about the service. Users and carers come to anticipate that they will be entitled to such information and that the arrangements will be regularly reviewed. I have also known this to make participants more proactive and assertive in requesting what they need from a service.

SUPPORT DURING SESSIONS

Boundaries of therapy can become very messy and distended if the therapist is seduced into trying to offer 100 per cent support to a client over the course of a session. Some clients with learning difficulties will (especially during the initial stages of therapy) find it impossible to stay in the same room as the art therapist for the whole session. This may be true even when the length of the session has been tailored to meet the individual's capacity in terms of concentration.

For some clients it may be appropriate for them to be left to their own devices, for example, going for a walk around and (hopefully) returning when they feel ready. For others this would pose an unacceptable safety risk. Such eventualities should be discussed with the carer when a contract is established. An interim review can always be called if unforeseen issues arise during the early weeks of therapy.

I have spent many a fruitless session chasing clients around the grounds of various establishments, feeling that I had to be totally responsible for their safety and well-being every minute of the session. I'm ashamed to say that I was quite a seasoned art therapist by the time I decided that this was an ineffective use of my skills and the client's time. It usually also meant that I was colluding with an avoidance tactic which disrupted the real work of the session.

Different situations require different solutions, although if you suspect in advance that something may be an issue, it is usually advisable to enlist the support of a well-briefed paid worker. In the past, I have used the services of care workers, mobility aides, key workers and art therapy assistants depending on availability. Such a person can be on hand outside the therapy room to provide support to the client when they choose to remove themselves from the session, and to offer them gentle encouragement to return as appropriate. Such supporters can also play a vital role for clients who need support with personal-care skills or with those who may pose a potential risk to their own or the therapist's safety.

There is really no benefit in playing the macho therapist, being able to absorb what is (sometimes literally) thrown your way. My view is that this stance merely colludes with the client's *modus operandi* and denies the client's inherent responsibilities within the therapeutic relationship.

INTERIOR OF THERAPY

What happens within art therapy sessions will be influenced by a myriad of factors. On the one hand, broader issues such as financial and organisation constraints can play a key role, whilst on the other, interpersonal issues such as the quality of the client–therapist relationship and the motivation of participants will be central. I would like to consider four factors which I feel are important to the progress or otherwise of therapy. I am also sure that many readers will be able to think of other equally important issues.

- The therapist's theoretical perspective
- The client's skills range and level of engagement in the therapeutic process
- The quality of the therapeutic space
- Adequacy of the client and therapist support-structure outside of therapy.

The therapist's theoretical perspective

In terms of theoretical perspective, most art therapists claim to work within a psychodynamic framework (Rees 1996). Obviously, in this case there will be greater emphasis on the power of the unconscious processes and the exploitation of transferential phenomena as a basis of therapeutic change. Unconscious processes are played out in the tripartite area – the space between client, therapist and image.

Both psychodynamic and object-relations theories have long since informed my work and practice as an art therapist. However, I have more recently been drawn (as it were) to the more humanistic end of the theoretical spectrum and in particular into the domain of person-centred approaches.

From my current vantage point, I am particularly interested in dynamics of power within therapy. Whichever theoretical model an art therapist employs, the relationship with any client will be an unequal one. The therapist has the magic mantle of professionalism and the client wants/needs something from her. All too often, it seems to me that the key to change is viewed as located within the therapist. Therapists are paid for their expertise, understanding and skills. In the field of learning difficulties, this split between the knowingness of the therapist and the not-knowingness of the client is heightened and emphasised. The psychodynamic model can, I believe, reinforce this power structure. The therapist runs the risk of placing herself in a quasi-medical role where diagnosis (interpretation) and treatment (therapy) becomes hers to impart. My fear is that such models can put the onus on the therapist to know, to understand and to barter unconsciousness with consciousness.

In contrast, whilst person-centred psychology does not deny the existence of powerful unconscious processes, it puts its faith in the client's own intuitive understanding of what they need to move on. I have heard numerous criticisms of this way of working, perhaps the most damning being that it is 'just being nice to people'. My own experience has been quite the contrary, having seen some highly effective challenges being made within a person-centred framework. These challenges are often successful because they are specific and direct yet offer support to the integrity of the individual being challenged.

Within a person-centred tradition, an art therapist becomes not a guide, but a co-traveller, a witness to the strivings of another human being. I have been taken aback, astonished and surprised by the wisdom and deep understanding of clients with learning difficulties often enough to know that I can never really know what they know, but that I can be an active witness to their profound experience and knowing.

The client's skills range and level of engagement in the therapeutic process

As has already been mentioned in the Introduction, art therapy is one of the few psychotherapeutic professions to survive and thrive within the field of learning difficulties. This must be at least partly attributable to the fact that art therapy can operate successfully at a number of cognitive and emotional levels. Correspondingly, the art therapy process can reflect this by its pitch and focus. At one end of the continuum, the physicality of the media can mean that art therapy may concentrate almost entirely on the experience of holding. This can be achieved on a very concrete and non-verbal level with clients who have no spoken or signed language and limited development of broader symbolic functioning. At the opposite end of the spectrum, one could argue that art therapy would resemble that with any other group of people, that is, where the client is engaged in art processes which both client and therapist subsequently reflect upon together.

However, it would be over-simplifying the case to present such a one-dimensional picture. Some clients who are non-verbal have developed advanced symbolic function in other areas of representation. Their language delay could well be attributable to specific neurological trauma or structural problems in the mouth and larynx. Whilst special signing systems such as Makaton for people with learning difficulties have been in existence for some time, not all those who could benefit have been offered training in their use.

It may be more useful to represent clients' positions with regard to the following grid (Figure 2.2); the two continuums are Verbal/Non-verbal and Symbolic/Asymbolic. The latter refers to the degree of broader symbolic functioning which the client has acquired, that is, how they are able to represent things and feelings to themselves and others. Below, I give a brief outline how hypothetical clients labelled A, B, C and D may organise themselves within art therapy sessions. I fully concede that by simplifying the situation in this way I am at risk of doing a disservice to the complexity and diversity of people's experiences and responses. However, it may be useful for readers who have no experience of art therapy with people with learning difficulties to gain a basic picture of the different ways in which the therapy can manifest itself depending on the presenting skills and needs of the client.

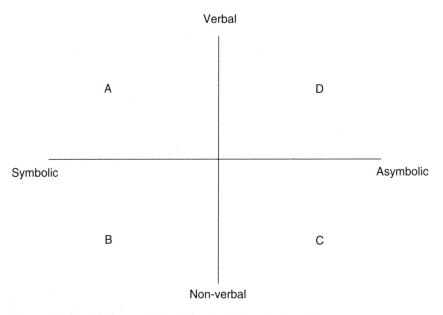

Figure 2.2 Verbal-Non-verbal and Symbolic/Asymbolic grid

Client A (Verbal/Symbolic)

David is referred to art therapy because of bouts of uncontrolled anger which he vents against anyone close at hand. Most of the time he is a quiet and demure young man who is polite to the point of unctuousness. He is articulate and is a skilled artist, he attended a special school and the level of his learning difficulty is usually referred to as moderate. He attends individual art therapy sessions for several months. At first he draws beautiful idealised images of his childhood, rolling green hillsides and shop windows brimming with goodies. Initially, his angry side is totally denied, but very slowly begins to find expression in the content of his work, for example, in a drawing of a cemetery. After about a year of working he produces a self-portrait in the full throes of a powerful rage. In line with the change in his images he has been able to use his developing relationship with the art therapists to touch on his angry feelings toward his mother, whose mental health needs he had to support when he was barely able to take care of himself. He also began admitting how frightened he had been as a young child by the arguments which had been a regular feature of his parents' stormy relationship.

Client B (Non-verbal/Symbolic)

Rhea is referred to art therapy largely because of her difficult behaviour. She is a strong-willed, determined young woman. She has no spoken language and often seems frustrated because she is unable to make her needs understood. Initially, she uses individual art therapy to test out the safety of the relationship. She deliberately picks up sharp objects in a cavalier fashion or tries to eat the inedible. At first, her drawings are all of a non-representational type (scribble). The art therapist is tempted into under-estimating Rhea's abilities but, during clinical supervision, checks out her hunch that there is more afoot. Gradually, Rhea's drawings change and she begins representing objects in a desperate attempt, it seems, to meet her own needs. The objects she draws are often food or soft toys. Later still, the developing relationship between Rhea and the art therapists enables them to explore sharing images and objects, to experience trust and coping with the sadness and frustration which can arise from unmet needs.

Client C (Non-verbal/Asymbolic)

Mary is a woman in her fifties who attends a small art therapy group for people with severe learning difficulties. In her early days of attending she is totally unable to settle and spends the majority of the time wandering around the art therapy room humming tunelessly. She avoids all contact with other people in the room. Mary sometimes gravitates to a space near the door, so the art therapist puts a chair and table with paints and paper there, indicating that this can her place if she would like it. Occasionally, she begins picking up a paint brush as she walks past and furtively making a quick dab on the page before continuing on her circuit of the room. Over time, she spends longer painting and becomes particularly interested in the edges of the page which she overlays again and again with paint. She also becomes absorbed with the edges of the table, which she also paints. As she explores the physical edges of her environment, she also seems to have a clear concept of her own boundaries within the group. There is an obvious reduction in her anxiety to the point where she is able to make fleeting eye contact with other people present. The physical containment of the room and materials seemed to have afforded her some experience of emotional containment.

Client D (Verbal/Asymbolic)

Ceri is a man in his thirties who is diagnosed as autistic. Whilst he has a fair vocabulary, much of what he says is insistent and repetitive. He seems to have great difficulty acknowledging the presence of other people. His relationships are generally very mechanistic. Whilst he will interact with other people present, this tends to be on a very instrumental level, for example, grabbing someone's arm to use their hand to open a door. In individual art therapy he is very concerned with routine and order and spends more time counting and organising the art materials than using them. He has to feel very, very safe before he can drop his defences enough to try any form of experimentation. After a very long time, there are a few tender moments when Ceri is able to use some of the found objects lying around in the art therapy room in a shared storytelling session with the art therapist.

The quality of the therapeutic space

The quality of the therapeutic space can have a major impact on the progress of therapy in a number of ways. On the most fundamental level, the space needs to be safe and private, that is, free from interruptions. This is not as easy to ensure as it might appear at first hand. As traditional hospital-based departments now move out into community bases, there is a growing expectation amongst management that art therapy will take place in shared-usage rooms.

This has a number of implications. First, a range of people, all with different needs and agendas will have claim on the space so, for example, may think nothing of interrupting a session to retrieve a piece of equipment. Second, items left in the room by other users may not be safe for some clients who are chaotic in their approach or who have challenging behaviour. Third, the therapist may find herself limiting the range of art materials on offer to the clients because of pressure by other people who use the room.

Whilst shared-usage rooms are perfectly adequate for many art therapy clients, there will always be a group of potential service-users with learning difficulties who will need a room which is accessible but set apart and where free use of materials is possible. This is important not only for the efficacy of therapy but also for the safety of both client and therapist.

Such rooms may be in a number of locations, including health clinics, community resource centres or community education establishments. The broader context may have very serious repercussions for the safety and efficacy of therapy. Clients whose behaviour may at times be erratic and unpredictable should not really be offered sessions where other vulnerable people (for example, very young children or the elderly) also use services. Not only is there a duty to protect other users of the resource but also to ensure that such clients with learning difficulties are not exposed to situations which would result in them being labelled further.

The previous life of a venue may still be very much in evidence. In Hilary Lomas and Penny Hallas' chapter (Chapter 3), they discuss an art therapy group which was held in a community education centre, part of which was still being used as a primary school. There may be powerful associations for a group of people who have been infantilised for much of their lives. One department where I worked as an art therapist had previously been used as a pathology laboratory: sometimes, new clients would clutch their arms as they entered the building, with the expectation of having blood samples taken. Heaven only knows what sort of dynamics were precipitated by this scenario!

Adequacy of the client and therapist support-structure outside therapy

Both client and therapist will require support beyond the boundaries of the art therapy session if therapy is to be useful, effective and sustained.

The client will need her carers (either family or paid workers) to be supportive of the concept of therapy, to provide the necessary practical assistance and goodwill to resolve any potential areas of tension. Good communication is vital and the manner in which this takes place can be discussed as part of the contracting process referred to earlier in this chapter.

If part of a broader organisation, the art therapist will require a clear supportive management structure where her authority as a professional and clinician is respected. There should be the opportunity for negotiating appropriate working conditions with regard to physical resources and caseload. Correspondingly, it is equally important that the art therapist familiarises herself with the tools of evaluation and assessment (see Chapter 12) so that she can set clear clinical objectives, prioritise an often scarce resource and provide a consistent flow of information to the broader organisation about the performance of the service.

Underpinning all this, it is essential that the work is sustained by good-quality clinical supervision (see Chapter 13) and that the art therapist has opportunities to meet with colleagues for informal support and validation.

CONCLUSION

This chapter has attempted to look at some of the broader issues to do with context, organisation and theory, which may either support or undermine the essence of the clinical art therapy work with clients who have learning difficulties. Even to the most conscientious art therapist, such details may at times seem troublesome or tedious when the 'real work' of therapy is often so pressing. However, if the frame is neither solid nor a good fit then the picture inside will be vulnerable and will not be viewed to its best advantage. If the basis for therapy is not sound and well supported then this will inevitably be mirrored within the dynamics of the therapeutic relationship itself.

BIBLIOGRAPHY

Rees, M. (1996) *The Supervision of Art Therapists*, unpublished MSc dissertation, University of Bristol.

TAITH Arts Therapies Service (1995) *Learning to Listen* – Analysis of Questionnaire for Service-Users and carers, unpublished survey.

Part 2

Art therapy at work

Chapter 3

It's a mystery

Accounts of an art therapy group for people with learning difficulties

Hilary Lomas and Penny Hallas

Central theme
- An account of a co-facilitated, community-based art therapy group for people with learning difficulties who were experiencing problems in their relationships with others.

Key points
- The stormy manifestation of the pivotal themes of autonomy, control and identity.
- A review of participants' personal experiences of the group, using a retrospective interviewing technique.
- A description of the co-therapists' experiences and recollections of the group highlighted by counter-transference phenomena.

INTRODUCTION

This chapter is about an art therapy group for people with learning difficulties who were experiencing problems in getting on with others. In the introduction we first outline the nature of the group, how it was formed, and something of the therapists' approaches. We then describe what we wanted to explore in this chapter, the process we went through to do it, and how this process informed the end result.

We were part of a new department and the Arts Therapies team had only been working together for a few months when planning for the group started. During the course of the group described, the team was also evolving. We were finding that, although our theoretical perspectives differed, we shared views on the ethics of practice and an interest in trying to develop a service which was user-friendly and respectful of people's rights and wishes (see also Chapters 2 and 12).

BACKGROUND TO THE GROUP

Referrals coming in to the Arts Therapies Department indicated that there may be a need for a relationships group, but as we did not have enough possible members, further referrals were sought by sending out information about the proposed group, its aims and who might benefit. We stated that we anticipated the main emphasis of the group would be on making links between the art work undertaken and the thoughts and feelings of people attending the group, with the aim of clarifying the interactions in the group, and helping people to find more satisfying ways of relating to others. We expected the group to contain people with a range of abilities, and thought it might include people who lack confidence in social situations, or who draw attention to themselves in ways which do not help them gain satisfying relationships. We did specify, though, that group members would need to have shown some wish to relate. These details were kept intentionally broad, as we felt that the referrals themselves would define the nature of the group. Departmental policy is to have a relatively long period of assessment before ongoing therapy commences. This has been found to be useful when working with people who may find the concept and details of what we offer difficult to grasp, as it allows them to get a clearer idea of whether they wish to pursue ongoing therapy.

Referrals came mainly from support staff, though there was one from a family member, and one self-referral. All but one came from the community. The referrers were contacted in order that some background information could be gathered, including reasons for referral, and whether the idea had been discussed with the client. Meetings were then arranged with possible group members, in an environment they felt comfortable in, preferably on their own, but with support from a friend, advocate or support staff if they chose. Our aims in these meetings were:

- to explain who we were, what an art therapy group is and what it might involve
- to gain more understanding of how the person felt about the referral, and whether they felt that they would be interested in the group
- to assess whether we felt this particular person might benefit
- to gauge who, from those referred, would be likely to complement each other in a group.

Following this stage, one person referred chose not to be further involved in the process, another seemed to us to be likely to benefit more from individual art therapy, and we felt that the remaining three men and four women might well benefit from working together as a group. All had some verbal communication, and happened to be within a similar age group.

THERAPISTS' APPROACH

We had not worked together before, but shared a basic psychodynamic framework and a non-directive style. The application of psychodynamic art therapy with people with learning difficulties had been described by Rose Hughes (1989) and Robin Tipple (1993). We both felt that this approach could be useful when running a group. Sue Strand's (1990) moving account of an art therapy group in an institution looked at the benefits the group offered its members in terms of gaining a sense of personal power and responsibility. She described how the group offered people the opportunity not only to make their own choices but also to notice and explore the effect they had on others. Thus group members could become more aware of themselves as social beings as well as feeling individuals.

We both shared this view that people could have the emotional maturity and sophistication to cope with the complexity of group therapy. We felt that people had experiences in common and could gain from sharing these. We wanted the group to be a place where people could feel they would have an effect.

SUMMARY OF THE GROUP

The group ran from November 1993 to June 1995 and was held once a week, for a period of one and a quarter hours. It was confidential, but there was an agreement that key carers would be given regular feedback. It was located in an Adult Education Centre, which had formerly been part of the primary school still occupying the floor below. A variety of art materials was available and people were free to use them as they wished. Though membership started at seven people, it dwindled to three after nine months, and though three new members were introduced, mysterious absences and departures were a pattern throughout.

The group was full and complex, with members sharing their experiences of loss and achievement, of living with handicap, of being bullied, and of the struggle to gain some control over their own lives. A very noticeable feature of the group was the energy that was put into a series of long-running disputes which underlay all other aspects of the work.

In contrast to the intense scrutiny to which we subjected all other group processes, we allowed our own relationship as co-therapists to evolve without a great deal of discussion. The group was not an easy one to be part of and encouragement and reassurance became our priority in our discussions of each other's work. Looking back, having written this chapter, we wonder if a more questioning stance might have led us to a greater understanding of the counter-transference issues, described with hindsight in our commentaries.

APPROACH TO WRITING THE CHAPTER

In writing the chapter we wanted to include feedback given by the group members, to consider how their memories of the group corresponded to or differed from those of the therapists, and to see if the responses would shed any light on some of the things still puzzling us about the group.

We knew that the group members would all need some degree of support in making their contribution, and decided to use interviews, conducted by a non-therapist member of the Arts Therapies Department. She wrote to group members to ask their consent to be interviewed, and also contacted support staff to explain the project so that they could help clients understand the implications of what we were asking. Of the ten who were involved in the group, it was only possible to approach six to be interviewed, and, of these, five agreed. A list of questions was compiled, though in practice these were used as a framework for the interviews, and were not strictly adhered to. Photographs of the building, rooms used and both therapists were used as reminders in the interviews. The therapists were interviewed using the same approach.

We had been afraid that either no-one would want to be involved in the interviews, or that no-one would be able to remember the group. It was a lesson to us that most people were keen to be heard, and that their memories were rich and vivid, with a wealth of feeling. For this chapter it has been necessary to condense the interviews, whilst trying to maintain the individuals' voices and viewpoints. It was decided to jettison the impossibly long therapists' interviews altogether, and to incorporate some of what was covered into our commentaries.

THE ARGUMENT

The argument previously mentioned was an aspect of the group that was vividly remembered in everybody's interviews and it was this that we chose as a focus for the chapter.

The therapists describe their perceptions of what it was about in their commentaries, but it may be useful to define more clearly now what we mean by what we call the 'argument'. Given that the group was for people who were experiencing difficulties in getting on with others, the therapists were obviously prepared for conflicts. However, there was something in the persistent, repetitive nature of this particular one that made it seem it was fulfilling a particular function, and almost seem to have a life of its own.

It was primarily between two prominent members of the group, a man and a woman, and first arose when male/female relationships were discussed. It was not confined to any specific issues however, but rather took the form of a constant bickering with and attacking each other. Other members took various roles, being drawn in to take sides, or to act as mediators and peacemakers. It was mainly expressed verbally, and through actions. Only occasionally did it seem to come out in the art work, and then partly in response to therapists' suggestion that using the materials might help.

In what follows we first present the abridged interviews (I. is the interviewer) then the therapists' commentaries, in which we describe how we have tried to make sense of the group and particularly the argument, now, in the light of the interviews. We have not tried to make the individual voices conform to an overall theoretical perspective, and the chapter reflects a process of exploration and discovery rather than a linear story of past thoughts and events.

INTERVIEW WITH GARY

Gary was in his mid-thirties. He lived on his own and received some support from Social Services. He was in regular contact with his family who lived in the same area. He referred himself to the group, as he found it difficult to get on with others. He came for the duration of the group, with some prolonged absences. He made his own way there. He was working part-time when he joined the group, but became unemployed after a few months. (See Figure 3.1)

G. I can remember quite a lot about art therapy group, in the sense it started November 1993. It made a lot of stops and starts. It finished, I think, in June 1995, exactly one year ago. You go there and you draw pictures with pencils and crayons and paintings also. You paint pictures with paint brushes and paint, while you're talking and explaining what's happened in the last week or so. Well, the main object of the exercise of going to these classes is so that it teaches you the art of painting and decorating and drawing you see.

I. Can you remember anything about the building?
[Shows pictures of rooms]

G. Oh yes. I remember that room when we first started out, then we moved to another room because of the noise of children at break-time, making so much noise. And this is the room we had when we changed around. Wooden chairs converted from plastic chairs, plastic tables, so it was splinter chairs.

I. What do you think other people think about the group?

G. The consistent ones who stayed on for the whole length of time, I think enjoyed it, but after a while it fizzled out and so they decided to pack it in because otherwise it just gets boring and tedious if it carries on. There has to be a time where something has to stop, where all good things have to come to an end.

I. What were Hilary and Penny like?

G. Well, I mean they were quite pleasant and polite, they were never rude and ignorant and, er, they did try to be reasonable, but they did have difficulties and problems sometimes handling some of the people who joined the group who were really disruptive and really I mean bad-tempered all the time.

I. So did they handle that as well as they could?

G. Yes, they did. Wasn't easy for them, but I mean . . . They just could not be aggressive and they just couldn't shout and lose their temper. They might have lost their job if they hadn't [sic], that was the trouble.

I. If they're getting worked up and everybody else is getting worked up . . .

G. You end up with a volcanic eruption and lava spilling everywhere, don't you? With a volcano in America or Tenerife as an example, around the world, exactly.

THIS IS A OF CLAPHAM JUNCTION
VERY SCRUFFY STATION: 2400 TRAINS IN 24
PICTURE OF hours

PASSENGERS: S.R. E.M.U.

THIRD RAIL D.C.A.V.

CLASS 7+2 LOCO. PLATFORM &
PASSENGERS: EMU. COACHES
STOCK.

LOCO.

PLATFORM & BUILDING.

Figure 3.1 Gary: Clapham Junction

I. What kind of things did you talk about?

G. Well, mainly we talk about, well, the last week or two weeks and what have you. What we've been getting up to, what we've been doing with ourselves, and other people always were talking about what was on television all the time.

I. Soaps maybe?

G. Yes. Typical *Sun* readers and *Star* readers and *Sport* readers, that are only interested in things that are drivel aren't they? . . . Things that are unimportant and rubbish, aren't they? . . . Everyday life, which we just don't want to know, do we?

I. Did you talk about other things like, erm, communication?

G. Well, the art of communication is expressing and explaining yourself in a certain and what d'you call – spontaneous way. Literally speaking then, while you're doing that you have to draw and paint at the same time to take your mind off things and to teach you how to draw at the same time as talk, which is not easy . . . that's something you have to do I suppose. That's the whole purpose and reason of the art therapy practice.

I. Did you talk at all about ways of coping with problems?

G. Yes we did, did that all the time.

I. Did you find that helpful?

G. It was indeed, yes. Except some of them are quite difficult, you see Sandie, so the problem is, I mean, it's just about how to win the battle and tilt the situation off into your favour. That is the problem, that was the frustrational side of it I found.

I. What did you think about your paintings? Did you think they were good or . . . ?

G. Well they were not 10 out of 10, I wouldn't say they were that spectacular but, er, most of them . . . I didn't do any paintings, mine were more drawings, but I would give them more than 5 out of 10, but not 10.

I. What did others think about their own drawings? Did they say?

G. They didn't, but I'm sure they were of the opinion that they did their paintings to the best of their ability and agility. That's all I've got to say about it for myself.

I. Do you think anyone found the group helpful?

G. The people who stayed on like me, the whole length of time did. And a few other people did too.

I. When new people joined the group, did it improve the group?

G. Well, it improved to start with and than after a while, something goes wrong and then some people get a bit intimidated and antagonized and er – the wrong way you know, by being obsessed by the whole thing, so they just pack it in and cut it out like that.

I. But there were a few people who stayed all the way through. Did you become close?

G. To what?

I.   To each other.

G.   No. No, that wasn't going to happen. Didn't expect it to and besides I didn't want it to. I would forgive and forget everyone else what they did, but this one person I wouldn't, that was Susan. She was a disgrace.

I.   So was it something you discussed?

G.   As this was an art therapy group and the information is confidential and private it's best if you don't, I felt, for safety reasons.

I.   On the whole, did you find anything about the group unhelpful?

G.   Well, a few disappointments and regrets I have about the group.

I.   Do you want to talk about these?

G.   Yes. I think I should because Penny Hallas and Hilary Lomas, I know they work at the hospital but I didn't get a chance to ask them one question. I didn't have time. I didn't ask them, I mean, where they were born.

I.   Where they were born?

G.   That – that was the problem. I never really got a chance to have my say in that matter or put myself forward, my best foot, forward, the right foot, because I just felt I didn't get a chance.

I.   In what ways would you say that going to the group helped you? Just a couple of points.

G.   I suppose, point number 1. It helped me meet new people who I hadn't met before who I didn't know anything about or because I hadn't met them, that's point number 1. And point number 2, I mean the difficulties when you do meet these people you find they have irritating faults and habits and problems and the group becomes very stormy and unpleasant, which isn't very nice is it, to say the very least about it.

I.   Anything else that should be said about the group?

G.   Finding different ways and means of – I suppose of allowing more time. Instead of starting at 10 until 11.30, try and make it a little bit longer, so that people can have their say, and also there was a bit of difficulty with the group because we couldn't have a – like – take it in turns, and some people, I mean, wouldn't say a word for an hour and a half, I found a bit strange and odd, and other people would just go on and on, hogging the conversation and, er, being a bit rude and ignorant and disruptive. So I felt we should have a quick programme, 5 or 10 minutes for someone to speak then once the time is up you stop speaking and come back and wait your turn, say half an hour later – so that's the rules that should be applied to the group. Everybody should have their fair say, every 10 minutes maximum or 5 minimum so that's another rule we need to query, check up you see!

INTERVIEW WITH MIKE

Mike was in his late thirties. He was living in a house with two other people and support staff. He had previously attended the local day centre, but was now involved in a variety of social and educational activities in the community. He made his own way to the group, which he joined in its ninth month. He subsequently had to leave when he was admitted to hospital on section. He was pleased to be able to return for the last session. (See Figure 3.2.)

I.   Do you remember anything about the group?

M.   Well, I really tried it. Susan was getting on my nerves. I mean, telling me to be quiet about Mr J all the time, but I never keep on about him. And that's why I was upset about it: so that's why I never enjoyed it.

I.   Do you remember what you did in the group?

M.   We had a chat, and drawing.

I.   Is there anything else you'd like to tell me about the group?

M.   I left the hospital. I said goodbye to them. I said goodbye to Hilary and Penny and all the group. I said thank you very much for having me to the both of them, and then that's it. And if I see you again, please give me [a ring in the meantime].

I.   What do you think other people thought about the group?

M.   Well, I spoke to a tutor, and he thought it would be a good idea to have a coffee break, about 11 o'clock. It's a good idea. You need a coffee break.

I.   Did the others say anything else about what they thought about the group?

M.   Well, I think the group was very nice.

I.   Was it noisy in this room? [Showing photos]

M.   It was, yeah. Noisy, it is. It's Susan. Susan, because she's noisy all the time. I said to her, I said, 'Susan, can you keep your voice down please, and never mind about Mr J all the time.' I said, 'Think about other people.' I told Hilary and Penny, I think that Susan's being noisy and I think . . . I said Susan's being noisy, and, well, they told her twice to keep her voice down, but it never worked out.

I.   What else can you tell me about Penny and Hilary?

M.   Well, I told what's his name, Gary. Gary told me I think Susan is very noisy. And she is very noisy. So I said, 'What do you think, Gary?'. 'I think Susan should keep her voice down' I said, 'Yes, keep her voice down.'

S.   Is there anything else you can remember about Hilary and Penny? Were they good at controlling the group?

M.   Well, them two, Hilary and Penny, I think they were good teachers.

I.   What did you think of your drawing and painting?

M.   I think I done it great, yes.

I.   What did other people think about your drawing and painting?

M.   Well, they think it's great, yes.

I.   How did the group help you? [Pause] Did you find it unhelpful?

M.   No, I really enjoyed it.

I.   It didn't upset or annoy you?

M.   [Becoming angry] Yes, it did. And I don't like Gary keeping on about when we're going to have a cup of coffee, and when are we going to have a break. I said to Gary, 'Why don't you mind your own business? It's nothing to do

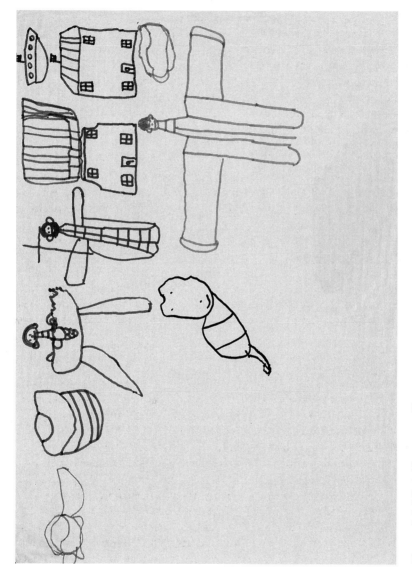

Figure 3.2 Mike: Figures and houses

with you. You leave Hilary and Penny to sort it out for themselves.' I said to him, 'Gary, you're not in charge, mind your own business. You're not in charge. Them two is in charge!' What I told him. And she said she's OK. She's OK. And Susan's annoyed with Gary because Gary's being cheeky to Susan. And that's why, if you have an argument . . . I know, I've done it before. No, Susan's done it before, in the day centre, on about Mr J all the time. I said [I don't want] 'any discussion, Susan. You go straight out. Straight out from the day centre.'

I. Did she leave the group too?

M. She should have done. And them two. I told them two, 'Why not, if Susan has a bawl out? With you, with me, or Gary, send her back out until she calms down and says sorry to everybody.'

I. Last question . . . If you think back, is there anything, apart from Susan, that stands out in your mind?

M. I talked about my feelings, and where I lived as well. Where I lived, what I was doing, and that's it. And my drawing as well, but I don't like painting. I don't mind drawing. I really enjoyed it. I said goodbye to them, because I don't see them anymore now. So if I ever see them, for coffee or tea or whatever.

INTERVIEW WITH SUSAN

Susan was in her mid-forties at the time of the group. She lived with her family, and attended the local day centre. She made her own way to the centre, but came by car to the group, together with Anne. She attended regularly throughout the duration of the group. (See Figure 3.3)

I. So can you remember anything about the group?

S. Um – there was a boy there, I never like him, and Penny knew that I didn't like him. He was using awful bad language at me, you know telling me to . . . and he laughs in my face, that's what I never liked. And I told Penny that.

I. Is there anything else you can remember?

S. Oh. We used to talk, you know, and it was private, and she said don't . . . . But every time I used to say something, he used to butt in, and one day I went and said to Penny, 'I've got to walk out or he's going to say something to me.' He didn't come in one day and it was marvellous, it was peaceful.

I. What other kind of things did you do in the group?

S. They used to do painting. We had pens and paints, you know. They done everything, you know. I did one of them and it was all right, but I can't do anything. I can't draw. I'm so dopey I can't do anything. I wash up, but I can't do drawing.

I. Do you remember anything about the building? [Shows photos]

S. It was right upstairs and I . . . . Oh, I said to Penny, 'I can't walk up all them stairs.' I said to her, I said, 'I wish I had a . . . lift' and I annoyed, I, er – Oh,

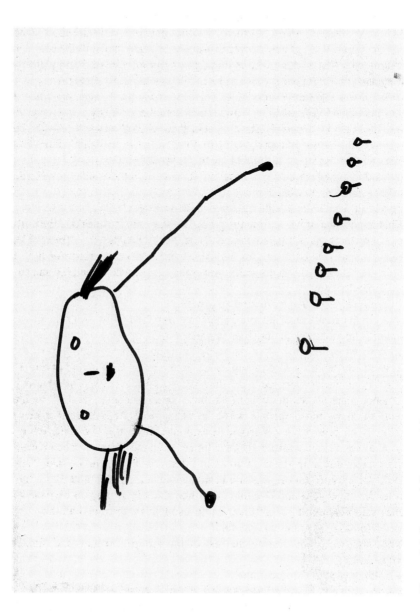

Figure 3.3 Susan: A figure and flowers

I remember that [room], I said to Penny, 'Oh, we're in a school now are we!' Oh and the walls – was really dirty. And I didn't like the chairs, they was too slippery.

I. So how many were there in the group? Can you remember?

S. Me, Anne, Angela, Mike and there was that boy you've heard about, who used to swear. We had new people in – one walks in and one walks out.

I. Imagine you had a friend who is thinking of going to an art therapy group. They ask you what your group was like. What would you tell them?

S. I think it was OK. It was very nice. The people was really nice, but where I goes now on a Tuesday, they're awful nice, and there's a boy always says to me – he's always laughing and it's better than where I was before – and he says to me, 'I'm not talking to you, I'm not talking to you. What's funny?'

I. What do you think people thought about the group?

S. We said to them why don't we have coffee here?, and they said they can't do it. They can if they wanted to.

I. So you all got on OK together, except for this one guy?

S. What annoys me, if we starting the group, he walks in. If I speaking, he butts in. Penny says, 'Don't be so damned rude, she's speaking' . . . '[h]er, [h]er there,' – that's what he said to me. Anne didn't take any notice of him. I remember walking down the stairs with Anne, and he said something and she just looked at him.

I. Did you feel frustrated by him butting in?

S. I did. I had to walk out. She told me to walk out, Penny.

I. So what did you think about Hilary and Penny?

S. Oh, lovely.

I. So what kind of things did you talk about in the group? What kind of topics?

S. Why do people start on you? And they just – you know . . . I – you know if somebody starts, then you want to know. I said to Penny, I said, 'Why are people making fun of people who's handicapped?' And she said 'I don't know.' And people . . . and people, if I go into, down here there's five boys from down the bottom and they say, oh this . . . to me, 'You're handicapped' and they're throwing stones at you and I don't, and I . . . and he said 'Why don't you piss off' and all this and I said I'm not having that, and they're not little, they're big . . . and I've told the police about it, so why do we have it? They said why don't you get their names, so I asked them and all they said was 'What do you want to know for?'

I. So do you talk about this to the rest of the group? Do they find similar problems?

S. No. No, they didn't say anything.

I. So, what other things did you talk about?

S. Oh, we was saying about him. I said, 'Why, why is he using bad language all the time, and butting in?' And he says 'She is, she is, she is' and I said, 'Just leave me alone will you.' He threw a pencil at me, and Penny saw him and said, 'Gary, out!' He got his bag and walked out. I said . . . . She said, 'I know you didn't say anything to him.' He threw the . . . right over from the table, he did it purposefully.

I. What did the other people in the group think about the drawing and painting?

S. Well, I think they liked it. When I was speaking to Anne, I said, 'How do you like it?' All she was doing was cats. Drawing cats, and her picture was marvellous. I told Penny mine's hopeless.

I. What did she say?

S. She said, 'It's not.'

I. Did you find the group helpful?

S. I did. They was all kind to you and they listened to you – they wouldn't just ignore you.

I. Did it help in any other way?

S. Making me calmer – to speak about it.

I. Did other people tell you whether they found it helpful?

S. No.

I. In what ways did you find the group unhelpful?

S. I used to like it.

INTERVIEW WITH ANNE

Anne was in her early thirties. She lived at home with her family, and attended the local day centre. She also spent one day a week working in a nursery, where a member of her family was employed. She came to the group by car with Susan, and attended regularly throughout. (See Figure 3.4.)

I. Do you remember anything about the group that you attended?

A. Yeah, I remember them.

I. And do you remember where it was, that you had to go?

A. Yeah, some old school, and up those steps!!

I. Is there anything else you remember about being in those rooms?

A. Emm . . . I remember there used to be paper on the tables. They used to put the two tables together, and all the chairs around like that one. Emm . . .

I. So do you remember anybody else who used to be in the group?

A. Susan, myself, emm . . . Gary, David, John . . . and Liz, I know that. But they didn't half get on, they didn't get on with Susan. She used to tell people . . . and be really horrible, and . . . she used to walk out, and then when she come back in she slam the door.

I. Did you get on with other people in the group?

A. Yeah, I used to get on with Liz, for some of the time.

I. So imagine that you had a friend that was interested in going to an art therapy group. What would you tell them?

A. Emm . . . I would say that they do talking, . . . [?] . . . give our names, tell the people who we are, what we do or something. No. Tell the people, the person, the people, our names and tell them where we're from. Then we'd paint and

Figure 3.4 Anne: A cat and the sun

talk. But if there was the people apart from Susan, it was lovely and peaceful. No arguing, no shouting, no swearing.

I.   What did you think about the other members of the group?

A.   They . . . well, this one man, Gary, used to say all this C's, F's and B's languages, but since Susan told him to shh, she used to get up and walk out, and then . . . . She used to upset a lot of people, not funny anymore, ignorant, made me cry.

I.   So what did you think of Hilary and Penny?

A.   They were both nice.

I.   What kind of things did you draw?

A.   Emm . . . I dunno, I could draw some things, not others.

I.   What sort of things did you talk about?

A.   Mmm [long pause] I can't remember.

I.   Did you talk about your drawings?

A.   Yeah, we talk about them, we talk about something else. Talk about our drawings and what they are, and, I can't think what else we did.

I.   Did you talk about friendship at all? Relationships, that sort of thing?

A.   We did talk about that, friendship and the other word. I can't remember what we talked about.

I.   So, did you talk to other people about their drawings and their paintings?

A.   No. We only had to talk about our own paintings. We didn't talk about anyone else's.

I.   Do you think the group helped in any way?

A.   Erm . . . Drawing, meeting other people, meeting friends, the group, friends . . . [?] . . . the people in there, Penny. Hilary. I can't remember now.

I.   Do you think anyone in the group found the group unhelpful?

A.   Yeah.

I.   Did they tell you why?

A.   No, but I could see by their faces.

I.   Is there anything you want to add about the group?

A.   Can't think really.

I.   Did you like the environment? 'Cos you mentioned it was a school and started laughing. Did it put you off, the fact it was a school?

A.   No. It didn't bother me a bit.

I.   Is there anything else you'd like to add?

A.   I thought it was good.

INTERVIEW WITH DAVID

David was in his thirties. He had lived in the local hospital for many years. At the time of joining the group he was planning to move out to a flat of his own. Preparations for this were taking up most of his time, and he spent many of his days going out from the hospital with the people who were supporting his move. He started at the beginning of the group and left after about six months. (See Figure 3.5.)

Figure 3.5 David: A house

I.   Do you remember anything about the group?

D.   Not really. It's a long time since I've been there. I remember doing some drawings, having a go at drawings and that. They said they were good but some of the people down there were making fun of my drawings and that, so I didn't bother any more.

I.   If I showed you some pictures perhaps it might help.

D.   I remember being in this room Yeah, I remember being in there. It was awful cold though. No central heating, none at all. They said the central heating wasn't working.

I.   Did you enjoy the group?

D.   Yeah. I enjoyed it but there was nothing much going on there. There was nothing to interest me.

I.   Imagine that a friend wanted to attend an art therapy group, like you. What would you tell them?

D.   I'd tell them to have a go at it and see what they think of it at the end, and see what happens.

I.   Do you remember the people in the group?

D.   No.

I.   Do you want to remember them?

D.   No.

I.   Would you like to comment about the sort of things they said about your drawings?

D.   They said they were a load of crap, and a stupid way of drawing, and they didn't like the way I'd done it. Some of the residents. So in the end I just give up.

I.   What did Hilary and Penny say?

D.   They said they were quite good. I was doing well, they said, but I didn't know if they were just trying to get me to stay, or something. In the end I just couldn't stay.

I.   What was the reason you went to the group? Why do you think you had to go to the group?

D.   To learn. About drawing.

I.   Do you think there was another reason why you went?

D.   No, it's just I was interested in having a go, see what I'd come out like.

I.   Did you find it easy to talk to other members of the group?

D.   No, I couldn't understand a word they were saying half the time.

I.   Did others enjoy the group?

D.   That I don't know.

I.   So nobody said anything to you about that, and you couldn't tell by their faces?

D.   Yeah, they were smiling, they were happy, you know.

I.   What about the people that ran the group?

D.   They were alright. They took their time. When they see someone having trouble with drawing and that, they just stuck with them and helped them. They helped me a lot.

I. So you spoke to them quite often?

D. Yeah.

I. Thinking back, did you talk about problems within the group, for example if someone was really being noisy, did you talk about why?

D. Well, we just said that the noise should be kept down a bit more, and Penny and Hilary agreed with it, and said they were going to see about it, that's all.

I. Did you talk about problems in communication at all?

D. I did, 'cause I couldn't understand a word they were saying and that, and they were worse off than me and they could hardly talk and that, and I couldn't understand a word they were saying. But Hilary said just go and listen, so I went and listened. Some of the words they said were interesting and I could understand, but when we got about their families and that they just got annoyed and upset.

I. Did you have to talk about yourself?

D. Yeah, I told them all about myself. About my family and that. Where I used to live and that. How I had a nervous breakdown and went to the hospital.

I. Did you talk about relationships at all? Making friends with people?

D. No.

I. Can you remember what you drew?

D. Houses, countryside, animals, people walking.

I. Can you think of reasons why you drew houses?

D. 'Cause I thought about living in a house or flat somewhere.

I. What about when you drew people? Were they people you knew?

D. People I used to be friends with, and people to help me around here, which they are doing.

I. Do you think anyone in the group found it helpful?

D. I found it helpful. If you had problems you could talk to Hilary or Penny, and I found it really helpful.

I. Was there any other way you found it helpful?

D. I just felt calmer and that, and more relaxing.

I. Can you think of anything that was unhelpful about it?

D. Just the noise and some of the screaming and that. It used to put me off.

I. Did it make you angry?

D. It didn't make me angry, but . . . your coffee's going cold. It's Tesco decaffeinated, I use decaffeinated coffee because of my tablets.

I. Is there anything else you would like to say about the group being helpful or unhelpful?

D. I think if they keep the group on it'd be more helpful for disabled people and people coming out of school and that. In the night-time or daytime for people like that, to help them get better drawers. I think maybe one day someone in the group will be a proper artist and that, and draw something good, and do well for himself or herself.

I. Thinking back, is there anything that stands out in your memory?

D. There was a young girl who could hardly walk, and people helped her upstairs. And she used to sing all the old war songs. Every time she drew, she drew something about the songs that she sang, and they were really lovely drawings. I liked her singing. She was really good. I do it now at the Karaoke, but it took me two and a half years to do it. It's good fun.

I.   Is there anything else you want to say?

D.   I just think the group was good. Pity I didn't stick it a bit more, but it just got too much for me, 'cause I was having problems then. It got too much for me and I just cracked up. So the hospital stopped me going because they'd seen something was wrong. They knew I was going to have a nervous breakdown or something again. So they stopped me going.

I.   If the group was running again, can you think of any ways they might improve it?

D.   They could try and keep the noise down, and play music for people to listen to. It would help them do their drawings better. I thought you wanted to know a bit about the community. It's going really well out here!

THERAPISTS' COMMENTARY: PENNY

Reading the interviews I was struck by how vividly they brought back the issues and dilemmas that were experienced in the group. I found them fascinating but also experienced a familiar sense of weariness and powerlessness.

I remembered how many ideas and theories the therapists had about the group, and the argument, and how difficult it was for us to find an approach that seemed helpful, that we felt would make any sort of difference. I now wonder if there might have been ways of approaching in a more direct way some of the most painful issues which it had seemed impossible to touch on at the time.

There was something about the group that made such directness difficult, and I think this may tie in with the most powerful feelings I experienced on reading the interviews. These were evoked by the references to the long-running argument, which I remembered as being more than the usual expressions of anger, or strong feelings; it felt destructive, punishing and relentless. Actual physical violence was held in check, but was threatened. All group members, in different ways, perhaps by crying, threatening to leave, actually leaving the room or even the group, showed that they found the intensity of the arguments hard to bear. My own feelings were those of the powerlessness and weariness already referred to, and these feelings held in them elements of anger, disappointment and frustration.

How do I make sense of these responses to the interviews and of my memories of the group, especially of the argument?

The interview format reminds me of patterns of exchange within the group. Although there were times when people responded to one another, frequently they didn't so much respond as seize opportunities to speak, often at the expense of others. Group members seemed to feel that others' contributions were irrelevant to them, were a distraction from what they wanted, or were even a personal insult. This happened even when they were apparently agreeing with each other. The exchanges frequently took the form of a series of monologues, with those not speaking waiting with barely concealed impatience for their chance.

At the time of the group the therapists had noticed that the members found difference impossible to tolerate, and had kept in mind Winnicotian and Kleinian ideas about separation, individuation and splitting (Klein 1957; Winnicott 1971). All members in the group were struggling in their lives with issues of lack of control and autonomy, and of identity. How could a need to belong, to be safe, to be accepted and loved, be reconciled with a simultaneous need to make it quite clear that they were a person in their own right, apart from all others? Complicating this was the need to disassociate from others in the group who reflected too clearly any sense of being different, or not good enough. Did the argument provide a way of reconciling contradictory needs?

Agazarian and Peters suggest that monopolising/being monopolised may be 'a group manifestation of individual early symbiotic refusal to discriminate differences, and may be in the service of the implicit individual goal of group fusion' (Agazarian and Peters 1981: 109). In this case, was the argument one of the ways the group tried to fuse whilst ostensibly maintaining differences?

Agazarian and Peters also refer to early phases of groups being 'flight' from the work of the group, to 'fight' within the group; these then form a basis for a challenge to the authority of the group leaders (1981). This group seemed to leap straight into the 'fight' stage, but with the argument also enabling a flight from, or denial of, the problems group members were experiencing. It provided members with a clearly defined, recognisable structure for escape.

What of the role of the therapists in this? An image I often associated with the group was of a nest of fledglings, all of whom needed desperately to get enough from the parents, even if the others died. I often found the group a struggle, and felt I could not do enough to help. Both therapists left sessions feeling starved. I think that in a way the image reflected group members' dream of getting rid of the others, and having a good group, and the therapists, to themselves. For example, the interviews convey a strong sense that if only other people would change then everything would be all right. It is also evident that people would have liked more, or different things from the therapists. Susan, Mike, Gary and David all have ideas about how they might have liked the therapists to act, particularly with regard to the argument.

I think the therapists had hoped the group would be a space for the members to be and to become themselves. Taking on responsibility can be a difficult and frightening thing to do, so responsibility and authority were often surrendered to the therapists, maintaining the infantilised state of group members. At the same time, the therapists were silenced and disempowered by the argument, which seemed to take control away from everyone alike.

There may have been another way that the effect the argument had on the therapists served to protect against the difficulty of the work the group was gathered together to do. The sessions were always very full and I remember experiencing a pressure upon me to think quickly, to understand and respond. It was hard to find a space for what Patrick Casement refers to as the 'internal supervisor' (1985). I felt stupid, but failed to connect this feeling, to find a place for it within the dynamics of the group. At the time, the therapists thought that the argument was a form of acting out – a defence against unbearable feelings – and made many attempts to reflect this back to the group, without it making any difference. Now, rereading the interviews, and re-experiencing my feelings of stupidity, I wonder if it is possible that the argument was there to make sure the therapists knew what it felt like to be silenced and disempowered. Perhaps I was colluding with the group's need to deny feelings of inadequacy, and perhaps if it had been possible for me to say how ineffectual I felt, it would have enabled these feelings to be acknowledged by the group, rather than being expressed in envious attacks, scapegoating others and the art media, a desperate jockeying for status, or a great smoke-screen of argument.

Feelings of stupidity are obviously related to the issue of learning difficulties itself, and this sort of dynamic may have been part of why this issue was so difficult to approach directly. That the group was only for people with learning difficulties was always made clear, and I'm quite sure was apparent to all the members, some of whom referred themselves. Topics such as physical disabilities, medication, facilities and activities exclusively for people with learning difficulties were talked about, but explicit reference to learning difficulties was rigorously avoided. At the time, I thought that people would talk about the issue in whatever way they felt strong enough to bear, and that for the therapists to do otherwise would be punitive, almost violent. Reading the interviews, I wonder if we were being over-protective, even in some way maintaining a sense of the facts being unspeakable, or shameful? By not overtly addressing the issue, were we closing the door on the chance for the group to feel we could be strong enough to bear their direct anger? I think of some of Valerie Sinason's courageous interpretations, how they were met with relief (Sinason 1992) and wish I'd found a way of being bolder.

Group members were, however, able to share much of the pain of their experiences with other people. The accounts of rejection and hatred they had suffered, the guilt, the powerlessness, and the constant struggle to hold onto any 'good' feelings were intensely moving. Casement points out that it is not necessarily therapeutic for therapists to try to provide what Alexander describes as 'the corrective emotional experience' (Casement 1985). We certainly tried to provide a counter-culture to the controlling, authoritative attitudes they had so often experienced. However, it may be that through our own reluctance to be identified with rejecting families or controlling staff, we were thwarting the opportunities the group needed to explore unresolved feelings about them. Another possibility is that in avoiding behaviours we felt had been destructive, we may not have recognised prompts from the group to act in ways that they would actually have found helpful.

Casement refers to the necessity of the therapist differentiating between wants and needs of the client (Casement 1985). The interviews suggest to me that all members wanted something special for themselves from the therapists. Mike and Gary both make it clear they would have liked a more personal relationship, and all interviewees show how they wished that the therapists had agreed with them, and acted on their behalf, as individuals, rather than on behalf of the group. Yet on the rare occasions when members somehow did have their fantasies fulfilled (for example, one week when there were only women) they realised their needs were not actually met. It seems to me that the argument played its part in keeping such insights at bay. It also seems an expression of members' desire that we act, protect, give a familiar, or idealised, kind of support, no matter how untherapeutic, whilst testing to the limits our ability to meet a simultaneous need, consciously and unconsciously expressed, that we resist this desire.

THERAPISTS' COMMENTARY: HILARY

I listened to the interviews with a wish to hear that the group had been helpful and wanting an answer to the unsettling question, could an art therapy group run with the best of intentions be unhelpful or even damaging to the participants? My first reaction was one of disappointment. The conflict was still so vivid in people's minds. Time had not resolved the feelings or altered the experience. I was surprised by my own strong reactions of grief and uselessness at this imperfect group. A second hearing revealed a more balanced view. Most people reported feeling positive about the experience and would recommend the group to their friends. Two people said they felt calmer as a result. Others felt proud of their art works. Above all, the liveliness of the group and the extent of people's involvement in the experience is borne out in their accounts.

Also in my mind had been questions about practice. Our sound theoretical understandings had not seemed to help us very much when faced with the experiences of those attending the group, and with our own experiences of it. Interpretations and ideas put to the group often fell flat and did not have the effects we had expected. Do we need to modify our approach when working with people with learning difficulties? When considering this I have found research carried out by psychotherapists at the Tavistock Clinic London helpful, in questioning the relationship of the disability to the person. Much of their work has explored ideas about how disability affects the development of the personality, and how the person copes with or uses his or her disability, as well as its social implications. I have found the distinction made by Stokes (1987) between cognitive intelligence and emotional intelligence particularly pertinent when thinking about the group here described. He notes that people who score low on cognitive intelligence tests can display considerable emotional intelligence and have the ability to recognise and describe feelings in a way that is indistinguishable from those without learning disabilities. Members of the art therapy group displayed a high level of sophistication and individuals showed themselves to be sensitive to non-verbal expressions of feeling, as well as able to convey complex emotions through straightforward verbal statements.

To return to consideration of participants' views, alongside the positive comments there were many complaints about the unsatisfactory physical environment, about the stairs, the dirty walls and the lack of coffee. Everyone mentioned being very upset by the noise and shouting, one person to the point of tears. Most group members picked out Susan as causing the difficulties in the group. The ongoing argument took place in the main between her and each of the three men in the group. In my memory Susan had been the most able to express her anger. At times I found her difficult and unreasonable, but I also felt she contributed honesty and energy to the group. In my attempts to be even-handed and understanding was I being too dismissive of others' distress at these expressions of anger and verbal aggression? We understood the role Susan was taking as a function of the group dynamics. At times we felt she was the scapegoat, holding the unreasonable and angry projections of others. We wondered if she enabled them to play out their everyday roles to the full, and to communicate actively their own difficulties in relating. We shared our observations, but we found that interpretations of the group dynamics usually produced little response. After a time we modified our approach to one of encouraging individuals to gain insight into the immediate origins of their anger. This was a little more helpful. The questions of how to understand and manage the argument and each individual's contribution to it preoccupied us throughout the course of the group. However, looking back I think we over-estimated our influence. It was group members who were often responsible not only for maintaining the argument, but also for containing and sometimes stopping it.

Two questions remain for me. First, why did people continue to attend such a stormy group? Second, why should this group engender such powerful feelings of despair in me, alongside the professional satisfaction and interest I gained from running it? Rereading our working notes and listening to the interviews provides some answers to the first question. People valued getting things off their chests. They acknowledged the importance of being able to express how they felt. It also seems that people gained far more from their individual expressions in their art work than we had appreciated.

Looking back, I expected the art work to be used in a particular way. This may not have matched the ideas of group members. I hoped the pictures could become more appropriate containers for the scapegoat transference, and thus diminish the scapegoating of individuals in the group. I hoped that the art could express the unbearable feelings of vulnerability and so become 'empowered' and the client could begin the process of acknowledgement and introjection of these feelings as described by Joy Shaverein (1992). I think it was the activity itself that became the scapegoat. Some group members felt that drawing would display their disability. This had the effect of limiting the amount of work produced. Individuals who dared to put pen to paper risked having their efforts sneered at by other group members. Thus the work was often done quietly without comment and placed in the art folder without being shown.

The experience of learning difficulty was a central theme in the group, although I cannot remember the terms 'mental handicap' or 'learning difficulties' being used by group members at the time. In recent years much has been written about the effects of society's attitudes to handicap on the person with learning difficulties' internalised view of themselves. Stokes (1987) writes that handicapped individuals are inevitably scapegoated, holding the handicapped and damaged aspects of their families and of society at large. Valerie Sinason vividly describes how an internal image of imperfection and damage is developed in the child with learning difficulties. 'It seems that if the first mirror of the mother's eye registers distaste, as Hera's did, and as most parents do when initially faced with the shock of a handicapped child, a sense of not being the wanted beautiful healthy child builds up' (Sinason 1988:96). A picture drawn by Anne (Figure 3.6) which she described as a smiling golliwog conveyed this sense for me. She drew the picture at a key point in the life of the group. We had been meeting for about nine months, the membership had dwindled to three and we were introducing new people to the group the following week. The session had started uncomfortably with a dispute between Susan and Gary flaring up almost immediately. Penny and I attempted to focus on feelings about the changes in the group. Susan said it was nothing to do with her, voicing a feeling that the group had of a lack of power and control. Gary felt the newcomers could be potential allies. Anne introduced her picture saying 'Welcome to our group.'. Talk of the picture united the group in lively discussion. The figure embodied the hopes and fears the three had concerning new members, what they would be like and what they would think of the group. I was interested that Anne described her man as a golliwog. The figure was obviously white and bore little resemblance to a golliwog as far as I could see, except for the black hair sticking out of the top of the head or hat. It was not at all clear whether Anne or any of the group members were aware of the racist implications of the term used. However, group members had alluded to black people in previous meetings, when discussing their fears of the 'otherness' of people who would be joining the group. All the current participants were white, including the therapists. In thinking about the possible meanings of the picture I am assuming that the group members carried an awareness at some level of devaluing images and terms, in common with the culture of which they are a part. The group described the 'golliwog' as funny and dumb, and as being made up of bits and pieces of different clothes. He was taken up as the group's mascot, and both liked and despised. People felt that the picture could be shown to prospective members to show them what the group was like. I think it is interesting that they used the word golliwog, a term that has both racially abusive and childlike connotations, when thinking about a figure that conveyed something of how those in the group saw themselves. I felt this illustrated the way individuals saw themselves as different and devalued members of society. Perhaps the conflicts in the group served as a distraction from such painful realities.

I ask myself why the meeting described above was one of the few times when there was a feeling of cohesion in the group. Why did people so often deny their common experience, rather than find strength in this? Whilst running the group,

Figure 3.6 Anne: A figure

I remember having a fantasy I hardly dared share, that the group was staying together for similar reasons to those for which a couple might remain in an abusive and damaging relationship. Thinking back on this odd and rather extreme image, I began to speculate about its possible counter-transference meanings. Valerie Sinason (1992) writes of the historical association of the learning-disabled with 'bad sexuality' and society's fears of damaged offspring. She suggests that the learning-disabled carry social and cultural fantasies about bad sexuality. She notes that these fantasies are also carried by those with learning disabilities, who may see themselves as a product of bad sexual activity between their parents.

The relationships between the men and the women in the group were not easy. There was a tendency for the group to split along male/female lines. The reasons why male/female relationships were so hard were not that clear. Difficult experiences concerning the relationships between men and women were sometimes described. If any member of the group had suffered sexual abuse we did not hear of it. At the time we speculated about the lack of opportunities for people with learning difficulties to develop the range of adult relationships with members of the opposite sex. Perhaps there was also an unconscious fear that any pairing in the group could only lead to damage. Could my image of the abusive partnership have been a reflection of this fear? Such fears could partially account for the group's tendency to pull apart, rather than come together. Valerie Sinason (1992) discusses the development of sexuality in people with learning disabilities. She points to the fact that children may have to be helped to wash and toilet themselves for longer than would be the case with their non-handicapped peers. Thus it may be difficult, for example, for the boy who is being washed by his mother in later childhood to develop an idea of body privacy. The lack of such a concept could lead to difficulties when trying to establish relationships in later life. A difficulty in maintaining appropriate boundaries did seem to be an issue in the group. From time to time the women would complain of unwanted touching, while the men would feel rejected and unlovable. The hopes of group members for girlfriends and boyfriends, both within and outside the group, were usually unfulfilled and often unrealistic. In the group there were further practical difficulties with boundaries in that the community of people with learning difficulties is small and group members knew each other in different contexts. Confidentiality was difficult to keep.

I return to my second question regarding my own feelings of uselessness when faced with descriptions of the group. Thinking about this with the theme of handicap in mind, I wonder if we were in part holding the uselessness for the group. We were certainly rendered helpless by the argument. Shaun Gravestock and Gill McGauley describe a group for adults with learning difficulties in which group members mounted envious attacks on those considered 'normal'. They write of the group, 'We felt that their anger at us for giving birth to an imperfect group reflected anger at their parents for giving birth to them, with their imperfections' (Gravestock and McGauley 1994:161). Perhaps we could understand the argument as being an attack on us for running such a disabled group. During the course of the group there was much dissatisfaction expressed about the rooms in which the group took place. Group members were sensitive to the fact that the building was an old school, associating this with being treated like children. With hindsight, perhaps these real concerns could have given us the opportunity to discuss the experience of living with disability with more openness in the group. The birth analogy is interesting. For the first nine months there was persistent uncertainty about its survival. After this point, once the group had been 'born' with the introduction of new members, it became possible to begin the process of accepting it as it was. It is interesting to note that the golliwog image, the drawn symbol of the group, was produced at nine months.

Much of this commentary seems to focus on interpretations we didn't make. It is difficult to let go of the role of useless therapist. Hopefully we can learn from experience. Undoubtedly the next group will bring its own challenges.

ACKNOWLEDGEMENTS

We would like to thank the following people for their help in preparing this chapter: Maggie Higgins, Sandie Taylor, Lyn Davies, and members of the group whom it is not possible to name for issues of confidentiality.

BIBLIOGRAPHY

Agazarian, Y. and Peters, R. (1981) *The Visible and Invisible Group*, London: Routledge and Kegan Paul.

Casement, P. (1985) *On Learning From the Patient*, London: Tavistock Publications.

Gravestock, S. and McGauley, G. (1994) 'Connecting Confusions with Painful Realities: Group Analytic Psychotherapy for Adults with Learning Disabilities', *Pychoanalytic Psychotherapy*, 8(2): 153–67.

Hughes, R. (1989) 'Transitional Phenomena and the Potential Space in Art Therapy with Mentally Handicapped People' paper given at Conference 'Art Therapy for People with Severe to Marginal Learning Difficulties' held 29 November 1989 at Leicester Frith Hospital, Groby Road, Leicester. (Not published.)

Klein, M. (1957) *Envy and Gratitude*, London: Tavistock.

Shaverien, J. (1992) *The Revealing Image*, London: Routledge.

Sinason, V. (1988) 'Richard III, Hephaestus and Echo: Sexuality and Mental/Multiple Handicap', *Journal of Child Psychotherapy*, 14(2): 93–105.

Sinason, V. (1992) *Mental Handicap and the Human Condition. New Approaches from the Tavistock*, London: Free Association Books.

Stokes, J. (1987) 'Insights from Psychotherapy', paper presented at International Symposium on Mental Handicap, Royal Society of Medicine, 25th February 1987.

Strand, S. (1990) 'Counteracting Isolation: Group Art Therapy for People with Learning Difficulties', *Group Analysis*, 23: 255–63.

Tipple, R. (1993) 'Challenging Assumptions: The Importance of Transference Processes in Work with People with Learning Difficulties', *Inscape*, Summer.

Winnicott, D.W. (1971) *Playing and Reality*, London: Tavistock Publications.

Chapter 4

On the edge

Art therapy for people with learning difficulties and disordered personalities

Simon Willoughby-Booth and Joanna Pearce

Central theme
- A reflection on the experience of working in an art therapy setting with clients who share the following characteristics:
    - Moderate learning difficulties
    - No identified mental health problems
    - Occasional serious anti-social outbursts.

Key points
- Exploration of our experiences as art therapists in the light of existing literature on the subject of borderline personality disorder.
- The employment of case studies to illustrate the progress of art therapy with such people.
- A consideration of the particular value of art therapy for these clients, especially with regard to its propensity for offering a containing physical experience where pre-verbal issues can be explored.

INTRODUCTION

In our work as art therapists in a large hospital for people with learning difficulties we have found a small group amongst our clients, who although all individually very different, have gradually come to display characteristics that have led us to start viewing them as a distinctive group. They do not have a specific mental health diagnosis but their behaviour presents significant problems for those around them and themselves. They have only a moderate degree of learning disability and present most of the time as polite, sociable and often eager to please; however, many of them are detained in hospital under Mental Health or other legislation for a variety of reasons and, on occasion, display seriously anti-social and sometimes criminal patterns of behaviour. One feature which they all have in common is that over time, sometimes for several years, they have maintained relationships with our department that are clearly meaningful to them but which often leave us feeling deeply confused, frustrated and at a loss to define what it is that we are attempting to offer them through the art therapy process.

Gradually we have found points of reference in the literature, albeit about a superficially different diagnostic group, that have rung bells for us, and it has seemed to us that our group displayed behaviours which corresponded with the diagnostic criteria for borderline personality disorder. In this chapter, we intend to follow the directions that have emerged from this, to explore causal factors as well as treatment theories and clinical practice, and to explore the implications this has for the way we approach our work with these clients. We will use case studies to illustrate how the work has developed in different situations and present an argument for developing new ways of working with such perplexing people, highlighting the need for further research and investigation.

DESCRIPTIONS IN THE LITERATURE

The descriptive classification and diagnosis of borderline personality disorder is a problematic field and it has been a reassuring discovery that experienced practitioners should be prepared to admit to feelings of confusion and frustration when faced with the needs of people whose lives are clearly disturbed by patterns of behaviour so unpredictable and unresponsive to conventional treatment approaches. The attempt to derive a coherent view of this group has resulted in an extensive literature, reflecting many different theoretical models from psychoanalytic and psychotherapeutic viewpoints and diverse treatment approaches. The term 'borderline personality disorder' was formally introduced into the system of psychiatric classification in the *Diagnostic and Statistical Manual of Mental Disorders – III* (1980) and was further revised in *DSM-III-Revised* (1987) and *DSM-IV* (1994). The literature of both descriptive and psychoanalytic views of borderline personality disorder is reviewed by Akhtar (1992) and by Berelowitz and Tarnopolsky (1993), who concur that the classification is valid although some questions remain. Akhtar describes the range of presenting behaviours and early psychic development that contribute to the classification and summarises the situation as follows:

> a borderline individual views himself as a victim, is self-righteously indignant and chronically enraged, is intensely involved in idealising and hating others, is superficially adapted to reality though highly impulsive, is transiently zealous about moral and ethical issues, is very romantic and sexually promiscuous, and is recklessly decisive and smugly knowledgeable. However, covertly he feels inherently defective, is frequently suicidal, is incapable of truly depending on others, is impaired in his capacity for aloneness, is unable to experience genuine guilt, is incapable of sustained love, and is vulnerable to magical thinking and psychoticlike episodes.

(Akhtar 1992:359)

Akhtar describes the range of presenting behaviours of the different personality disorder classifications and traces the early personal development that may contribute to each way of being. A new system of classification is postulated that refines and extends the nosology, grouping the disorders into a 'hierarchical scheme of character organisations' of higher, intermediate and lower levels. See Table 4.1.

The prognosis for the individuals we have identified is 'guarded' under this classificatory system; this reflects our experience and also our view that our intervention is not to be seen in isolation but as a component of a whole treatment programme.

We have been able to find few references to working with clients who have personality disorders in the art therapy literature. Hughes (1986), Cole (1986) and Goldsmith (1986) describe work with clients who had learning difficulties, were described as having personality disorders and who presented major challenges to their carers. Henley (1991:69) also describes work with a client who had been diagnosed as having a personality disorder, though the client did not have learning difficulties. Lachman-Chapin (1979) describes Heinz Kohut's view of personality development, its relationship to art-making and creativity and its implications for art therapy. She asserts the particular contribution of the art therapist to work with clients who

> lack a cohesive sense of self because of its failure to develop during the pre-oedipal period. This is typical of a great many psychiatric patients (particularly those classified today as borderline or narcissistic personality disordered rather than neurotic).
>
> (Lachman-Chapin 1979:8)

DIAGNOSTIC CRITERIA

The *DSM-IV* (1994) criteria for borderline personality disorder are as follows:

> A pervasive pattern of instability of interpersonal relationships, self-image, and affects, and marked impulsivity beginning by early adulthood and present in a variety of contexts, as indicated by five (or more) of the following:
>
> (1) Frantic efforts to avoid real or imagined abandonment. *Note*: Do not include suicidal or self-mutilating behaviour covered in Criterion 5.
> (2) A pattern of unstable and intense interpersonal relationships, characterised by alternating between extremes of idealisation and devaluation.
> (3) Identity disturbance: markedly and persistently unstable self-image or sense of self.
> (4) Impulsivity in at least two areas that are potentially self-damaging (for example, spending, sex, substance use, reckless driving, binge eating). *Note*: Do not include suicidal or self-mutilating behaviour covered in Criterion 5.
> (5) Recurrent suicidal behaviour, gestures, or threats, or self-mutilating behaviour.

Table 4.1 A hierarchical scheme of character organisations

	Higher level	Intermediate level	Lower level
Diagnostic categories/ Treatment/Prognosis			
Corresponding diagnostic	Obsessive	Narcissistic	Borderline
	Hysterical	Masochistic (Type II)	Infantile (histrionic)
	Phobic (avoidant)		Paranoid
	Masochistic (Type I)		Hypomanic
			Antisocial
			As-if
			Schizoid
			Schizotypal
Treatment of choice	Psychoanalysis	Psychoanalysis/	Psychoanalytic psychotherapy/
		Psychoanalytic psychotherapy	Supportive psychotherapy/
			Medication
			Other adjunctive measures
Prognosis	Excellent	Good	Guarded

Source: Akhtar, 1992:373

(6) Affective instability due to a marked reactivity of mood (for example, intense episodic dysphoria, irritability or anxiety usually lasting a few hours and only rarely more than a few days).

(7) Chronic feelings of emptiness.

(8) Inappropriate, intense anger or difficulty controlling anger (for example, frequent displays of temper, constant anger, recurrent physical fights).

(9) Transient, stress-related paranoid ideation or severe dissociative symptoms.

(*DSM-IV* 1994:654)

It is apparent that many behaviours of our client group match these criteria and some have in fact been diagnosed as having a personality disorder, though many have no formal diagnosis. We are not pretending to achieve conclusive or differential diagnosis, but to explore the implications that viewing the needs of this discrete group of individuals from a different perspective may have for art therapy practice. There is much discussion among practitioners about the appropriateness of any psychotherapeutic intervention for clients with lower-level personality disorders, for example, borderline, paranoid, anti-social, schizoid; and clearly there are issues of containment with chaotic and dangerous behaviours that pose problems for the therapist and may necessitate changes in approach and role during the course of therapy. This is not unusual in working with clients with learning difficulties where the role of the therapist may have to change within the space of a therapy session.

RECONSIDERING OUR CLIENT GROUP

On the basis of descriptions in the literature, we have been encouraged to review the characteristics displayed by our clients, to establish if there are elements of commonality and categorical links between them. Some of the characteristics of this group appear to closely echo those found in the literature: the formation of a false self is very apparent in the gap between overt and covert presentations; the use of splitting as a defence mechanism; the very clear absence of an integrated identity; the inability to present a clear picture of events; a mismatch between direct and reported feelings and weakness of superego function. We had always been aware of these presentations but had not viewed them as indications of a discrete group, nor had we accounted for the impact on our approach of the knowledge that these clients have limited cognitive development.

How much are the presenting behaviours accepted as the inevitable result of being learning-disabled? Are we falsely making serious assumptions such as equating intellectual impairment with distorted psychic development which inevitably results in dysfunction of personality and behaviour? Are our clients incapable of learning new behaviours because of their lack of understanding and experience? Will they never be able to take responsibility for their actions? Is art therapy offering a space for these individuals to express how they feel and to develop a fuller acknowledgement of themselves and their worth, where they can gain confidence and personal satisfaction? Or, fundamentally, are we saying they are how they are and real personal growth is not an option? Is it possible that we are therefore blinded by received perceptions about our clients, guilty of failing to explore the reasons why they may be behaving the way they do, and failing to create opportunities for significant change within the art therapeutic process?

If it is probable that the seeds of personality disorder are found in failures in the early environment of the infant with normal physical, perceptual and cognitive development, then it is possible that the behaviours we have observed in our client group owe something to similar early developmental experiences; it is more likely that the needs of an infant whose development is erratic and unpredictable may not be fully recognised or met. Akhtar (1992:132) reviews the concept of 'cumulative trauma', that is, where there is no apparent major trauma in early life and yet the environment is constantly failing to meet the needs of the infant. How easy must it be for the best caregiver to get it wrong when there are so many unknowns in the development of a baby with a disability, where physical problems may necessitate hospitalisation, where the physical and the emotional development are unsynchronised and where problems may not be recognised until quite late on. During the crucial separation–individuation stage of the development of object relations, difficulties may well arise for an infant whose development is delayed in ways that are not clearly understood. The increased dependence of the child with a mild degree of learning difficulties seems to present a situation where to get a good-enough balance between dependence and independence is almost impossible.

According to Akhtar's nosology, there is correlation between the levels of personality disorder and heredity and early childhood environmental factors; between the successful attainment of psychological development in terms of preoedipal and oedipal factors, and those derived from latency and adolescence, and psychostructural characteristics. We have begun to feel that we need to explore more fully the failures of development in our clients that may be due to environmental factors in early infancy and childhood, rather than to the inherent impact of their disability, and to review our treatment models accordingly. In order to do this we have reconsidered the presenting behaviours of our defined client group and attempted to link these to the diagnostic criteria of *DSM-IV* (1994). The following short descriptions outline and introduce some of the significant presentations which we have encountered amongst our clients:

1   A man in his mid-thirties, first seen when admitted for a psychiatric report after he carried out an actual physical assault. He is eager to please, polite and apologises for things that are clearly not his fault; he has trouble sequencing events and has an unexpected difficulty with the concept of time, embarking on long and complex tales that are almost impossible to comprehend. He expresses paranoid ideation and conveys his anger with loss of control, terrifying grimaces and gestures. He is obsessed with horror films and, to frighten people, acts out some of the things he has seen on screen. At times

he is very child-like and obedient but describes his frustration and rebellion about his lack of independence.

2   A man in his mid-twenties, very sycophantic and charming but self-infantilising and resorting to teasing and giggling. He is very demanding of attention and manipulates others so that he appears to be in the right. He attempts to make those who work with him feel that they are special to him. He has a good sense of time but sometimes gives very distorted versions of events. He is very seductive and sexually opportunistic and has a history of sexually offending behaviour.

3   A woman in her thirties, who has a child about which she is very ambivalent and who is very demanding of help but is unable to use it. She constantly fails to keep appointments, gets herself into dramatic difficulties and makes impossible demands on the Health and Social Services. She has a history of alcohol abuse and of putting herself at risk sexually. She is very labile in affect and attempts to be emotionally manipulative.

4   A young man who has developed a pattern of withdrawal and refuses to travel except by car. He makes impossibly high demands on his carers and threatens destructive or self-abusive behaviour if thwarted. This is carried out often enough for it to be a serious challenge. His mood changes rapidly and he switches from idealisation of a person or situation, to attempting to destroy or attack it. He complains of boredom while sabotaging every offer of occupation. He presents a recurrent pattern of engineering his own rejection so that people give up on him.

THE CONTRIBUTION OF ART THERAPY

Stokes and Sinason define 'secondary Mental handicap' to indicate the 'emotional sequelae of the primary impairment' (Stokes and Sinason 1992:48) and, if we accept the impact of environmental factors on the already vulnerable development of these clients, we are striving for real reparational work. What are the ideal conditions and how does art therapy help in this process? It is clear that, working as we do currently with these clients, we are unable to form any very clear picture of their early history; they themselves for a variety of reasons cannot relate incidents always clearly or chronologically ordered and many of the relevant facts will never be known. This means that it is only from observing their behaviour that we can surmise the degree to which developmental goals have been attained. Often we can only see in retrospect what our clients have been asking from us.

If the failure of the early caring environment has led to failed object relations formation, then what we are attempting is to provide a holding space with the possibility of regression; where containment is concrete and where pre-verbal work can be achieved. Art therapy is able to provide all this and also the opportunity for safe acting-out, for the experiencing of object survival through the materials and the important use of the made objects at the different stage of the developmental journey. Lachman-Chapin points out that

Art and the art therapist can be used by many patients in finding ways to express *without shame* those grandiose, exhibitionistic wishes which have not been integrated into the personality and sense of self. As artists, art therapists are particularly suited to performing this task because they share, to a greater extent than the average person, their patients' need to exhibit themselves and receive attention, or to meet grandiose expectations of parental figures.

(Lachman-Chapin 1979:8)

Because of the fundamental nature of art-making and its role in symbol formation, it is possible for clients to establish a profound relationship with themselves through the art work, leaving them greater flexibility in the way they choose to use the relationship with the therapist, who as a person is almost bound to be dangerous in some very fundamental way. The versatility of the art-making process is very important in the range of possibilities offered so that 'patients after a long period of messing-around find a way to begin to symbolise and restate something about their past in one art medium or another' (Lachman-Chapin 1979:7). There have been times in working with these clients that one's importance has become that of enabler or witness while the important work is done through the art-making process, and other times when the focus of the work seems to be on the roles that the therapist is being asked to play. The experience of being utilised is another of the distinguishing characteristics of this work, which is reminiscent of Winnicott's comment about adolescence: 'Parents can help only a little; the best they can do is to survive, to survive intact . . . without relinquishment of any important principle' (Winnicott 1971:171).

THE ART THERAPY SETTING

The case material described in this chapter is drawn from our work in a learning disabilities service in a large urban area. Clients are usually seen in one of three situations: an Art Therapy Department in a traditional residential hospital for people with learning difficulties on the outskirts of the city; a small residential centre for people with learning difficulties and challenging behaviours, or a small residential and day hospital unit for people with mild to moderate learning difficulties that provides assessment and treatment for forensic and mental health problems.

The hospital Art Therapy Department has been established for more than twenty-five years and, though the hospital is now closing down, the department is well equipped, has big studios and is a welcoming place in which to work, enabling clients to feel safe and supported. It is integrated into the pattern of life in the hospital and is part of a range of multi-disciplinary services available on the site. Clients have, in some cases, maintained their relationship with the department over many years, so that art therapy plays a very significant role in their lives. The two residential units are part of a new service for people who face problems additional to their learning difficulty. In both, art therapy is an integral part of the treatment programme and each has a well-equipped art room as part of the day hospital service. The art therapists are part of a multi-disciplinary team which includes medical and nursing staff, occupational therapy, communication therapy and clinical psychology. Several clients who were formerly seen in the hospital setting are now seen at one of the new units and we have been able to maintain continuity of treatment.

In each setting, the art therapy room offers a safe, holding environment for our clients which is essential for their successful involvement in art therapy. Clients are referred to art therapy for many overt reasons, including poor socialisation, communication difficulties, mental health or behavioural difficulties or for 'assessment' but amongst this group we have identified a significant number who fit into the group we have identified and meet the diagnostic criteria for personality disorders.

CASE STUDIES

The following case studies reflect some of our experiences with this group of clients and their experiences of art therapy.

Jean

Jean is a 32-year-old woman who is under a guardianship order; she was referred to the Treatment Centre where I (J.P.) work, for a possible depressive state and because she was constantly breaking the terms of her order by returning to her family home. She was then living in a group home where there was a programme of activities and shared domestic responsibilities, a home with a particular ethos. She was seriously self-isolating with disturbed sleep patterns, low motivation and low self-esteem. She presented as extremely confused, unable to maintain a coherent conversation and with appalling short-term memory.

Jean is an only child and went through normal school without apparent problems although she left without qualifications. Her grandmother lived with the family. The first record of illness was at age 18. At this stage she was self-isolating, had lost her job and was being severely infantilised by her mother, being fed and dressed. The family seemed to have a fairly chaotic lifestyle with patterns of heavy drinking but though Jean was discovered to have a mild learning disability, no further action seems to have been taken and she was returned home from hospital. At the age of 28, she referred herself to her GP with a 'secret'; she had severe weight loss and the family situation was found to have deteriorated considerably. She was placed under a guardianship order to ensure that she moved out of the family home.

During her art therapy assessment she painted with enthusiasm, making swirling lines and filling in the areas between: this pattern of working seemed very fixed and seemed to be a kind of self-maintenance. She would talk with extreme distress about problems in her current living situation, confusing the past and present. She would often retreat into morose silence and forget from one minute to another what she was talking about and who the people around her were. The 'old bat' was interchangeably her grandmother or the woman who currently cared for her. She rarely referred to her parents directly and never in any way negatively.

I have continued to work with Jean both individually and in group sessions. The work of the groups fed into her 1:1 sessions and she began to make images and talk about her schooldays. Her home placement eventually broke down and she moved to what seemed far from ideal temporary accommodation in a mental health hostel, where there was a less interventionist style of support. Here, though her personal care dropped, she throve emotionally. In her artwork she continued to try out new ways of working but often returned to her maintenance style, here she began to comment on what she was doing with great excitement and almost with surprise at the smallest variations. She still never spoke of her family as anything other than caring but her unscheduled visits lessened, she became more willing to stay at the centre for full days and engage in a full programme of activities. Her memory was greatly improved but with certain problem areas, as she appeared to be unable to recall menstruation from one month to another and continued to have problems of self-care generally. Eventually she moved to a single flat with a very high level of support and at about this time both her parents and her grandmother became unwell and her mother subsequently died.

Her 1:1 sessions became a focus for any grief work she might need. For a while she did not want to do any art work, even her safe patterns were too difficult and she would sometimes start one only to break off, but she used the time to talk about missing her mother. Next she began, at her own instigation, to work with paint on a pre-wetted paper; this work became very bold and really quite messy, only just being contained within the paper. It was dramatic and impressive and she was keen to mount and display it publicly and it received a lot of attention and appreciation. The essentially physical nature and potential messiness of this work has been a safe form of regression and the acceptance and affirmation it has received have, I think, marked an increased acceptance and valuing of herself. Her sense of identity and self-worth has developed recently to the point where she has been gradually able to relax some of the complex defences and begin to acknowledge the previously unacceptable facts and feelings of her life so far.

Soon after she began attending, a clinical psychologist did a memory assessment test with her; I remember the verbal report as being 'she appears to have no memory'. As a clearer picture emerges from Jean one can see why she chose not to remember.

Up till this recent work, her relationship with me has been almost impersonal; the objective nature of the work has given her something to trust deeply when people who got too close were potentially threatening. Now she is beginning to challenge what she sees as my coercive role, and is able to link this with working through her feelings about her grandmother. There are also links with her loss of her mother in terms of a loss of mothering when she was a child.

The art therapy is part of a complex pattern of care; the environment of the Treatment Centre has allowed her to work at her own speed and to access a wide range of approaches. While containing her, it has allowed her a great deal of control over her involvement.

Alan

Alan was sent to the Treatment Centre after being charged with an assault on a worker in his supported housing. He has a moderate degree of learning difficulty and no confirmed mental health diagnosis. His mother left his father when he was small and went to America to remarry; this marriage did not last long and she returned with Alan and a new brother to live with her own mother. The second son also has learning difficulties but not to such a degree.

From his history, it would seem that from early on Alan's mother and grand-mother constantly asked for help with his difficult behaviour, comparing him unfavourably to his brother, while the professionals reported an engaging child trying hard to conceal the level of his difficulties. As he became older his behaviour was reported as becoming problematic and he was taken into various placements with brief returns home. He spent some time in a large institution which became a focus for much of his anger. He has no contact with his brother but his mother is still involved with him and visits him regularly. Since his admission he has had 1:1 art therapy and any suggestion of group work has been strenuously opposed.

His presentation is very much of someone in control; he is verbal and likes the trappings of authority, meetings, briefcases, etc. He has many physical problems and it is on these that he has focused any problems in the past and he expresses his mood often through them; his outbursts of temper are violent and damaging and he has a history of absconding.

When we first began work he was almost constantly angry with the authorities who sent him to the centre and it became clear that running away was his response to most situations. This was not only in his actual attempts to leave but, in his inability to engage with the present, he constantly listened to what went on outside, planned for his meetings with more important people who could sort things out, or went to sleep. He frequently refused to co-operate with treatment, escalating the situation till medication or restraint were required. His attendance at art therapy, as with everything, has been patchy but enough for definite changes to be observed.

It was clear from the start that his image-making was very much more immature than his speech would have lead one to expect: this alerted me to how successfully he has come to conceal his difficulties. He has a great fear of ridicule and of letting people see what he perceives of as bad drawings; some of his extremely ambivalent attitude to me is based on his fear of having trusted me with this secret. He constantly checks the confidentiality of the sessions now and I feel this has more to do with a fear of ridicule about the work than specific concern about the content. His drawing does engage him, often briefly but very intensely. During one phase of work he made a series of swirling, roughly egg-shaped drawings, working quite hungrily through sheet after sheet of paper. Just prior to this we had evolved a conversational way of working, reacting to each other's marks, seeing how close we could get and playing, and this seemed to be a quite important stage in the work.

On occasion his work has been a direct portrayal of his desperately low self-esteem: when he was using boxes to construct possible new homes, he made one that was a kennel for a fat dog. When attempting once to draw the anger he was feeling with a fellow resident, he made a swirling shape and placed a very tentative dot inside; he has recognised this as an image of himself and his need to protect the hurt little boy inside.

Lately his behaviour within the centre has become more reliable, he has been able to explain his feelings a bit more and seems to be taking a bit more respon-sibility about attending his work places. In his art sessions the art work has lessened but he has begun to talk more freely of his difficult feelings about his family and to try to describe his pain. His relationship with another resident has focused him back to his feelings of jealousy towards his brother and his grief at his rejections by his mother.

Very early on in our work I told Alan that I thought he would find this place (the Treatment Centre) the one place he could not run from and that would not throw him out. He has constantly tried to force me into situations where I would be cross with him and could be seen as coercive. When he used to sleep in the sessions and again when he has arrived just plain furious, I have tried to react neutrally and, when it seemed right, asked him what reaction it was that he wanted from me. The way he perceives our relationship is constantly changing and I have often been surprised by his reaction to the situation.

For Alan, the use he has made of me has been as important as the use he has made of the art work. I have attempted to maintain the sessions and to recognise and, where appropriate, to question his range of coping strategies. But the engagement of the art work with his feelings has been the starting-point for the relationship. The art work cannot be manipulated but it is also something over which he does genuinely have control; through it he is very tentatively looking at the reality of himself. The work with him has only been possible within the structure of the secure unit and the supportive work that has been offered to him. It has been the view of the team that it has made a necessary parallel to the ongoing more cognitive and behavioural work he is being offered.

Both these people face the world with selves created in response to negative aspects of the early caring environment. These 'selves' are no longer able to main-tain them – they have let them down. This 'failure' has lead to them receiving 'treatment', but treatment to what end? The old self has to be dismantled and a new development of self encouraged; supportive, cognitive work gently demonstrates and enables new ways of being; art therapy can offer the chance to return to early ways of sharing time with another and rebuilding a relationship with the world.

CONCLUSION

There is a little-recognised group of people with learning difficulties who can be more easily understood when viewed in a frame of reference which acknowledges the concept and nosology of personality disorders. We do not feel that their needs have been fully explored, nor has their potential for achieving significant personal change. The predominant treatment approaches in this field are behavioural, cognitive and pharmacological; psychotherapy is not widely used or, so far, very well documented. We feel there are grounds for further investigation into the effectiveness of art therapy and its place within a structured treatment programme.

In writing this chapter we have provoked more questions than we have answers but it has been enormously illuminating for us and has confirmed us in the belief that art therapy has a specific role. This lies in enabling the client to side-step elaborate defences and to work on the gradual rebuilding of a true self, establishing self-trust and object-trust in both non-verbal and verbal ways. This clearly involves a degree of regression, which is often seen as a potentially dangerous process to be avoided. Because in the process of art-making some dissolving of conscious control is involved, we as art therapists are familiar with a dipping in and out of the potential chaos of undifferentiated experience and of trusting the objective nature of the art work itself to hold this safe, and in therapy to make it available for recognition and acceptance. In this lies the core of the potential value of art therapy for this client group.

BIBLIOGRAPHY

Akhtar, S. (1992). *Broken Structures: Severe Personality Disorders and Their Treatment*, New York: Jason Aronson.

Berelowitz, M. and Tarnopolsky, A. (1993) 'The Validity of Borderline Personality Disorder: An Updated Review of Recent Research' in Tyrer, P. and Stan, G. (eds) (1993) *Personality Disorder Reviewed*, London: Royal College of Psychiatrists/ Gaskell.

Cole, P. (1986) 'Psychopathology Illustrated through Art Therapy', *Inscape*, February: 10–14.

Diagnostic and Statistical Manual of Mental Disorders: III (1980); III Revised (1987); IV (1994). Washington DC: American Psychiatric Association.

Goldsmith, A. (1986). 'Substance and Structure in the Art Therapeutic Process – Working with Mental Handicap', *Inscape* Summer 1986:18–22.

Henley, D.R (1991) 'Facilitating the Development of Object Relations Through the Use of Clay in Art Therapy', *American Journal Of Art Therapy* 29(3): 69–76.

Hughes, R. (1986) 'Destruction and Repair', *Inscape*, February: 8–10.

Kernberg, O.F. (1976) *Object Relations Theory and Clinical Psychoanalysis*, New York: Jason Aronson.

Khan, M. M. R. (1963) 'The Concept of Cumulative Trauma', *Psychoanalytic Study of the Child* 18:286–386.

Khan, M. M. R. (1974) *The Privacy of the Self*, New York: International Universities Press.

Lachman-Chapin, M. (1979) 'Kohut's Theories on Narcissism: Implications for Art Therapy', *American Journal of Art Therapy* 19(1): 3–9.

Masterson, J. F. (1976). *Psychotherapy of the Borderline Adult: A Developmental Approach*, New York: Brunner/Mazel.

Stokes, J. and Sinason, V. (1992) 'Secondary Mental Handicap as a Defence' in Waitmann, A. and Conboy-Hill, S. (eds), *Psychotherapy and Mental Handicap*, London: Sage Publications.

Tyrer, P. and Stan, G. (eds) (1993) *Personality Disorder Reviewed*, London: Royal College of Psychiatrists/Gaskell.

Waitmann, A. and Conboy-Hill, S. (eds) (1992) *Psychotherapy and Mental Handicap*. London: Sage Publications.

Winnicott, D.W. (1971) *Playing and Reality*, London: Tavistock.

Chapter 5

Lost in space

The relevance of art therapy with clients who have autism or autistic features

Lesley Fox

Central theme
- A reflection of my own understanding of the term 'autism' based on personal experience as an art therapist and insights gained from a broad range of academic sources.

Key points
- A review of current thinking around autism and its relationship with art therapy.
- A consideration of the potential therapeutic needs of people with autism.
- Case examples illustrating how art therapy may catalyse a reclamation of symbolic function for clients who have autism.

The question of autism is so vast that this chapter cannot be a comprehensive review of the subject. It will be based on my fifteen years of experience working with adults with learning difficulties, predominantly in community settings. In the first part of the chapter, I propose to draw together some theoretical perspectives on the subject, selecting what has been illuminating for my own understanding of clients with whom I have worked. In the second half of the chapter I will discuss some aspects of my work with clients who have autism, attempting to show a connection between the theory and my practice.

AN ART THERAPIST BECOMES AWARE OF THE CONDITION

There are many art therapists working in this area, but as yet their experience does not seem to be readily available. What is available in print about art and autism seems usually to be written by members of other professions, and tends to refer to those whose ability to use art materials is already established – sometimes exceptionally so, as in the case of Nadia (Selfe 1977), and Stephen Wiltshire (Sacks 1995:186). Historically, the National Autistic Society has been sceptical about psychodynamic modes of treatment, which may in part have been a reaction to the one-time theory that parents were somehow to blame for the condition. My experience may reflect that of other art therapists: I found that carers and families valued input from the psychology profession involving assessment and provision of guidelines for the constructive management of clients, which to some extent was assumed to conflict with the art therapist's contribution. Paradoxically, this appeared partly to be due to the realisation that a feature of autism is a difficulty in using symbols, and with developing the imagination.

My first autistic clients tended to be those who were undiagnosed, or had fallen through the psychologist's net or who, rarely, had shown exceptional artistic abilities, or who were very institutionalised. Over the years of working with a mixed group of clients under the umbrella term 'mentally handicapped' which has now become 'learning disabled', I gradually became aware that a significant number of clients exhibited autistic features to some degree. I now have more direct referrals of clients with this condition and it has become increasingly apparent to me that art therapy can make an important contribution to their treatment. At the moment, over one-third of my caseload are at some point on the autistic spectrum.

SOME THEORETICAL PERSPECTIVES FROM OTHER PROFESSIONS

As indicated, there is a valuable body of work from other professions, notably psychology, psychoanalysis and psychotherapy. Although there has been much speculation about the different causes of autism – genetic, emotional, biological, traumatic – the aetiology of the condition is still not clear-cut, with no single cause identified. It appears to develop at a time when the organism is still very obviously functioning as a holistic unit and can logically be likened to a basic primary defence, so that it appears as a handicap due to abnormal development, affecting the higher functioning of the brain.

How this manifests is described by psychologist Uta Frith, who has found that the condition appears to be due to 'a deficit in information processing systems' (Frith 1990:100) and concludes that the common denominator in autistic people of all ages is 'the inability to draw together information so as to derive coherent and meaningful ideas. There is a fault in the predisposition of the mind to make sense of the world' (Frith 1990:187). She considers that this explains the essential features of autism, with all other symptoms secondary.

Autism was originally defined by Kanner (1943:217). Since then different writers have focused on different sets of diagnostic criteria. That issued by the World Health Organisation in 1987 is as follows:

- That the condition is present or onset prior to the age of three years.
- That there is a qualitative impairment in reciprocal social interaction.

- That there is a qualitative impairment in verbal and non-verbal communication and in imaginative activity.
- That there is a markedly restricted, repetitive, stereotyped pattern of behaviour, interests and activities.
- That it is not attributable to any other pervasive developmental disorder.

The associated 'Asperger's Syndrome' (Asperger 1944:76) has a less devastating effect on general development and is consequently very much less prevalent in clients with learning difficulties, the main difference between the syndromes being that with Asperger's Syndrome there is no speech or cognitive delay.

The prevalence of autism in the population appears to be between 2 and 4 per 10,000, and for people with learning disabilities with autistic features to be 22.5 per 10,000. Although the sex ratio of incidence is higher in males than in females, females may be more severely affected. There appears to be no reliable correlation of the incidence of autism to social class or cultural factors (Frith 1990:57).

There are specific conditions which can occur in conjunction with autism, for example, epilepsy. The majority of people with autism remain disabled and unable to live independently due to the nature of the condition, the pervasive effect of autism on development and to associated difficulties.

There is considerable evidence from psychotherapy that in some cases the condition can be amenable to this treatment. There is much to be gained from reading case studies and explanations from psychotherapy and psychoanalysis of what might be happening internally for a client who exhibits the deficits described by Frith. Tustin tried to explain why this deficit in functioning might arise. She distinguishes between 'organic' and 'psychogenic' autism: 'organic autism can be a reaction to brain damage or sensory defect, whereas psychogenic autism is the reaction to a delusory traumatic situation which seems to threaten life and limb' (Tustin 1992:11). Tustin considered that the dividing line between the two types of autism was not necessarily clear-cut. She believed that psychogenic autism is due to an infant becoming aware of its separateness before it has the resources to cope with it, the result being a perverse development rather than an arrested development, with an attempt to shut down the 'potential space' (Winnicott's term).

> The delusory state of fusion which existed prior to the catastrophic awareness of bodily separateness was not a normal early infantile stage but an abnormal state with which both mother and child had colluded, and for which there may have been a genetic susceptibility in both of them, as well as environmental pressures which provoked it. Inevitably, since there was felt to be no space between them, this undue closeness *hampered* the development of 'object relations'. This *meant* that cognitive and emotional developments *were* impeded. The 'closing down' nature of autism is a further impediment.
>
> (Tustin 1992:12)

Tustin further distinguished between autistic and psychotic children by their use of objects: 'autogenerated encapsulation' in which a hard object is used to plug the hole where a missing person is denied existence; and 'confusional entanglement' in which self and not-self are inextricably confused and a child is entangled with outside objects. She found that these two types could be easily confused, with their therapeutic needs quite different (Tustin 1992:46, 74).

Anne Alvarez, working with clients at the Tavistock Clinic, has observed that the condition is not necessarily post-traumatic but can be a result of a less dramatic scenario where communication is interrupted, or never set in motion, for a variety of reasons (Alvarez 1995).

Although the potential outcomes and the treatment interventions vary with what Tustin terms both psychogenic and organic autism, the area of difficulty remains the same. With the 'potential space' unavailable or shut down, the ability to use symbols is not developed, so that a person can be fixed in a world where all experiences are new, unpredictable and uncategorisable, that is, essentially fixed in the here and now, without access to memory or anticipation and living with fear of attack by projections of unmodified instinctual feelings. This is the extreme end of the spectrum. Others are able to negotiate the normal developmental stages but inadequately so, so that there is a markedly uneven psychological, emotional and cognitive development, affected by the existence of authentic early developmental states.

THE IMPORTANCE OF SYMBOL FORMATION

I consider that the common denominator which Frith finds in clients with autism, namely 'the inability to draw together information so as to derive coherent and meaningful ideas' (Frith 1990:187) seems to indicate that a client has failed to successfully negotiate, for whatever reason, that stage of development where the ability to use symbols is acquired. This could account for many of the features which are frequently described as belonging to the person with autism.

Using Klein's concepts of the paranoid–schizoid and the depressive positions, Hanna Segal (1988:49–65) shows disturbances in symbol formation are reflected in an individual's early object relations. Early symbols formed during the process of projective identification and feelings of omnipotent control are experienced by the infant not as symbols but as the original objects. In the later depressive position, external objects surviving omnipotent destruction are experienced as real, whole and autonomous. Winnicott (1986:106) suggests that the first impulse in relation to an objectively perceived object is destructive, and that there is an ongoing destruction in unconscious fantasy relative to objective object-relating. The process of developing realistic rather than omnipotent thinking, and of modifying primary instinctual aims is dependent upon the development of the ability to use symbols. Segal (1988:49–65) writes that it is only after the establishment of good symbolic relations to body products, essentially valuable recreations of the breast, that art materials can be used to carry projections which can then be used for sublimation.

THE ROLE OF ART THERAPY

It is apparent that where there is potential for development, the earlier the treatment, the better the prognosis. When people with these kinds of problems reach adulthood and are found in a clinical setting, it can be assumed that any treatment they may have had has been unsuccessful or only partially successful, and that their emotional and cognitive development has been impeded. To anticipate a 'cure' may be over-ambitious and courting disappointment. However, there is a great deal which can be offered to enable people with autism to reach their potential and to live less fearfully and more fully.

It is important as always that clients are accepted as they are, and that unconditional regard and respect are available in principle from the start. As artists we can celebrate diversity, and it is essential to be aware of our own conditioning, so that others are not forced into moulds of 'normality', the door remaining open to an appreciation of different ways of perceiving and processing the world.

Despite the great differences found in each client, the overall treatment aims can be quite similar: to promote communication and trust, and to encourage the ability to use art materials to further creative expression, emotional integration and intellectual development.

I have tried to set the scene with a view to becoming more aware of the potential meaning of what might happen within an art therapy session with an autistic client. In my service, the ideal for clients with autism is a structured day which also caters for individual needs as far as possible. Within an art therapy session, the client is provided with a regular boundaried time which has the quality of being more unstructured. It is structured by the therapist on the edge of a client's needs, so that there is always potentially a little more space to explore. This is the space which Tustin describes as unavailable. The therapist will support a client within the space as necessary. The space is essentially Winnicott's 'potential space' (1986:106) where the therapist will seek to provide that adequate supporting presence which is essential to renegotiation of early developmental stages. I find the potential space extends beyond my person to the physical boundary of the studio space.

It is important that the studio space is welcoming, with the sense of an ordering presence. It is possible to present a space which can be apprehended instantly as belonging to another realm of experience. It is essential that the client is there by choice. Respecting a move towards the door is a successful two-way communication which often gives the client the confidence to return. Using simple language, I speak about the issue of choice together with the proposed programme even when a client appears to be unable to communicate. Almost invariably, clients subsequently show a greater understanding of language than is initially apparent, even if their own speech is very limited. It is also the case that this is an area where there may potentially be the opportunity for further speech and language development within the context of a meaningful environment. It is known that creative experiences and development of creative abilities can affect overall functioning in terms of cognitive intelligence (Gardner 1989:167–82). Clients who are silent, vocalising on a pre-linguistic level, or using a limited vocabulary, may need the experience of hearing language addressed to them and others and the opportunity to distinguish sounds and meanings within a potentially meaningful environment, together with the opportunity to develop the understanding that there is space for a response of some kind which will be valued. However, it is necessary to remember that clients may be responding to speech less in terms of content than in terms of sound, tone and intent, and that for clients who are often acutely sensitive in terms of their personal space, sound can be either intrusive or supportive (Fox Coyne 1992:60).

JASON

Using a pseudonym, I am going to introduce an autistic client who I consider to have benefited from art therapy. Jason is a young man in his early thirties. Following an out-of-borough placement at a boarding school, he attended a behavioural therapy unit within a large institution for clients with learning difficulties. As a result of changes in the moral climate, public opinion, and eventually legislation which have taken place in recent years, the institution has now closed and the philosophy of community care is now a practical fact. The Day Therapeutic Care Unit where I work was set up specifically to provide treatment and care for young adults like Jason who might at one time have expected to spend their lives in institutional care.

Jason lives in a small unit in the community with other clients who suffer from autism. They have lived together for a number of years, with staff who appreciate their particular needs and demands. The behavioural therapy unit in the institution had a very structured programme which did not include art therapy, and was rather separate from the larger institution. Jason was referred to the art therapy department when he moved to the community therapeutic care unit, as it was then the policy to refer all clients for assessment, and he was seen by a colleague for two years.

An art therapy assessment usually takes between six and eight weekly sessions, individual or group. It is a process of exploration with the purpose of evaluating whether a client would benefit from receiving the service. Clients are assessed for their expressive, emotional, creative, psychological and physical needs. Developmental stage assessment is also carried out from the client's drawing level, and an assessment made of the client's cognitive functioning. This enables the formulation of an appropriate type of treatment plan and sets the foundation to plan realistic aims. It also acts as a form of communication to other staff as to the client's well-being.

Jason looks much younger than his years. Initially he seemed very timid, moving slowly and carefully when not making repetitive rocking or jumping movements. Sometimes he bites his hands, or pulls his hair. Jason suffers from epilepsy which is not completely controlled by medication. His spoken vocabulary is very limited, although he seems to understand more than he says, and his comprehension appears to be developing. Jason's words include 'yes' and 'no', and it is possible to present ideas to him. Jason can be persuaded to give, typically, one-word responses, but seems to prefer not to use speech, and does not instigate verbal exchange.

I became involved when my colleague and I decided to open our adjoining door, and Jason tentatively came through into my room for tea, and sometimes sat with me and my clients when my colleague was absent.

When I first met Jason I intruded upon his personal space, which was a larger area than is normal. In desperation he threw an article that he habitually carried out of the window, and ran out of the room to fetch it. I acknowledged his communication by becoming more aware of how much space he needed to feel safe, by slowing my movements and speech, and by speaking about what I was doing, if I needed to pass behind his chair for example. I noted that Jason was able to use art materials mainly at the level of controlled scribbling, but that moments of voluntary art work were few. He regularly brought a child's storybook to the session, and eventually I was allowed to handle it, and read it to him, which provided some opportunities for interaction. A drawing of the anthropomorphic hero (Figure 5.1) shows that he was unable to reproduce the character as a whole, and he is made up of unconnected parts. Space was given to Jason's keen interest in a

Figure 5.1 Jason: The anthropomorphic hero of a children's story

science-fiction cartoon by obtaining a tape of the series and sharing his pleasure in listening to it, often. Another client present was helped to make a vehicle from the programme out of junk packaging, which had the nature of a shared interest.

At this point my colleague was redeployed, and the family situation we had paralleled was ended. Jason became my client and I began to see him regularly as a member of a group of four in all. The other group members were all fellow residents from his home. The session length was gradually extended to ninety minutes, more like real time, the equivalent of a working afternoon at the unit.

Treatment aims for Jason, in line with our departmental philosophy were: to encourage spontaneity, independence and choice within an informal, non-threatening atmosphere conducive to fostering creativity and self-expression; to encourage him to gain confidence and self-esteem; to build on his abilities; to eventually take responsibility for his actions; to develop interpersonal skills and social interaction; to develop self-insight and self-reflection; to bring about long-standing emotional change; and to develop an ability to learn through role modelling. Art therapy can work on different levels simultaneously so that art work can also be used as a tool for communication in the development of a psychotherapeutic relationship effecting psychological change and emotional well-being. Jason's developmental stage of drawing development would be monitored. Changes in this area would be likely to indicate development towards his full potential, which may involve regression to, or renegotiation of early developmental stages, which could indicate his level of functioning.

Jason reacted to the change by sitting silently in the same place every week working on a small piece of clay which was kept pliable in a plastic bag between sessions (Figure 5.2). Jason worked on it for several months, wetting his finger and slowly and tentatively rubbing a groove in it, which activity he seemed to find comforting. He seemed to have regressed, during the sessions, to an early stage of development where experiences involving rhythmic sensuousness, smoothness and moistness were being recaptured or enacted. Although Jason worked in silence, he seemed to be observing what was happening around him.

Jason was helped to move on from his clay work by a change which was suggested to the group in the form of a large piece of paper spread over two long tables which were pushed together. He was able to use a roller and paint to join in the group activity, where previously he had rejected offers to try other materials. He transferred the basic backwards and forwards motions from his clay-smoothing to the new activity. This development occurred at a point when I was seriously querying the benefit he was receiving from attending sessions, wondering whether his clay-smoothing had become a repetitive activity which could continue indefinitely. This seems to be an example of a situation whereby we silently negotiated between us that it was time for him to move on. My expectation or impatience may have been giving or confirming in him the confidence that it was possible, or perhaps giving him the impetus to avoid my potential displeasure and abandonment. The change happened after several months, and could be likened to a kind of weaning process.

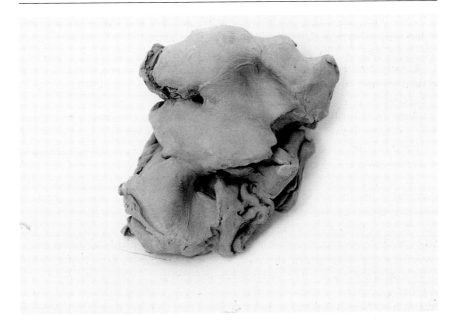

Figure 5.2 Jason: Clay comforter

At its largest, the group to which Jason belonged had five members, an art therapy trainee (Penelope Wilson) and myself. Wilson has perceptively encapsulated the life of the group sessions in her unpublished training study (1994), in which she describes the different ways each client used the group and the materials according to their differing needs, the group interactions which were encouraged, and the benefits of group work in this area.

I decided to introduce what became a succession of long-term art therapy trainees into this group partly because it rapidly became very busy, with constant potential chaos which needed containing practically as well as emotionally. It also reinforced my ability to be objective whilst working in a very subjective area. Each client seems to have felt secure and enabled with two therapists, and in terms of the group being like a family situation with young children, having two 'parents' made sense. The demands on a lone therapist seem to be not unlike the demands on a single parent in the equivalent situation. I was also aware that for this client group change was an important issue.

People who are autistic often seem to make their reference points outside themselves, in concrete areas, displaying some lack in the ability to communicate within themselves on a symbolic level so that anxiety, panic, disorientation, confusion, anger and denial are typical responses to external change. For people with learning disabilities generally, change is ever present, with constant movement of care staff over shifts and between posts. Most clients seem to experience difficulty in discerning between social and professional relationships and often express strong feelings about staff movement. Permanent change of care staff with autistic clients at my unit is dealt with on a practical level, by the change occurring quite quickly with emphasis on what is remaining the same.

Introducing a succession of trainees into the group for a limited time span of an academic year has been helpful. It has provided an arena for clients to experience change over time, and loss, whilst ensuring continuity of support. It has enabled clients to develop concepts around these issues, and the group has become one which can encompass change. We have used simplified calendars to assist with the concept of time, and have been very aware of the need to deal very thoroughly with the issues around trainees joining and leaving.

The week following Jason's move to paint with other group members, he returned to his clay work, but the next session after that, he started to draw. In order to support himself he instigated intense eye contact which felt as if it had a potentially dual purpose: of reflecting and confirming his presence, and of attempting to become one with the therapist. Jason sought intense relationship by the strength of his gaze and his helpless needy presence. Art therapy trainee Simon Hastilow described how towards the end of a session Jason became agitated. He stopped work, frowning. Standing up he began repeated flicking motions with his arm. Eventually he hit the trainee on the side of the head. On impulse Hastilow asked Jason if he needed the toilet, and Jason replied 'Yes', and was then able to go independently. It appeared that Jason felt that Hastilow should already have been aware of his needs. This incident prompted the unpublished study 'Symbiotic Relationships in Art Therapy with Autistic Adults' (Hastilow 1995).

If Jason is presented with an issue which he finds hard to process he has sometimes resorted to what have appeared by their rapidity to be instinctual, unpremeditated, physical reactions, that is, spitting, hitting, and throwing objects. When hitting he often seemed to hold back his hit as if struggling to contain it. It has been important to discourage unsocial acts whilst offering interpretations which can be simply expressed in terms Jason can understand. Over time, Jason appears to have been able to build up some concepts about his actions.

Some of Jason's physical expressions are directed towards himself rather than others, for example, biting his hands, pulling his hair. Actions around the perimeter of his body can seem to have different and multiple functions, for example, reinforcing his sense of self and preventing dissolution; containing aggression towards another; locating pain on a physical level. Jason has been able to accept concern that he is hurting his hands and acknowledge pain as being inside. Acknowledging feelings and helping him to name them seems to help him to hold his feelings and not be swept away by them.

Initially, it often felt precarious to be sitting next to Jason, relating for the most part in silence, trying to promote a secure and non-threatening presence, being aware of when interest has been needed, and when it has rapidly become intrusive and feared to the point where Jason seemed to be experiencing the need to attack or to defend himself. As Jason seemed to be projecting some of his own feelings onto whoever he was with, it was important to sense when this was happening and find a way of communicating to him that he was in no danger from us. Much of the early work with Jason was in this area, negotiating a way of being together in the same space.

It seemed important to try to encourage the feeling in Jason that he is a separate person and that I don't magically know what he is thinking or feeling – for example, when ready to draw, Jason usually looks at the pens and then at me. Whilst responding to his communication I also ask if he needs help, and tell him how I know that he might want to draw, that I have seen him looking at the pens and then at me. Jason is sometimes surly when this concept of being separate is placed before him, but I try to compensate for this by showing that it can be fun to have a two-way exchange, and that a group together can also interact pleasurably. This involves being aware of Jason's feelings, for example, when the other client is receiving attention, and of his feelings about not being so verbally fluent as the other client, interpreting these issues as appropriate, and ensuring that Jason is presented with the opportunity to be included in interactions.

Whilst the low incidence of Jason's seizures hasn't changed, he has recently started to rest his head on a pillow on the table, sucking his thumb, and falling into a deep sleep, with eyes flickering open from time to time to look at me. It feels as if he is not checking that I'm still there, but knows I will be. Arising from his rest he has surprised us by seizing a pen and drawing freely, expansively and independently.

Whilst Jason was developing his drawing and his ability to relate he was also enabled to investigate the studio space. I had been told that Jason was unable to tolerate photographs or mirrors, and the reasons for this became apparent as this line of enquiry was pursued, at his instigation. A museum visit with another group was recorded in the studio with photographs taken by the group members. Jason indicated his interest and recognised some of the people in the photographs, including myself and an art therapy trainee. At first we thought he was unhappy about sharing us with other groups but it later occurred to us that he was also puzzled about the nature of photographic images, and appeared to think that the clients in the photographs were also in the room. At this point he appeared to enjoy handling a photograph of a previous trainee (Penelope Wilson), even kissing it.

Having shown interest in the photographs, Jason initially refused when asked if he would like a photograph of himself. Weeks later he changed his mind, due partly to his ongoing interest in the photographs and also to his interest and pride in his clothing, which was reflected back to him and supported. We have a collection of photographs of Jason wearing different T-shirts. I felt the interest in his clothing might be part of a developing awareness of skin boundaries and identity, and of the passage of time.

The first photographs I took of Jason were of him with a trainee art therapist, Hastilow. Whilst making the venture less risky for him he was also later delighted to have images of the two of them together. It also seemed to make it easier for him to understand where the real person was located. Although neither group member (there were two in the group at this point) was able to operate the camera, both now wanted photographs of themselves with their art work and with myself and the trainee. Cameras and photographs had been introduced into the group much earlier following a request from another client's key-worker, who was compiling a pictorial timetable, and also to record more ephemeral work, but Jason had shown no interest. Now he was discovering them for himself. Initially, when Jason was presented with photographs of himself it was apparent that his fragile sense of self was flowing away. When I thoughtlessly presented him with several photographs at once, he deliberately tipped his drink onto them but seemed to regret it immediately, saying 'Oh no'. He was able to cope with this feeling with support, and spent many sessions looking at and handling photographs.

As part of the process of learning about images and self we decided to introduce a mirror, and found at first that both clients were immediately confused. I asked the other group member to address Jason, and he referred to the mirror image rather than to Jason himself. Jason replied to the image in the mirror. Although they were puzzled, it seemed less frightening and more like fun, and we played and talked around the mirror for a number of sessions until they became at ease with it and it lost its fascination.

Jason also seemed concerned about the family group nature of some of the photographs, and was able to indicate that he would like to have a photograph of a member of his own family who had recently died, even though he had had a photograph which he had destroyed. This request was passed on and fulfilled. That Jason could now own this photograph seemed to show a shift in his understanding of images. Although we were aware that Jason had suffered a bereavement – indeed, at one point his behaviour had deteriorated – it seemed important to leave it to Jason to bring it up, which eventually he tentatively did. Once he had done so it was possible to help Jason to be with his feelings about this as necessary, in a more focused way. To be able to mention the name and to grieve legitimately seemed a great comfort for him.

With regard to the trainee art therapists it became clear that Jason had no way of telling if they were still alive, once they had left, but we were able to refer to photographs and assure Jason that they were still alive and might be thinking about him sometimes in the same way that he was remembering them. From his relief it seemed that he might to some extent have been operating at a level where he considered his own wishes and fantasies to be very potent, as well as illustrating his difficulty with abstract concepts.

An incident which seemed to help Jason to integrate concepts of death occurred when he and I were working alone together. He noticed a dead bumble-bee at the beginning of the session. Pointing to it, horror-stricken, he looked around for something to throw. He chose a carton of milk, which may have had some meaning, and hurled it across the room. It seemed important not to put the bee in the waste bin but to try and indicate that the bee's death was part of a cycle, that its life had meaning, that it would be disposed of with respect and gratitude, and that I wasn't too afraid. With Jason holding my hand throughout, I scooped up the bee, and we took it downstairs and buried it in the grounds. I said a few words over the grave, speculating about a life spent amongst flowers, giving thanks for a productive life and saying goodbye. This episode had the feeling of a childhood experience of death in the animal world, and I was also conscious that for Jason, death was a recent reality, painfully present in some form. Jason kissed me affectionately on the cheek at the end of the session.

At the same time, the other remaining member of the group, Tom, was investigating in parallel, following his own needs which seemed partly precipitated by reaction to family events involving feelings of separation and loss. He regressed from a stage where he could just about represent himself in bed 'with monsters underneath' to a stage where he used colour sensuously, revelling in the colour and in the experience of using materials for their own sake. His mood changed drastically from manically cheerful and busy to extremely depressed, restless, weepy and clingy. Single brush strokes became identified as people he knew. Tom often cut them in half or obliterated them with paint, expressing both anxiety and pleasure in his 'Oo-er, I've cut her in half. Oh dear'. Play and conversation around this visible symbolic destruction of important figures in his life seemed to help him to integrate his conflicting feelings about them and the location of those feelings in himself, confirming inevitably the figures' independent existences. Hiding with paint and relocating images was also done by Tom around the time a trainee was leaving. His moods, once described as a bi-polar illness, are now stable. Medication prescribed to help him through this difficult time has been reduced.

Tom's appetite for image-making is voracious. His images have more conviction than before his regression and they are produced with lots of chatter about what is happening in the pictures with lots of laughter and play. As yet, Tom appears oblivious to the effect this has on Jason, whose ability to communicate verbally is less developed. Interaction is promoted by acknowledging Jason's feeling about his inability to communicate verbally at the same level as Tom; by being aware of the need to offer Jason the opportunity to be included in the exchanges; by encouraging Tom to be aware of when his chatter might be intrusive for Jason. Exchange of space, silence and power are paralleled in the concrete world by negotiated sharing of equipment and attention.

Tom is very curious about the world, and for both clients the question of death is raised again when, for example, he asks of a worn-out pen 'It's dead, isn't it?' Although the subjective nature of his experience is apparent when he kisses a paintbrush or table, says 'Hello' to a new electric fan or sees death in an empty drinks can, it feels as if he is touching on a difficult subject, admitting the possibility of death into our space. We have been able to talk simply about the difference between leaving and dying, and about one's limits of influence, acknowledging that there would be feelings about these issues.

Whilst studying the photographs displayed on the wall alongside his seat,

Jason also continued to work slowly on his drawings, which at this point consisted almost invariably of small patches of colour, using controlled scribbling, predominantly in shades of his favourite colour, red. In colour therapy, red is acknowledged as the dominant colour of the base chakra, and is considered to be very grounding: 'Children tend to love this colour because, until they reach puberty, they are not fully earthed' (Wills 1992: 76). Jason's drawing was recognisably a continuation of his earlier clay-smoothing operations, which in turn seemed to be based on the earliest experience of comfort and communion. He needed total intensive support to become able to draw.

Over an eighteen-month period Jason worked on a limited number of drawings which he built up over months (Figure 5.3), and on two occasions destroyed in what seemed like savage acts of vandalism and blind rage. These acts of destroying his own work as opposed to a fantasy destruction of a person seem to indicate that the drawings he built up were perhaps functioning as transitional objects (Winnicott 1986:1–30), which he created and destroyed. This urge to destruction acted out with materials is likely to be familiar to others working with this client group, and is a process I have witnessed several times with different clients.

Although Jason could previously attempt to reproduce characters from fiction if directed, his drawing now is more coherent, less rigidly produced, is meaningful within a context and is seemingly developing in a way which parallels the usual developmental phases. Jason is less rigid with regard to his drawing, and

Figure 5.3 Jason: Transitional object drawing

is happy to choose a fresh piece of paper, frequently completing a piece of work to his satisfaction in one session. Whilst using the same technique of controlled scribbling in small patches, with lots of rests in between, he has also interpreted pictures of rocket ships from his favourite cartoon and has independently tried some free and rapid circular scribble, influenced to some extent by the work of the other group member. Figure 5.4 shows an occasion when his backwards and forwards motion became exploratory. Figure 5.5, Santa Claus and Dog, shows Jason integrating the backwards and forwards motion with a style which gives him more symbolically expressive possibilities. His drawing of a puppet character 'Brains' from a children's science-fiction television series (Figure 5.6) seems more holistic than the earlier attempts at a figure (Figure 5.1), with an emphasised mouth and an inside.

Interpersonal dynamics are coming more obviously to the foreground, as indicated earlier, and unconscious symbolism has appeared in a recent work in a new medium, collage. His first collage presented a formal image of a child sitting on his mother's knee, both smiling and looking happy, gazing towards the viewer. Having noticed that Jason was very drawn to this image, I asked him if he would like to make a picture with it. Although Jason has limited dexterity with the scissors, in cutting out this image, whilst I held the paper, he managed to cut several times across the little boy's head, stopping precisely at the edge and not cutting into the mother at all. It felt as if he might be expressing the feeling of being damaged, possibly by his own feelings projected into the mother image,

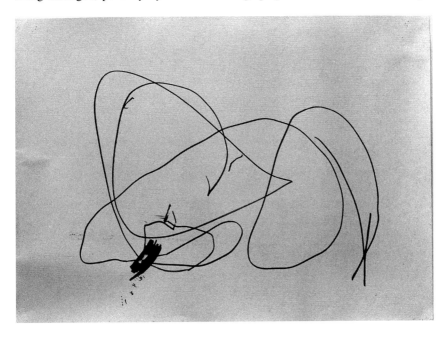

Figure 5.4 Jason: Starting to explore

Figure 5.5 Jason: Santa Claus and dog

Figure 5.6 Jason: 'Brains', a puppet in a children's TV series

with the mother protected, or all powerfully vengeful. Jason has acknowledged that the little boy is hurt, and that he feels like the little boy inside, even though he is a grown man.

Concepts of inside and outside have been around with our communication about the location of pain, and with Jason's new awareness that some pens have barrels which are a different colour from the colour inside.

Tom also began using collage at around the same time – pictures of young furry animals awake and asleep, including a photograph of a young kangaroo asleep inside the mother's pouch. Increasingly, there seems to be a productive correspondence between their work.

Work with Jason and Tom is long term and ongoing and has proved rewarding. However, not all clients can use the opportunities available in art therapy, and not all art therapists work the same way. As with any client, their personal needs and agenda direct the response. Some individuals I see alone for shorter periods of time. Clients who are functioning more independently whilst still using immature modes of relating may benefit from being in a group of people who do not suffer from autism, where the difficulties arising in their daily lives can be explored in microcosm whilst developing an ability to relate and to set in motion a healing relationship with art materials.

My title referred to the perception I have been able to develop through working with Jason as to what it might feel like to be unable to process information into meaningful concepts, how frightening and confusing the world might seem, how important is our ability to use symbols. I began the chapter by indicating the vastness of the subject and have, of necessity, limited my illustrations. By presenting some of the work with Jason in particular, and with Tom, I have tried to show how it might be possible, through developing a therapeutic relationship within a tangible potential space, to enable clients to renegotiate or negotiate very early developmental stages. This is done by promoting the use of art materials symbolically to develop an understanding of symbols which parallels the development of their ability to conceptualise and have successful meaningful relationships with the world as developing individuals.

BIBLIOGRAPHY

Alvarez, A. (1995) Lecture 'New Developments in the Psychotherapy of Children with Autism', The Tavistock Clinic 75th Anniversary Conference: *Mind in the Balance: Issues in Mental Health*, London: Tavistock Clinic.

Asperger, H. (1944) 'Die autistischen Psychopathen im Kindesalter', *Archiv für Psychiatrie und Nervenkrankheiten*, 117: 76–136.

Fox Coyne (1992) 'The Display and Exhibition of Art Work done in an Art Therapy Setting', unpublished MA thesis, University of Hertfordshire.

Frith, U. (1990) *Autism: Explaining the Enigma*, Oxford: Blackwell.

Gardner, H. (1989) 'Project Zero: An Introduction to Arts Propel', *Journal of Art and Design Education* 8(2): 167–82.

Hastilow, S. (1995) 'Symbiotic Relationships in Art Therapy with Autistic Adults', unpublished PG Dip. A.Th. Clinical Training Study, University of Hertfordshire.

Kanner, L. (1943) 'Autistic disturbances of affective contact', *Nervous Child*, 2: 217–50.

Sacks, O. (1995) *An Anthropologist on Mars*, London: Picador.

Segal, H. (1988) 'Notes on Symbol Formation' in *The Work of Hanna Segal*, New York: Aronson.

Selfe, L. (1977) *Nadia: A Case of Extraordinary Drawing Ability in an Autistic Child*, London: Academic Press.

Tustin, F. (1992) *Autistic States in Children*, London: Routledge.

Wills, P. (1992) *The Reflexology and Colour Therapy Workbook*, Longmead: Element Books.

Wilson, P. (1994) 'A Group of Five Autistic Young Adults', unpublished PG Dip. A.Th. Clinical Training Study, University of Hertfordshire.

Winnicott, D.W. (1986) *Playing and Reality*, Harmondsworth: Pelican Books.

World Health Organisation (1987) *Mental Disorders: A Glossary and Guide to their Classification in Accordance with the 10th Revision of the International Classification of Diseases (ICD-10)*, Geneva: World Health Organisation.

Chapter 6

Humpty Dumpty's shell

Working with autistic defence mechanisms in art therapy[1]

Margaret Stack

Central theme
- A detailed account of individual art therapy over a two-year period with a man who displayed many autistic features.

Key points
- Description of a long-term process of art therapy within an institutional context.
- Use of relevant literature, especially Tustin's concept of 'autistic encapsulation' to further illuminate the process.
- The importance of art therapy as a 'holding mechanism' supporting the possibility of exploration and change.

BACKGROUND

This chapter focuses on a two-year period of individual art psychotherapy with an institutionalised client diagnosed as having severe learning difficulties. The process of working with a client who displayed numerous autistic-like features is described within the context of the institution, with reference to relevant art therapy literature on this client group. The insight gained through tolerating extended periods of 'not knowing' and inertia has been supported by relevant theoretical models which eventually shed light on the nature of the client's predicament.

INTRODUCTION

> Shape without form, shade without colour,
> paralysed force, gesture without motion
>
> ('The Hollow Men', Eliot 1925/1982)

'The Hollow Men', by T.S. Eliot, succinctly describes the terror of a condition where meaningless voices, sightless eyes and unformed shapes remain paralysed within an inert form or shell. The poem echoes Tustin's definition of 'autistic encapsulation', a process she describes as a 'freezing of life giving propensities akin to a living death unless these tendencies can somehow be released' (Tustin 1990:153). The primary function of autistic encapsulation is one of protection; however, when over-used exclusively (as with certain institutionalised or autistic individuals), it has 'handicapping consequences', the effect of blocking our feeling, communication and life (Tustin 1990:133).

In 1943, Kanner's pioneering paper descriptively differentiated the syndrome 'early infantile autism', from 'inherent mental defect' as being characterised by profound social aloneness, an obsessive desire for sameness with occasional isolated areas of ability. Although the subject of this case study has been diagnosed as mentally defective and may not be autistic in the classical Kanner sense, he does display many of the autistic features outlined by Kanner and subsequent writers within this field. However, it is not my intention within this case study to debate the controversies surrounding the diagnosis and definition of autism: rather, I intend to use the insights provided by the theories of Kanner (1943), Tustin (1990) and Sinason (1992) as a means of understanding the complex nature of Dillon (a pseudonym) and his use of a 'protective shell' (Tustin 1990).

In order to gain a sense of Dillon, his complex behaviour and functioning, it will be necessary for me to trace his extensive institutional and personal history in chronological form. I shall commence with a review of British art therapy literature related to the field of mental handicap, which reflects the changing philosophies that have influenced Dillon's art therapy treatment to date. I shall then discuss his early personal and medical history, pre- and post-institutionalisation, including a detailed behavioural profile. Having completed my extensive introduction to Dillon, I then intend to focus on the impact of the art therapy environment on his treatment, with special reference to his two years of individual art psychotherapy. I have found it necessary to describe my individual work with Dillon within the context of two phases, thereby portraying an overview of the relationship with some specific insights. Each phase will be reflected upon and discussed in relation to relevant theory. My conclusions will draw from the material presented and focus on the effectiveness and future of art therapy with Dillon.

My intention is to introduce Dillon via relevant, but extensive historical and medical background information. His lengthy history records his institutional experience and mirrors the philosophical trends which have influenced his art therapy treatment to date.

EARLY HISTORY

But that I am forbid
to tell the secrets of my prison-house
I could a tale unfold whose lightest word,
would harrow up thy soul

(Shakespeare, 'Hamlet', 1. v. 13–16)

Dillon has lived within the confines of a large Victorian institution (established in 1870 for the feeble-minded) since his admission at eight years old. He is now forty-four. Although the hospital was officially closed in September 1994, in accordance with the philosophy of 'care in the community', Dillon continues to reside in a group home within the hospital grounds specifically built for individuals deemed behaviourally disturbed.

Dillon was adopted at five months and according to his medical records, he had contracted measles and whooping cough within his first two months of life. Although not stated, these illnesses may have had a bearing on his subsequent placement for adoption. His case notes record his first 'attack of fits' and his adoptive parents' first inkling that 'there was something wrong' as occurring when he was two years old.

He attended school for a short period at the age of four years, but was disruptive and considered unsuitable for mainstream education. A statement on his file from this period declares that 'he wanted to kill everybody, children and adults alike'. As his fits increased, he was diagnosed as having epilepsy, and was admitted in 1960 aged eight years. On admission he was described as 'a wild child', inclined to scream, cough and steal. The psychology report suggested that he 'expected opposition from adults' and 'queried mishandling during his early years'. They also noted that he liked solitary play, making jigsaws, block-building and often sang nursery rhymes to himself.

His diagnostic labels from this period described him as a 'high-profile imbecile' or 'high grade' and 'epileptic'; these altered in the 1980s in favour of 'severely subnormal', a label which still persists today under the umbrella term of 'learning disabled'. Dillon's diagnostic labels do not include 'autism'. However, I feel he exhibits many features synonymous with autism in terms of language retardation, the exclusive use of the personal pronoun 'he' for 'I', ritualistic compulsive behaviour and difficulty in developing social relationships; I will expand on these in the next section.

Despite the volume of records accumulated over the last thirty-six years, it became apparent, on examination, that there was a sparsity of factual historical information in relation to Dillon himself. The bulk consisted mainly of repetitive nursing records, continual medication reviews, the monitoring of fits, behavioural programmes and incident reports.

The few personal or social details recorded can be found in letters from his father to the consultant, and vice-versa, with regard to Dillon's educational performance. Throughout his recorded history there remains consistent contact between Dillon and his adoptive father but little mention of his natural or adoptive mother or siblings.

BEHAVIOURAL PROFILE

Dillon has had a history of disturbed behaviour – breaking windows, attacks on staff, self-mutilation and provocative swearing. He displays a number of idiosyncratic and obsessional behaviours, for example he constantly talks to and frequently reprimands himself in a parallel fashion: 'He's just cut his hair . . . Dillon, don't do that . . . '. Dillon always refers to himself in the third person 'he' instead of 'I', and incorporates conversations with others into his monologue in a sing-song manner.

He walks on tip-toe and usually clutches a tightly rolled up piece of paper which he constantly flicks. Dillon replaces this piece of paper several times a day as it falls to pieces with constant handling and chewing. He avoids social integration with his peers and remains autonomous and isolated even within a group. His body seems to be engaged in constant movement whether walking in circles or flicking his paper stick when sitting. Unlike autistic people in the Kanner sense, Dillon does not 'avert his eyes' from others, but stares in a rather intrusive way.

Dillon has no sense of time in conventional terms, that is, day, month, year or season, although he seems to have established an idiosyncratic sense of time based on a learned sequence of events and a rigid adherence to routine. Hence he remains obsessional about routine, finding any alteration difficult to tolerate or adapt to.

ART THERAPY HISTORY

Dillon has been attending the Art Therapy Department since September 1982, that is, for fourteen years at the time of writing. The referral form from this period states that he had 'attended every unit in the hospital during the previous 6 years, since completing special school'. The reason provided for his termination in the various units was in relation to 'his continuous disruptive behaviour' which the medical officer infers may have been 'related to mishandling'. He suggested that Dillon 'could do with a gentle, consistent and firm therapist to guide him out of his shell' (medical officer's 1982 referral).

The philosophy of the Art Therapy Department at that time reflected the general prevailing medical orthodoxy, with emphasis on behavioural and developmental models. Its founder, Bruce Males, pioneered in 1973 a specific way of working with mentally handicapped individuals, adhering to 'developmental principles' within the context of the 'creative environment' which has permeated the practice of art therapy within the department. Described as the non-directive proach in an open studio, emphasis was placed on spontaneous creativity the therapeutic value inherent in the art-making process (Stott and Males

1984:18). This philosophy formed the core of Dillon's treatment for many years, providing consistency of time and place and the opportunity to express, in a concrete and symbolic way, that which had previously been 'acted out'.

In the latter part of the 1980s, evidence of a more 'directive' approach emerges from Dillon's case notes, recording his introduction to a variety of media, plasticine, paint and clay, with 'appropriate interventions' by the therapist, in an attempt to 'broaden' or 'work towards the next developmental stage' (Stott and Males 1984:119).

The directive and non-directive approaches used within the department were equally used depending on what was deemed appropriate for the individual. Their use was validated by the outcome of a research programme undertaken as a collaboration between the Psychology and Art Therapy Departments in 1977. The outcome indicated the effectiveness of both approaches dependent on individual needs and circumstances (Males and Males 1977).

A report in Dillon's file dated 1987 states that 'his behaviour is becoming more obsessional, never wavering from his painting routine', which involved Dillon 'systematically emptying the palette and filling each sheet of paper in sequence with just one colour'. This was followed, in each session, by a series of line drawings; these were occasionally varied in content, but images were produced in a repetitive manner incorporating 'clocks, dogs, numbers, the alphabet and houses'. In 1990 and 1991 the first evidence of planned individual work with Dillon emerged in the form of two consecutive student case studies; one was 'observational' in nature and the other claimed to be 'non-directive' (Ogle 1991; Thomas 1990). The latter, a more detailed study, demonstrated Dillon's ability and eagerness to relate on a one-to-one level.

> I feel an enormous amount of material was produced in these sessions and that this was indicative of the growing relationship which facilitated this work to be expressed. Dillon has managed to break from his old routine of repeated images . . . manifesting in a new theme of boy/man images.
>
> (Thomas 1990)

The student recommended that provision be made for Dillon to continue with individual art therapy sessions. Unfortunately, this was not possible due to changes within the department at the time. Dillon was subsequently placed on a waiting list, and reverted to his repetitive image-making. The 1990s reflected a more psychodynamic orientation, brought about by an influx of new therapists (evident in the work of Strand 1990) and coincided with a changing emphasis within art therapy training.

When I commenced work in the department in September 1992, Dillon was attending two open studio sessions per week, working in a prolific but repetitive manner, producing up to forty images of cats in any one session. I first became aware of Dillon as his youthful appearance and boyish good looks (which belied his chronological age) differentiated him from other more elderly clients within the session. Despite this obvious difference, his independence, self-imposed isolation and seemingly 'undemanding ways, made it easy to overlook him' (Ogle 1991).

Being aware that my caseload encompassed the waiting list, I began to observe him within the open studio session. He responded to my silent attention by making eye contact, smiling and voluntarily bringing his images to me when completed. Eventually, he began to work beside me, moving his large mound of paper to wherever I happened to sit. His ritualistic way of working continued, but the content of his work altered in my presence as he introduced me to a large vocabulary of images ranging from fish, boats and trees to animals and inanimate objects. As contact between Dillon and me became more established, so too did his territorial dominance in my presence within the studio. He began to act out his aggression and possessiveness with other clients by breaking their pencils or crayons or provocatively flicking his paper stick in their direction. Subsequently, I reviewed my timetable and made provision to see Dillon weekly for an individual art therapy session.

I have now been seeing Dillon individually for two years. Despite inevitable changes in our timetable during this period and his eventual weaning from the remaining studio session, Dillon continues to turn up at the new and the original session times for extended periods.

ART THERAPY WITH DILLON

Because of the volume of notes accumulated on Dillon over the last two years and the limitations of space within this chapter, I have found it necessary to be selective with the case material presented. Therefore I intend to focus on the major recurring themes, describing these within the context of two phases. This format should provide a general overview of the two-year relationship, with some specific insights into the process employed by Dillon as a means of surviving his situation.

Whilst reflecting on Dillon's notes, it became apparent that the themes introduced in the first ten sessions were those that preoccupied us in the first phase/year of therapy. Hence, the content of these sessions, provide, in a condensed form, the primary concerns which were addressed during this period. However, one must bear in mind that the links and interpretations made now with regard to these early sessions, are from the perspective of hindsight and with two years' experience of deciphering Dillon's idiosyncratic verbal and pictorial language, and not to my original state of 'not knowing' and unfamiliarity with him.

I shall briefly describe the relevant themes as they occurred, sequentially, during the first ten sessions, followed by a discussion connecting these themes within the broader context of the first phase of therapy and with reference to relevant psychodynamic theory. I intend to use the same format for the second phase, but shall make the relevant links between the two phases in the discussion.

ART THERAPY: THE FIRST PHASE

Let me also wear
Such deliberate disguises

('The Hollow Men', Eliot 1925/1982)

The first session involved Dillon exploring the individual room in a manic but ritualistic manner, scrutinising each shelf, cupboard and contents, accompanied by circular body movements. During the exploration, Dillon discovered a pair of scissors, handed it to me saying, 'I don't know why he cuts his hair, he always does that every week . . . you shouldn't cut your hair . . . ' and continued reprimanding himself in the third person.

I interpreted that he seemed to want me to keep him safe (by handing me the scissors) and to help him understand why he cut his hair. I also reiterated the need for mutual safety within the room. Dillon resisted any further exploration on the subject of hair cutting and lapsed into a series of his familiar cat drawings. I acknowledged his need for something familiar within the strange new environment, and stated that it would take time to adjust to the new routine.

Subsequent sessions shed light on the significance of the scissors and his hair cutting. The themes of boy/man emerged in the fourth session, accompanied by images of houses and scissors. The boy, which sometimes turned into a man and vice-versa, differed from each other only by the inclusion or omission of hair. Whilst producing these images Dillon continued a verbal barrage, with accounts of hair cutting peppered with references to home. The depiction of a yellow car which he described as his father's car, later came to represent a metamorphic image for visits home or a symbol of his father, depending on the context. He then went on to reveal in the fifth session, that 'his dad always cuts his hair' (a practice that continued until recently, dispensed with as the result of an increased use of community services). Dillon appeared ambivalent about this practice; he smiled, stroked his head aggressively, whilst castigating himself continuously for cutting his hair. The symbols of scissors, father, car and phallic-like aeroplanes appeared in his drawings (see Figure 6.1).

The fifth session also marked the first occasion in which Dillon referred to me as 'Christine'. (Christine it transpired, was the name of a favourite cousin, who had worked in the hospital many years before my arrival.) Dillon drew two trees, joined together at the base, and asked how to spell Christine. This seemed to represent Dillon's idealisation of me as Christine which lasted for approximately a year, fluctuating in the latter phase between Christine and Margaret, depending on whether he perceived me as a good or bad object. The Christine theme re-emerged in the next session. Dillon drew 'my house' and wondered aloud 'where Christine lives'; he then drew a 'brown cat who lives in Christine's house'. Dillon's cat images seemed to be associated with feelings of loss, envy and displacement. For example, he talked with ambivalence about the 'nice kitty at home', then reprimanded himself for 'kicking her and pulling her tail'. It would

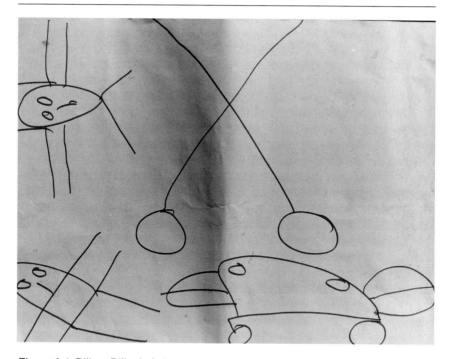

Figure 6.1 Dillon: Dillon's father, scissors, an aeroplane and a car

appear that the family cat became a receptacle for his feelings of displacement, a symbol of his own replacement, allowed to live at home when he cannot. The 'cat in Christine's house' seemed to contain elements of envy and desire in the transference.

The following session (number 7) Dillon introduced a new image, Humpty Dumpty (his most potent self-image) (Figure 6.2). The Humpty Dumpty occurred when I had informed him about the cancellation of the following session, due to a bank holiday. Dillon had looked perplexed and said he 'had a bad fit', fell down and vomited on the floor. He then drew a series of Humpty Dumpties, repeating the nursery rhyme line 'he couldn't be put back together again'. I acknowledged his distress and said that perhaps my news had felt like a 'blow'. He replied, 'He always falls and there is blood on the wall and on the floor'. I reassured him I would return and stated that things seemed to hurt him very easily, which was why he needed a strong 'shell' to protect himself, so he would not break like Humpty Dumpty. Dillon stared at me, drew another Humpty Dumpty and asked, 'Where does the "hat" go?' I pointed towards the head and Dillon subsequently drew a hat on Humpty Dumpty's head (Figure 6.3). He drew two more Humpty Dumpties with hats on, before the end of the session, perhaps for extra protection against separation or an attempt to block out thinking and listening.

Figure 6.2 Dillon: Humpty Dumpty

Figure 6.3 Dillon: Humpty Dumpty with a hat

The eighth session followed the break. Dillon appeared preoccupied with his hair, talking continuously to himself, whilst investigating and rearranging the contents of the room. He located a pair of scissors, drew a ball and proceeded to cut it into little pieces, handing them to me. With the same speed and proficiency Dillon cut a chunk of hair from his forehead and handed me the scissors while severely berating himself. This was followed by an uninterrupted series of twenty Humpty Dumpties. The anxiety within the session seemed to have been precipitated by the break. In retrospect, Dillon seemed to be demonstrating in every conceivable way how disturbed and unheld he felt; by chopping the paper, his hair, drawing twenty Humpty Dumpties and handing me the pieces to 'hold'.

Similarly, Dillon arrived at the ninth session and produced a handful of hair, having managed to cut it before the session commenced. The ensuing session reflected Dillon's mania, as he talked about 'how his dad gave him a lot of hair' and 'he had pulled loads out yesterday'. He drew a boy which then turned into 'bear with lots of hair'. He then revealed that he frequently plucked his secondary body hair from his neck, chin, eyebrows, nose, tummy, legs and bottom.

This disclosure was followed by several more hairy bears (Figure 6.4) and a Humpty Dumpty. Dillon sang the nursery rhyme as he worked. The singing seemed to pacify him; and he proceeded to sing his repertoire of nursery rhymes, including 'Jack and Jill' and 'Three blind mice'. Despite his resumed composure, I was struck by the inherent cruelty of the nursery rhymes. The 'broken crown' and 'cut off tails' were resonant of his own attempts at self-mutilation. I suggested

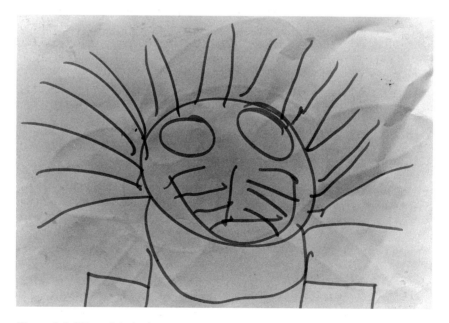

Figure 6.4 Dillon: A hairy bear

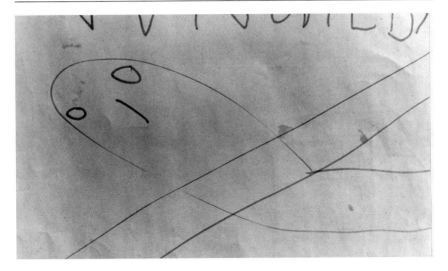

Figure 6.5 Dillon: An aeroplane with a man in it

to Dillon that he was trying desperately to show me the lengths he had gone to in order to try to remain as a boy within a man's body. Dillon stared at me, then drew an aeroplane with a man in it (which resembled a castrated penis, see Figure 6.5).

The following session (number 10) Dillon arrived with a shaven head. He seemed subdued throughout, and had difficulty in executing images, producing only three, 'a boy with lots of hair', 'Yogi Bear' and a painting which disintegrated under the weight of paint and handling. Dillon constantly rubbed his bristly head throughout the session, appeared confused and lethargic, repeating 'He doesn't know why he does it.'

I suggested that it must be difficult to remember the reason why he cut his hair as, having become so ritualised, the meaning must sometimes get lost.

Reflections on the first phase of therapy and theory

The first theme to emerge from the material presented was that of 'hair cutting'; this later became linked with 'home', his 'father' and the interchangeable 'boy/man' images. Sinason suggests that in many families where there is a handicapped child, the only way of managing the hurt is 'to demand that the child stays a baby' (Sinason 1991:21). The child internalises these wishes and fears that 'growing up to the best of his/her ability and differentiating, will lead to rejection or death' (Sinason 1991:21). In Dillon's situation he had already experienced rejection twofold, both by his biological and adoptive mothers. Hence, his fear of 'rejection or death is not necessarily a fantasy' (Sinason 1991:21). Dillon came to equate not only the arrival of his secondary body hair with adulthood but all hair, and concentrated mainly on attacking his head, the area associated with his handicap. His attacks of self-mutilation seem to have been desperate attempts to try to remain as a hairless boy in order to secure his visits home and the love of his father. His father's self-imposed role as barber seemed to be the origin of Dillon's fantasy and subsequent self-mutilation. For Dillon, this practice was inextricably linked with his home visits and familial acceptance.

Bicknell (1983) discusses the infantilisation of the mentally handicapped individual: '"The Peter Pan and Wendy" syndrome occurs, the child is infantilised, the "child" is accepted, but the handicapped adult to come at a later date is far less easily accepted' (Bicknell 1983:71). The 'infantilisation' permeated the transference and my counter-transference to such an extent I found I often had to struggle to remind myself that Dillon was in reality a 44-year-old man and not a 4-year-old boy reciting nursery rhymes.

Dillon's self-mutilation and sexual repression was graphically symbolised in the ninth session (and numerous others) as a 'man inside an aeroplane'. This image had the appearance of a man being trapped/castrated, inside a dis-connected, broken or dismembered object. The dilemma facing Dillon was a complex one. If his status as an adult male was acknowledged he feared he may risk the loss of his father and home; however, if he remained stuck in this time-warp he risked further frustration, self-injury and ambivalent feelings towards his parents.

According to Wheeley (1992), Freud's interpretation of the Greek myth of Oedipus focused solely on his deeds, isolating them as inevitable stages in childhood development. She states that Freud's theory omitted the parental act of abandoning him on a hillside to die in order to outwit the prophecy of the oracle. Wheeley suggests that if Freud had acknowledged or applied the same principle of inevitability to the entire myth, the parental wish for infanticide would be accepted as a universal step in the Oedipus complex and as a precursor to the child's preoccupation with incest and murder. Freud's theory was later modified by Klein and Winnicott to allow for the infant's fear of annihilation as a 'manic defence' subject to their defenceless state. In Dillon's situation, the first part of the myth, the parental wish to abandon or kill the child remained most relevant, in the light of his history of adoption and institutionalisation. Therefore, it would appear that the 'terror of infanticide' may have been the precipitating factor for many of his manic and autistic-like defences.

Similarly, Dillon was fearful of therapy, of getting in touch, of being wounded, of opening the shutters of his autistic-like shell and spilling out uncontainably. Tustin (1990) maintains that 'emerging autistic children experience their body as being in two halves, one half seemed to represent the mother and the other half the baby. The danger is that the two halves will fall disastrously apart, never to be put together again' (Tustin 1990:46). This helped me to understand Dillon's reaction to the bank-holiday break, his introduction of Humpty Dumpty who 'couldn't be put back together again' and his subsequent disturbing description of his experience of having fits and falling down. Tustin states that treatment brings to the fore their many bodily fears which have been 'kept at bay by feeling that they were protected by a shell' (Tustin 1990:46). Similarly, I feel Dillon's shell is a complex construction involving numerous mechanisms, through which he attempts to 'hold' himself together.

This echoes Symington's (1985) succinct description of the 'primitive omnipotent processes' the baby resorts to in order to survive when the mother is absent or emotionally unavailable to him. She maintains that the baby attempts to hold himself together in a variety of ways by focusing 'his attention on a sensory stimulus – visual, auditory, tactile or olfactory. When his attention is held by this stimulus, he feels held together' (Symington 1985:481).

Dillon's various survival mechanisms, which ultimately form his 'protective shell', encompass his constant bodily movement in the form of his ritualistic walking on tip-toe, several times around the room, as if to form a physical boundary of 'self' or 'second skin' (Bick 1986:114). When his attention is not engaged in this way, Dillon resorts to flicking his paper stick, in close proximity to his face, as a 'visual stimulus' and as a means of blocking out external stimulation and communication (Symington 1985). Similarly, Dillon's constant talking to himself, flitting from one subject to another, incorporating conversations with significant others into his monologue can be seen as an omnipotent attempt to control or deny separation, and are also related to the primitive defence of 'constant movement' (Symington 1985). 'All this movement feels like a continuous holding of skin; if the movement stops, this may feel like a gap, a hole in the skin through which the self may spill out' (Symington 1985:481). This resonates with Gardner's (1984) theory of 'spatial intelligence' and Rees' (1995) research into the powerful motivational urges of deprived individuals 'to maintain internal consistency and control', in order to provide some 'definition of self' (Rees 1995:132).

However, like the function of any of the defence mechanisms, the processes employed become pathological if they cease to be flexible, concealing the individual inside a rigid barrier. The focusing on a sensory stimulus to hold the self together is seen in its 'most extreme and unmodified form in infantile autism' (Symington 1985:483). According to Tustin, the construction of the 'autistic shell' encases the individual 'in their own sensation-dominated "straitjacket" or "asylum" to the exclusion of almost everything else' (Tustin 1990:31). Therefore, she maintains that 'effective work with these children depends upon their being "held" (psychologically) by a therapist who has some inkling of the peculiar world in which they "live and move" and have their precarious sense of being' (Tustin 1990:32).

Thus the early work with Dillon mainly concerned the deciphering of his idiosyncratic verbal and pictorial language and its layered meaning in order that he would feel understood and therefore psychologically held.

THE SECOND PHASE OF THERAPY

Oh, dreadful is the check – intense the agony
– when the ear begins to hear,
and the eye begins to see;
When the pulse begins to throb, the brain to think again;
The soul to feel the flesh, the flesh to feel the chain.

('On becoming', Anne Brontë 1972)

I consider that the second phase of therapy commenced once Dillon ceased to self-mutilate. The cessation of his self-destructive behaviour occurred towards the end of the first year of individual art psychotherapy and followed many months of acting-out behaviour. The themes of destruction and repression continued (to a lesser extent) but were now confined to his image-making. In this second phase, I intend to focus briefly on Dillon's reaction to a break in routine. The disruption will be described in the context of two sessions, seven months apart. These two vignettes embody much of the chaos caused by the external uncertainty which predominates Dillon's present existence and the latter phase of art therapy.

Following the two-week Christmas break in 1994, Dillon arrived early and in an agitated state. During the session he talked in his usual disjointed manner about 'Xmas' and drew a house with Xs on the doors and windows. This was followed by a 'cat and Cherry' (the latter a horse and former hospital pet). I commented that he seemed to be feeling the loss of people and things he loved since his Christmas visit. Dillon stared at me and asked, 'Did you break your head?' I was momentarily stunned, unsure how to answer and then reassured him that I had not broken my head. I tried to explore if that was how he had experienced the holiday break, but met with resistance. In retrospect, I realise I had been too direct by answering instead of exploring the meaning of his question. My mistake became apparent as mania ensued; the session deteriorated into a masturbatory production of Humpty Dumpties, blocking out both me and thinking. Dillon produced thirty-two Humpty Dumpties in this session, ten with hats on, occurring in rapid succession. Whenever I tried to make a link or explore the meaning of his images, the hats seemed to appear, indicating that thinking had become too unbearable. Although the subsequent two to three sessions enabled Dillon to re-establish his routine, his withdrawal from his shell and a decrease in anxiety took many more sessions.

Seven months later, Dillon experienced another period of separation due to a planned three-week break which also coincided with the physical move of the Art Therapy Department and the closure of the hospital.

On my return from the break, I encountered a very manic Dillon who seemed to reflect the chaos of our new environment. Aware of his previous reactions to breaks and separations (which seem to resonate with the catalogue of rejections he had experienced in the past) I felt it necessary to be more directive in order to try to contain his anxiety. I interrupted his pacing ritual and asked him to sit and try to listen to me. Dillon complied and stared intently. I acknowledged the disruption

Figure 6.6 Dillon: A bus full of people and animals

of the holiday break to his routine, the many changes within the hospital and the very limited space within our new department. I explained the difficulties we all experienced in trying to adjust and suggested that we could work together to make it easier. Encouraged by Dillon's attentiveness, I continued and suggested using smaller sheets of paper (due to the lack of storage space) and to try and think together about each image before going on to the next one.

Dillon pointed to the paper and said, 'Cut it'. Using a halved sheet of paper Dillon produced one detailed image in this session: 'a bus full of children and animals' (Figure 6.6). For the first time, Dillon gave me a coloured marker and asked me to draw a snowman inside one of the windows, which he proceeded to copy. This symbolic mirroring continued throughout the session, filling in the windows on the bus. The subsequent sessions continued to encompass this new routine, Dillon favouring the use of smaller sheets of paper and my pictorial participation.

My drawing in the sessions continues to date, with me following Dillon's instructions and his attempts to copy these new images, thus increasing his pictorial vocabulary and my understanding. The latter half of these sessions usually reverts to his ritualistic Humpty Dumpty drawings as separation at the end of each session remains difficult for him.

Reflections on the second phase of therapy and theory

In her interpretation of Klein's paranoid–schizoid position, Segal describes the early ego as being: 'largely unorganised . . . in a constant state of flux, its degree of integration varying from day to day, or even moment to moment' (Segal 1988:25).

Similarly, Dillon's emotional state oscillates under the influence of intolerable anxiety, causing defensive disintegration in the form of 'splitting' and 'projection' (Segal 1988). Dillon's use of art reflects his various states of being mirroring his internal disintegration through images produced in rapid succession, recording his degree of anxiety like film stills.

This was reflected in the first session following the Christmas break. Dillon's ability to symbolise in the initial stages of the session was graphically illustrated in his depiction of houses and animals. However, as his anxiety increased, his images became more obsessive and repetitive, blocking 'me' (the writer) and 'thinking' out as his resources to deal with thinking depleted.

Symington maintains that 'misunderstanding the survival mechanisms might well lead to their reinforcement as the patient feels that he does not have available to him someone who can understand and therefore hold these primitive anxieties, so he must hold on to himself' (Symington 1985:484). Hence Dillon's increasing anxiety and mania throughout the session, as he was not initially understood by me and therefore he had to resort to the physical holding of himself in the form of an obsessive production of images.

Dillon's comment, 'Did you break your head?' and its implications needed to be explored before offering it back to him. My direct reply, as the resulting mania indicates, must have felt like an attack. Dillon seemed to equate the holiday break with a physical break or pain. This was verbalised by the broken head and symbolised by the subsequent Humpty Dumpties, his reference to falls/fits within the session and my counter-transference feelings of dizziness, headache and an inability to think.

According to Sinason:

> Where there has been organic damage to the brain or trauma, the actual apparatus for thinking has been affected and I consider that a thought then becomes an uncomfortable physical sensation. Some head banging, for example, is a way of knocking a bad feeling out of the head; sometimes it is a desperate attempt to knock a thought into shape.
>
> (Sinason 1992:225)

Sinason's theory highlights the extent to which Dillon has resorted to blocking out thinking. His history of attacking his head by hair-cutting, his frequent falls and fits and his constant movement, which forms his protective shell, are attempts at blocking out communication and thinking. McCormack illustrates the pain involved in reactivating the thought processes of a 35-year-old man with mild learning difficulties. The patient states that 'If somebody sits and listens it opens the "claw" in my head'. At first McCormack felt he was being attacked for not listening to the patient; however, it emerged that the 'real pain was in being listened to, which is also to be thought about'. Over the two years he saw this patient McCormack says that much of what they 'thought about was indeed very painful. Thinking and memory can lead to a knowledge of trauma that is unbearable' (McCormack 1991:61).

Bearing in mind these various theories, I resorted to a more directive approach in the session following the three-week break in order to provide some concrete containment. As psychological holding was proving inadequate at this point (due to Dillon's attack on his own resources to think), I needed to bypass this inert and painful position. Thus the concrete adaptation of the art materials to the new environment somehow enabled him to shift from his manic retreat and adjust to a new and healthier routine, involving another live object. This new phase appears to have enabled Dillon to open up to the possibility of learning a new pictorial vocabulary of being able to take things in and think for short periods at least.

Tustin (1990) maintains that autistic patients need a therapist who is in touch with their autistic states and fears of emerging from them, 'who is endowed with common sense' in order to help them 'come down to earth', in the metaphorical sense: 'such patients need to feel that there is a nurturing person who cares deeply whether they live or die and who affirms their existence by talking to them as if they exist' (Tustin 1990:47)

CONCLUSION

Come away, O Human child!
To the waters and the wild
with a faery, hand in hand,
For the world's more full of
Weeping than you can understand.

('The Stolen Child', W.B. Yeats 1986/1990)

W.B. Yeats' description of the 'faery child' or 'changeling' draws upon Irish folklore for its inspiration and on the many myths that existed to explain alterations or mysterious change in the human spirit. Many such myths have evolved throughout history and in other cultures in order to explain the alienation and mystery surrounding conditions like autism.

Kanner and subsequent writers within the field have shed light on the nature of autism, but Tustin's theory of 'autistic encapsulation' provided the most appropriate framework for me when thinking about the complex defence mechanisms employed by Dillon as a means of surviving his predicament.

Dillon's most prominent symbol of self, the Humpty Dumpty, aptly depicts his own fragile condition. He lives in fear of his eggshell protection breaking, the contents spilling out uncontrollably and never being put back together again. However, the egg can also symbolise birth and new life and is, I feel, representative of the second phase of art therapy with Dillon. Here he has demonstrated an ability to move in and out of his shell by interacting with me in the first part of each session then subsequently retreating, through his repetitive Humpty Dumpty images, as a means of holding himself together (Symington 1985). This physical holding which forms his protective shell is vital for his continued existence and survival.

Dillon has shown how art therapy provides a safe and appropriate means of communication, without its damaging his innate defence mechanisms. Dillon's use of art permeates his shell structure in an osmotic manner, allowing movement in and out, while maintaining its protective function, thereby preventing Dillon becoming prey to his own 'sensation-dominated "strait-jacket" or asylum' to the exclusion of almost everything else (Tustin 1990:31).

At present, Dillon's main preoccupation concerns external change regarding the hospital closure and relocation of clients and staff. These external conditions mirror a similar internal metamorphosis and remain juxtaposed to his need for consistency and sameness. Despite his omnipotent shell-like protection, his depleted resources to deal with change leave him more vulnerable than most. The prevailing *status quo* has abruptly altered from a period of stasis and inertness. However traumatic and dramatic these changes have proven to be, they equally provide an unprecedented opportunity to help redress and establish anew Dillon's boundaries of self.

Rees states that 'we all possess a powerful motivational urge to make sense of situations, often with very limited tools at our disposal. By ordering our experiences we ensure psychological continuity and our emotional survival' (Rees 1995:119). The outcome of her art therapy research with people who have severe learning difficulties validates this hypothesis. Rees' astute observations in relation to this client group have proved insightful and relevant to my understanding many of Dillon's spatial behaviours, as their repetitiveness and apparent resistance had often appeared to be against the therapeutic relationship.

My own process in writing this case study has equally proven invaluable as it allowed me the opportunity to reflect, evaluate and value my work, which in normal working practice becomes filed away and forgotten about. The process of reflection has also highlighted the areas of change which I had taken for granted, as I often became caught up in the resistance and frustration of extended periods of inertia. However, the effects of good supervision together with the theories of Tustin (1990), Sinason (1992), Symington (1985) and Rees (1995), have helped guide me through this 'primordial quagmire of unlabelled emotion' (Rees 1995:119). This body of knowledge has forearmed me with the necessary tools to help 'order Dillon's experiences' and thus provide 'psychological continuity' and 'holding' through this period of flux.

NOTE

1   A version of this essay first appeared as 'Humpty Dumpty Had A Great Fall' in *Inscape*, 1(1), 1996.

BIBLIOGRAPHY

Bick, E (1968) 'The Experience of Skin in Early Object Relations', *International Journal of Psychoanalysis* 49: 484–6.

Bicknell, J. (1983) 'The Psychopathology of Handicap, *British Journal of Medical Psychology* 56: 167–78.

Brontë, A. (1972) *Poems*, ed. Denis Thompson, London: Chatto and Windus.

Conference proceedings (1984) *Art Therapy as Psychotherapy in Relation to the Mentally Handicapped*, 29–30 November 1984, St Albans College of Art and Design, Hertfordshire.

Eliot, T.S. (1925/1982) 'The Hollow Men' in *T.S. Eliot – Selected Poems*, London: The Chaucer Press Ltd.

Gardner, H. (1984) *Frames of Mind – The Theory of Multiple Intelligence*. London: Heinemann.

Gray, J., Hughes, R., Cole, P. and Pearson, M. (1985) 'Art Therapy as Psychotherapy with the Mentally Handicapped', *Inscape*, 2.

Hughes, R. (1988) 'The Application of Object Relations Theories to Art Therapy with Three Women with Mental Handicap', *Inscape*, Summer.

Kanner, Leo (1943) 'Autistic Disturbance of Affective Contact', *Nervous Child*, 2: 217–50.

Males, J. and Males, B. (1977) Unpublished survey, Psychology Department, St Lawrence's Hospital, Caterham, Surrey.

McCormack, B. (1991) 'Thinking, Discourse and the Denial of History Psychodynamic Aspects of Mental Handicap', *Irish Journal of Psychological Medicine*, 8(1): 59–64.

Ogle, J. (1991) Unpublished essay, St Albans College of Art and Design, Hertfordshire.

Rees, M. (1995) 'Making Sense of Marking Space – Researching Art Therapy with People who Have Severe Learning Difficulties' in *Art and Music: Therapy and Research*. Gilroy, A. and Lee, C. (eds), London: Routledge London.

Shakespeare, W. (1987) *Shakespeare's Complete Works*, W.J. Craig (ed.), Oxford: Oxford University Press.

Segal, H. (1988) *Introduction to the Work of Melanie Klein*, London: Karnac Books.

Sinason, V. (1991) 'Interpretations that Feel Horrible to Make and the Theoretical Unicorn', *Journal of Child Psychotherapy* 17(1): 11–26.

Sinason, V. (1992) *Mental Handicap and the Human Condition – New Approaches from the Tavistock*, London: Free Association Books.

Stott, J. and Males, B. (1984) 'Art Therapy for People who are Mentally Handicapped' in *Art as Therapy – An Introduction to the Use of Art as a Therapeutic Technique*, Dalley, T. (ed.), London: Tavistock Publications.

Strand, S. (1990) 'Counteracting Isolation: Group Art Therapy for People with Learning Difficulties', *Group Analysis*, 23: 255–263.

Symington, J. (1985) 'The Survival Function of Primitive Omnipotence' in *Journal of Psychoanalysis*, 66: 481–7.

Thomas, G. (1990) Unpublished case study, St Albans College of Art and Design, Hertfordshire.

Tipple, R. (1992) 'Art Therapy with People who Have Severe Learning Difficulties', in *Art Therapy, A Handbook*, Waller, D. and Gilroy, A. (eds), Buckingham: Open University Press.

Tipple, R. (1993) 'Challenging Assumptions of the Importance of Transference Processes in Work with People with Learning Difficulties', *Inscape*, Summer.

Tipple, R. (1994) 'Communication and Interpretation in Art Therapy with People who Have a Learning Disability', *Inscape*, 2.

Tustin, F. (1990) *The Protective Shell in Children and Adults*, London: Karnac Books.

Wheeley, S. (1992) 'Looks that Kill the Capacity for Thought', *Journal of Analytical Psychology*, 37: 187–210.

Yeats, W.B. (1886/1990) *The Poems*, Daniel Albright (ed.), London: Dent.

Chapter 7

Rape! The violation of integrity and will

Rose Hughes

Central theme
- An account of individual art therapy sessions with a woman with learning difficulties who had been raped.

Key points
- Some observations about the nature and social perception of rape, in particular how the right to protection is not always highly valued on behalf of people with learning difficulties.
- The manner in which art therapy can replace the experience of disempowerment and deception with an increasing familiarity with self-determination and trust.
- The power of creating a supportive therapeutic alliance in this most sensitive of areas.

This chapter is about the rape of a woman with learning difficulties. It considers her use of art therapy and the broader legal and social factors which compounded this tragic life-event. To begin with, some observations about rape form a backdrop to an introduction to Beatrice.

RAPE

'Rape' defined in the *Longman English Dictionary* includes three facets which are:

1   An act or instance of robbing, despoiling or violating.
2   The crime of forcing a woman to have sexual intercourse against her will.
3   An outrageous violation.

In common parlance, point 2 is immediately understood as being the meaning of rape, with points 1 and 3 seen as yardsticks by which to measure the crime and the victim. That this value system of victim integrity and worth is real can be seen by the recent reporting and acknowledgement of male rape and the rape of prostitutes. For quite different reasons these two sections of the community were seen as virtually unrapeable: males perhaps because they are expected to never become subjugated by physical or mental force and prostitutes because they were somehow seen as forfeiting free will and therefore could not be violated. However progressive these developments are, it is only in extreme circumstances that they are given credibility as, for example, in the following two cases reported in national and local newspapers recently. In one a number of prostitutes were forced to have unprotected sex with a man with Aids and in the other a young man was homosexually raped by strangers in a London park. Thus it was only because of the Aids virus and the stranger rape of the man that these two cases spoke loud enough to be heard over the prejudicial status of the victim.

How many newspaper headlines do you see expressing the horror of rape of a woman with learning difficulties? Very few, if any! This is because will and violation are not commonly estimated highly for and on behalf of such women. However, attempts in law have been made to protect their interests. In *Butterworths Police Law* (English and Card 1994) it states that rape is non-consensual intercourse and, in particular, the Sexual Offences Act of 1976 adds: 'where the female is so mentally deficient or young or drunk that her knowledge or understanding are such that she is not in a position to decide whether to consent or resist' and English and Card comment:

> An apparent consent by the woman in such a case is not a real consent. In a fairly recent case, the Court of Appeal has stated that there is a difference between consent and submission, that is, that a woman who submits does not necessarily consent.
>
> (English and Card 1994:601)

That rape occurs is accepted, and it is reported more as there is believed to be a less collusive environment legally, with derogatory perceptions of women and women's human rights. However, high-profile rape trials over recent years reveal that the tabloid press and popular cultural views are ambivalent about male guilt and justice for women. A stark example can be seen in the case of the American boxer, Mike Tyson, jailed for rape but welcomed back to his public and professional world upon his release so unquestioningly that women in Britain waiting at bus stops late at night were confronted with a large close-up photograph of his face on the advertisement screens of the bus shelter. Across his neck was written the word 'challenger', referring to his forthcoming fight with Frank Bruno. The insensibility of a convicted rapist's face confronting women and girls at bus stops was mute. Within weeks Tyson was again being questioned about another sexual assault.

Another perspective was voiced by the business tycoon Owen Oyston, convicted and jailed in May 1996 for the rape of a 16-year-old girl, 46 years his junior. He described this rape as an 'affair', revealing the deception to self and others to conceal or validate this abuse.

All sexual abuse is perpetrated in a context of its calculated invisibility. As we can see, there are many ways of assisting this invisibility. One way of keeping something unseen is to not give it a name. To assist this, perceptions which confine rather than clarify understanding create ambivalence and become a tool of the abuser. Rape is often inflicted upon a known person by someone in a role of responsibility, care and protection of their victim, or by a member of their peer group.

It is not difficult to grasp the compounding of vulnerability of people with learning difficulties whose will and integrity are already demoralised. The term learning difficulty refers to people whose difficulties lie in part in concept formation. Thus, much can be felt but remains unnamed, invisible to words. Rape is defraud, and the rapist a trickster. This trickery is not executed simply by physical violence but by emotional and mental means. Women with learning difficulties may be tricked about the emotional relationship they have and can be guileless about other people's motives.

Confusion at the very least is created as a precondition to rape. This confusion can be emotional and physical. With so much past denial in the education and maturational guidance of people with learning difficulties, sensations and emotions are not named, understood or explored. The subjected are so, before they are raped. They are vulnerable physically and psychologically. The trickster rapist manipulates confusion and disempowerment of self-control, of thought, feeling and sensation to secure the invisibility of what he does and to deceive and confuse all.

BEATRICE

Beatrice had sex. She knew the words for sexual intercourse. She did not know the word rape. However, she could name some of her feelings, recount events and act out her distress. In this chapter I will explore her case, initially referred for ten sessions of art therapy to support her during the trial of a 'normal' man for her repeated rape. The following paragraphs give a brief portrait of Beatrice. Then aspects of her art therapy sessions are considered, plus the paradox that is evoked intrapsychically by public enquiry into private pain. To conclude, the damage of rape is named.

Beatrice has a learning difficulty; she can read and write a little and now in her mid-forties she has been learning to cook and care for herself in a supported environment. She is the eldest of three siblings of retired parents. She regularly takes holidays with her parents in their caravanette. These are for her the high-light of life and the camps she stays at provide her with an opportunity to dance and play, and also play with young children whom she both cares for and identifies with.

Her day-to-day life comprises a voluntary part-time job in a crèche and attending groups at a social education centre. Her social life is otherwise inconsistent contact with friends who, like herself, have learning difficulties. Beatrice often expresses a need for more company and within her home environment she will actively seek it out. She can appear very agitated at times and this distress seems to emanate from this need for company and attachment. She likes to talk and does so with a lot of insistence if she feels unseen. She can become very attached to people in her environment when she feels heard and valued.

Because of the limits to personal autonomy and social integration and because of the probable delay in meeting primary needs and achieving a balanced and mature achievement of narcissistic needs, some people with learning difficulties, including Beatrice, find happiness and comfort in activities usually confined to childhood. This is not to imply that she is a child but that she is not able – for a whole matrix of social and emotional reasons – to do, to the same extent, the 'adult' things to create security and happiness. With this compromise, naïvety is the price paid for an assumed safety – an assumption that does not always work for the individual in reality and which can perpetuate vulnerability.

Beatrice's need for fun, stimulation and social engagement can be seen in her drawings of herself playing in the swing park and in the paddling pool. Her joy in life is still symbolised for her in these childhood safe places. They are a regular, sustaining inner resource for her.

I first met Beatrice when she joined the art therapy group I ran during the winter evenings for the residents at the respite and training unit where she lived. The manager wanted an art therapy group to improve the self-expression and interpersonal relationships of the client group. The unit worked to help clients develop independent living skills and was for some geared towards a future of minimum staff supervision, possibly living in their own flats in the local community. The achievement of a level of tolerance, of independence and practical domestic skill was the main focus of the unit. The art therapy group was intended to enable clients to express and explore any difficulties arising out of this training process and for them to experience themselves intimately amongst peers.

The group was non-directive with a structure which allowed time to draw and paint and time to discuss with the group. The drawing and painting sessions took place around large tables; the discussion was held in a circle around the pictures placed on the floor, with group members seated in comfortable chairs.

The group members had quite diverse needs. One who had many autistic features seemed to enjoy the being together of the group and the use of paint. Another had a history of schizophrenia and many griefs and concerns. Another young and capable young man of a sensitive nature needed space to explore his interpersonal anxieties.

Beatrice developed a pattern of drawing what she called a 'good' and a 'bad' image. Memories of holidays filled with playful activity usually represented the 'good' and the 'bad' usually reflected daily worries and tribulations. She seemed to use this process to create emotional balance, and within the group she worked on sharing her own stories and giving space and listening time to deepening her awareness of others.

THE RAPE

It was some months after the group ended that her key worker became aware that something was wrong. Beatrice was seen less and less around the unit, or coming and going from her flat (which was situated in the suburban street in front of the unit). She was apparently withdrawing and was, unusually, refusing to allow her key worker to enter her flat, not even opening the door. After eventually allowing contact, she disclosed the deeply distressing sequence of events to which she had been subjected.

A small group of local 'normal' teenage girls had befriended her and visited her in her flat. They convinced staff and Beatrice that they cared for and liked her, a friendship she readily accepted. However, after a time they brought a 'normal' young man to visit her and began debate around sex and babies. Despite Beatrice having had a hysterectomy, they convinced her that she could have a child and encouraged her to fantasise about becoming a mother. They said this boy would give her a baby. They set the stage so to speak and left. The young man remained and in her misguided and confused state he moved from a vaguely consentual proposition for sex to a violent and non-consensual assault. It is very doubtful that Beatrice would have been capable of an informed mature choice, given her learning difficulty and her susceptibility to manipulation.

Despite her saying 'No' to sex he penetrated her vaginally and anally over several visits, causing bleeding and pain to both areas. The police were informed and the young man was called for trial at the Old Bailey. Beatrice wanted the man to be punished. She was upset, angry and confused.

THE THERAPY

Ten individual sessions of art therapy to help her with her distress, both about the assault and the imminent court case, were funded by the local council responsible for her unit. However, I felt that this did not give enough time to explore and work through her feelings or to receive an internally sustainable sense of support from me as her therapist. Beatrice knew me already, so trust was remaining from that previous time. However, I felt guilty that so few sessions now would not allow her to develop a sense of safety and sanctuary and that the beginning, middle and end of therapy would rush by all too quickly. I was aware that feelings expressed and explored would have to be experienced with the end of support from her therapist being clearly in sight. There are cases when short-term therapy is useful in that it lets the client avoid the dependency and the lowering of defences that longer-term therapy allows. Longer-term therapy allows the client to re-experience and explore, through the transference within a continuing relationship, the weaknesses and strengths of earlier significant relationships. This longer therapy would, I feel in Beatrice's case, have helped her more to strengthen her inner resources and more completely marginalise the harm done to her. But processes within us and resonant experiences are not weighed and measured by time alone. James Mann in his book *Time-limited Psychotherapy* says:

> The link between time and reality is insoluble. We can divorce ourselves from time only by undoing reality, or from reality only by undoing the sense of time. Categorical time is measured by clocks and calendars; existential time is that which is experienced, lived in, rather than observed.
>
> (Mann 1973:3)

Thomas Wolfe spoke of the meaning of time when he wrote: 'Each moment is the fruit of forty thousand years. The minute-winning days, like flies, buzz home to death, and every moment is a window on all time' (Wolfe 1952:3).

I am still not completely at ease with the briefness of this course of therapy and Beatrice clearly expressed her wish that it could continue. We can only live with this.

The sessions began. They were held in the art therapy room at my home, this being a small room equipped with a large table, chairs, a variety of art materials and a telephone, with a second door out to the garden. The contract with Beatrice was made verbally and it covered mainly practical considerations such as her confirmation of the days and times she would be able to attend, her transport arrangements and also her perceptions of the purpose of therapy. We also discussed the ways she might like to structure her sessions, between drawing, painting and talking. These options remained fluid.

It very quickly appeared that Beatrice was objectifying her experiences. She drew pictures of the assaults (Figure 7.1) and spoke of her anger with the teenage girls who created the conditions for it to happen. She recalled how the man had laughed despite her requests that he stop. She said she had not wanted sex but that initially she had felt physically stimulated. It seemed that after much police questioning and disclosure to carers and family that she was now numb and that occasionally panic and anxiety overcame her. She would raise her voice and talk in a dissociated way of her wish for justice. She began to discuss the police interviews and said that she both wanted to forget what had happened and to get in touch with her feelings. It seemed that the horror of the assaults coupled with the police enquiry was making her deny and split off from her feelings. She was using the therapy as sanctuary, a shelter in the storm. She began to draw pictures of holidays and all the happy times in the past that she had enjoyed so much. As with her former use of words and art in the therapy group she was now, in the language of one-word responses and simple sentences combined with the elucidating use of images, retaining a sense of 'good' and 'bad' in life, but was having to cut off and hold down feelings to avoid being overwhelmed.

There was much confusion expressed. Was she as frightened by the forthcoming trial as she had been by the assaults? It seemed so and she sought an

Figure 7.1 Beatrice: The rape

escape into denial and depression. Anthony Storr writes of depression and creativity that the liability to depression can act as a goad:

> prodding the potential victim into undertaking the solitary, difficult, painful, and often unrewarding work of exploring his own depths and recording what he finds there. As long as he is able to do this, he may escape being overwhelmed.
>
> (Storr 1988:143)

The struggle to repress was harboured and fought, its harmfulness expressed by her as she spoke of one or two individuals who embodied her projected thought and were telling her to 'Forget about it'. She was angry.

Later in the therapy she drew the assault again. As before it was made up of matchstick figures, almost diagrammatical in its depiction of the series of assaults. The images seemed extraordinarily emotionless but, unlike the previous occasion, she seemed to feel upset and did not want to look at the picture once it was completed. She turned it face down on the table and continued by drawing happy memories of visits to the swing park. She said words to the effect that she could only face the painful feelings in small bouts. The next week she came saying that she did not want to look at the incident and she lost herself in drawings of happy times. Unconscious representations were not explored verbally. She was clearly trying to defend against the emerging emotional pain and, I felt, after so much loss of control of her own processes – physically and emotionally by the assault and thinking and feeling through the legal process – for the sake of her integrity it was desirable that she, so to speak, take the helm of her own ship, in order to restore her faith in herself first. Storr, again writing of creative processes, explains how self-mastery is the precursor to overcoming depression. Beatrice's use of art therapy seemed to enable her to begin this essential journey.

> We can now go a step further, and understand that the creative process can be a way of protecting the individual against being overwhelmed by depression; a means of regaining a sense of mastery in those who have lost it, and, to a varying extent, a way of repairing a self damaged by bereavement or by the loss of confidence in human relationships which accompanies depression from whatever cause.
>
> (Storr 1988:143)

The next session she arrived upset and angry, talking in a very loud voice as if she could contain herself no more. Sorting through the jumble of thoughts and feelings it emerged that the taxi driver bringing her to the session had been unable to find the address and so had ejected her a street away. (This incident was taken up by her carers with the taxi company.) This rejection and lack of support triggered access to anger. She felt that the briefness of art therapy sessions was due to lack of commitment from her staff and that they were going to force her to move on to see a counsellor (that is, disclosure would be starting all over again). She also believed that she had been threatened with being thrown out of her flat if any males, including long-standing friends, came to visit her. She was clearly feeling very vulnerable and abused by all around her, and within these feelings were details which conspired to suggest and encourage a belief that she was being punished. More carer control of her and more isolation may have been deemed to protect her, but in fact implied that she was doing something wrong for the assault to have happened. It was again a feeling of loss of appropriate care, of autonomy and self-control which seemed to create distress and a frenetic state within her.

This emotional frenzy and chaos led on to a drawing of a deep red sunset (Figure 7.2). It looked a little like female genitalia to me, which I interpreted to her. She spontaneously went on to talk about how sore she had been after the assault and of her bleeding from 'front and back passage'. It seemed that the pain brought to the session, projected on to her feelings within her current life and relationships, mirrored the feelings evoked by the attack. More and more of her images began to look bloody, as if the violence physically and emotionally was being let out, both deliberately and unconsciously.

I have seen this before in the works of people who have been abused. A systemically beaten child produced drawings in art therapy unconsciously littered with bruises, bumps and elements of fragmentation. This releasing of previously repressed feelings is, I think, a process like grief. It can begin to resolve depression and protect the individual from further depersonalisation and confusion. This painting-out of abuse – by which I do not simply mean graphic illustrations but the spontaneous and unconscious painting-out of horror and pain in tone, colour, texture, mass and line – is deeply cathartic. The 'letting-out' resolves the internalisation causing depression, the isolation contributing to depersonalisation and the confusion caused by thoughts and feelings stuck between repression and expression.

This process can remain unnamed to the client, but the sense of facing, sharing and releasing the pain assists the healing process like tears soothe an aching heart. Adrian Hill, a founder of art therapy in the 1940s, observed that the art work of patients often expresses an emotional depth when they are most unwell. 'Indeed it is difficult to reconcile the lyrical and visionary outpourings of the sick person with the banalities which often issue from the self-same hand when health is on the mend' (Hill 1945:41).

After this drawing of a sunset she went on to draw a picture of a 'happy family', with a house (Figure 7.3), flowers, a newborn baby and herself playing with large hands – powerful or cumbersome was not clear. It seemed as if she was trying to move away from the distress of the first part of the session. The image of a newborn baby reminded me of the theme used in the coercion by the teenage girls, the belief in the idea that Beatrice could have a baby. In her drawing the baby seemed to represent a new beginning for the small family unit of 'mum', 'dad', Beatrice and another similar figure.

To reconstruct this ideal, depicted by baby and family, seemed a reclamation of the human love and bonding that that been spoiled and stolen. Baby and family represent good inner objects for Beatrice as the swing park and paddling pool

Figure 7.2 Beatrice: A deep red sunset

Figure 7.3 Beatrice: A happy family

represented a joy and freedom in life and in herself. The baby and family internally represented intimacy, security, bonding and love. These interpretations are based on her verbal associations as well as visual observations. Beatrice is interestingly somehow inside and outside of this family. The cruel cynicism of the rape, both of her body integrity, but also of her higher emotional and spiritual aspirations, personified by baby and family an inner sanctity already marginalised for this woman who knew intellectually she could never have or be this baby.

She recalled angrily someone calling her a baby and telling her to grow up. Her anger expressed the exasperation she could not name, that of being restricted in so much in life, of having lived the brutality of rape and then been challenged and mocked for any surviving remnants of her expression of need and emotion. She spoke in general and specific terms of feeling pressurised into accepting decisions and points of view that were not her own and did not feel right to her, again amplifying the disempowerment and indignity of her rape. She was particularly upset that a carer had used a key to enter her flat: the association with rape is obvious. The focus of her anger seemed to be clear in what this entry represented for her emotionally and the expression of anger seemed a way for her to demonstrate her need to reclaim and restate boundaries and personal power.

Free will to name and define boundaries is sometimes overlooked and marginalised for people with learning difficulties. This disempowerment can overtly and subtly silence them, leaving them vulnerable to abuse. Her anger was, I felt, her great motivator to be heard, to overcome rather than be overcome. As with all her expression of thoughts and feelings, I endeavoured to be and to be seen as hearing, acknowledging and validating her. This was not difficult because my counter-transference relationship with her in part created the understanding ally that she wanted to make real inside herself and in those around her.

The therapeutic alliance meant that she did not have to undergo this journey of overcoming pain and injustice alone. She expressed her trust in me and the alliance seemed defended when it could have so easily have become lost in the myriad of projections of betrayal, invisibility and lovelessness. A total breakdown of trust would have made this short-term therapy counter-productive. Likewise, the love of her parents seemed dependable, but she was clearly taking this journey of recovery as an independent person.

Rape with profound brutality had initiated a maturational journey whereby sexual identity, sexual relations and social independence would have to be integrated again. This journey she approached tentatively, reservedly and with wounds. The rape threatened to destroy her relationships interpersonally and intrapsychically. Through her pictures and her relationship with me, she was I believe, reclaiming and realising her personality. Anthony Storr describes this mature relatedness and the perils to it which, as in Beatrice's case, seek to destroy. Her personality and inner good objects where both threatened with being over-whelmed and destroyed by the rape. It was not only a violation of her physical integrity, but also intrinsically her inner integrity.

> the personality can cease to exist in two ways – either by destroying the other, or by being absorbed by the other – and maturity in interpersonal relationships demands that neither oneself nor the other shall disappear, but that each shall contribute to the affirmation and realisation of the other's personality.
>
> (Storr 1960:43)

THE COURT CASE AND THERAPY

Before the case came to court I received a telephone call from Beatrice's key worker informing me that the case had for some unknown reason been postponed. Two weeks later, another four art therapy sessions were funded in view of this. Beatrice and I discussed the most useful way to proceed, given this turn of events. We decided that it would be most helpful to divide the remaining sessions equally between the weeks immediately prior to the court case and the weeks immediately afterwards. This necessitated a three-week break in therapy. This was a difficult decision and was destabilising at a time when continuity of support and safety in exploration and expression seemed very important.

When Beatrice returned after this short break she again, as with her first session, drew in simple forms the assault but, unlike in the initial drawings, the use of colour now revealed feelings formerly repressed. The bewilderment and pain were present. She was also able to explore a little further into the confusion caused by momentary ambivalence at the level of sensation and free will. For a moment during the assault she had felt some sexual stimulation. It was this fact – that she disclosed to a member of the unit staff who subsequently informed the police – which I was informally told led to the case being thrown out of court. Her intellectual and emotional refusal to consent to sex was not seen as evidence strong enough to over-ride a moment's responsiveness to touch. This issue will be returned to by way of conclusion.

What was painfully lost and which she began to attempt to restore during the remaining sessions was her hope, trust, belief and joy in the belief of romantic love which, for her, seemed a primarily non-sexual intimate relationship. During one session she began to sing a medley of songs:

> Daisy, Daisy, give me your answer do. I'm half crazy, all for the love of you. It wont be a stylish marriage, I can't afford the carriage, but you'd look sweet upon the seat of a bicycle made for two . . . Edelweiss, Edelweiss, every morning you greet me. Small and white, clean and bright, you look happy to meet me. Blossom of snow, may you bloom and grow, bloom and grow for ever. Edelweiss, Edelweiss, bless my homeland for ever . . . If you were the only girl in the world and I was the only boy. Nothing else would matter in the world today, we would go on loving in the same old way. A garden of Eden just made for two, with nothing to mar our joy. I would say such wonderful things to you and there would be such wonderful things to do. If you were the only girl in the world, and I was the only boy . . . I'm for ever blowing bubbles, pretty bubbles in the air. They fly so high, nearly reach the sky, then like my dreams, they fade and die. Fortune's always hiding, I've looked everywhere. I'm for ever blowing bubbles, pretty bubbles in the air.

The overall sentiment of these songs was of a hopeful and loving relationship between male and female and with the world. This spirit of desired transcendence was evident within Beatrice as within the songs. Even the last song, where a dream is seen to fade, it is only in sight of the foreverness of trying for something beautiful. As with Pandora's box, opened in curiosity and letting out all the sins of the world, hope follows. For Beatrice the box was forced unwillingly open but as with Pandora, hope springs eternal, eventually.

Beatrice went on to draw a linear, grid-like pattern in red (Figure 7.4) and within each self-contained space she wrote the following words: Troubled, Angry, Shaky, Noisy, Cannot sleep, Joy, Hope, Love. The picture looked like tangled threads, the words describing her inner pain and distress alongside the emotionally satisfying feelings of joy, hope and love. It seemed as though the duality of 'good' and 'bad' in life, previously kept separate as images, were being brought more explicitly together in this one image. It was as if aspects of herself formerly split off from each other were being forced to find their peace together within her. The overwhelming psychic distress brought about by the assault could no longer be compartmentalised to contain a sense of unity. The 'bad' forced into

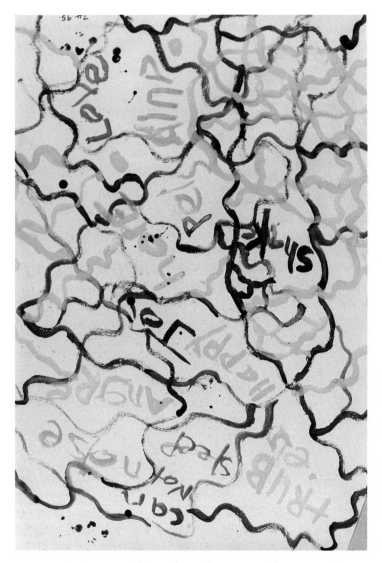

Figure 7.4 Beatrice: Grid of feelings

her in every sense by her rapist now had to become integrated by her. She would have to learn to cope with her own ambivalent feelings in a more intense juxtaposition. Brown and Pedder describe splitting as it

> involves the complete separation of good and bad aspects of the self and others, as illustrated by the perennial interest of children in heros and monsters, good fairies and witches – in modern form, Dr Who and the Daleks. Clinically we see it in splitting between good and bad feelings, between idealisation and contempt of self and others.
>
> (Brown and Pedder 1979:28)

It was some weeks later, after the court date, that she began to want to explore through imagery the possibility of uniting male and female characters, but before this a lot of despair was released. This is particularly difficult in the context of Beatrice's institutional life home life, where order and tepid and consistent emotions are preferred. Her emotional expression was, she felt, being rejected. Beatrice's sleep pattern became erratic, as did her eating. She was caring for herself less well and active emotions of anger and sadness were, she felt, being received by her carers as signs of her 'unpleasantness and bad behaviour'. This, I can confirm, was not just her fantasy and had a strongly compounding effect on her despair in human love and relatedness. People around her had difficulty understanding her emotional life.

Two sessions before the trial she drew a camping holiday, but this diversion could not block her prevailing worries regarding the trial. A central motif in this image was a flesh-coloured, spitted roasting pig (Figure 7.5). Her words conveyed her legal argument and no doubt not a little coaching, whilst her picture and all her other subtle communications suggested her feeling of loss of control, vulnerability and nakedness, as if the trial was another abuse and she was bravely trying to conceal her fear.

During the session prior to the trial she was more successful in her attempts at emotional avoidance, absorbing herself in a picture of the 'good times'. Before leaving she said to me in a calm voice that she wanted the defendant to go to jail because she had said 'No' and because she didn't like what he had done to her.

On the day of the court case she spent the morning in the lobby of the Crown Court with no information about where and when her case would begin. She was accompanied for a cup of tea in the court canteen by her key worker whilst waiting for news. He later told me a man rushed over to her while she waited in the queue and shouted at her, 'I'm going to get away with this'. Beatrice did not seem to recognise her abuser or understand his words! Some minutes later a notice was chalked on to the board that her case had been thrown out of court. No formal explanation ever seems to have been given to Beatrice, but the issue of consent on the basis of momentary sensory arousal superseded the violence of the repeated attacks and the ego integrity of her saying 'No'. So, in the legal sense, he *did* get away with it. My counter-transference when I heard this outcome was a

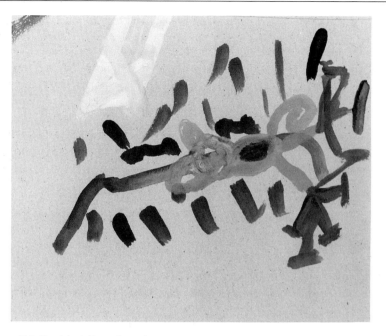

Figure 7.5 Beatrice: Roasting pig

feeling of rage at the abuser for approaching her to boast of his 'getting away with it' and at a legal system ill-equipped to defend Beatrice. I also felt sad and worried for her.

Despite the implications for Beatrice of not being heard, she expressed relief that the case was over legally, but at times her frenetic confusion seeped through. She decided she would like to use the remaining sessions to look at relationships between men and women. It was as if the end of the court case gave her permission to move on, to heal the split. But this mature and speedy adaption to outward changes in events concerned me. What had she done with any angry feelings? I wondered how much distortion of her emotional processes had been orchestrated by the focus on a rape trial. I wondered, as with the rape, if she had been steered and confused. I felt this particularly when she spoke with an untypical preciseness and contextual clarity about issues appertaining to her legal argument. I was saddened that this apparent 'focus' and 'strength' was not her own but a transient ego transplant set up to fail.

In her next session she said she wanted to be quiet, which I understood as her wanting to be quiet inside, perhaps this being her resolve to transcend her hurt and anger. She drew from her chosen theme of male and female relationships. Both man and woman were shown as safely and separately encased in a containing shape, keeping them securely apart!

This clearness of boundaries was amplified by her drawing a pelican road-crossing showing a red and green man. This image suggested the clarity and boundaried world in which Beatrice feels safe. The mature-sounding statement made by her of 'getting to know a man well' was belied by the image which suggested she wanted to feel safe. Getting to know well in the intimate sense that this phraseology is generally used was not, I feel, her inner reality at this time: it was a paradoxical, conscious aspect brought about along with other ideas and views pertinent to her court case and the pressure to 'grow up', interplaying awkwardly with her feelings about being raped and being on trial.

In her sessions I used the paradoxes between words and images to try and help Beatrice to find what was a more accurate and complete picture for her. I did not always interpret pictures openly so as to not take them from her, so to speak, but tried to gently open up areas to more consideration as they were brought up by her.

Since working with Beatrice I have been working for another brief period of therapy with a 20-year-old woman with learning difficulties who was raped by two 'normal' young men in the basement of her college. These men are currently serving a jail sentence and my client, at times with great humour, is trying to extend her resolution of overcoming her trauma and to achieve greater physical empowerment and greater independence. However, these men's convictions are unusual and invisibility is still the order of the day. Without much searching, I can recall disclosures of past abuse from clients and suspicions of abuse voiced by carers of people with learning difficulties but dates, places, times are lost.

SUMMING UP

There is a popular assumption that 'real' rape and sexual abuse has a uniformity of perceived and demonstrable horribleness, but confusion is created for the abused when mixed feelings are stirred up of love, fear and hate along with manipulated sensations and actions. This matrix is in conflict with the very integrating and unifying experience of loving human relationship which it shatters. Legally, it seems paramount that the abused person should be allowed substantiate their physical and emotional resistance to abuse.

Chronological age is equated, it seems, with an assumption of acquired personal accountability in cases of rape. I believe that Beatrice's middle age did not evoke the defence of innocence that a young woman with learning difficulties might receive. Beatrice, like most people with learning difficulties, has uneven development both in terms of functional skills and conceptual functioning. Beatrice does however have real ego integrity, true to her needs, thoughts and feelings. Despite manipulation and domination by her abuser, she knew that her 'No' meant 'No'. The invalidation of her ego integrity by the legal system sees her to be the worthless sub-humanity that the rapist endorsed by his violation of her.

What Beatrice was unable to find social confirmation of legally was the unequivocal truth that she had been wrongly hurt. Anthony Storr writes that it is through truth that inner security is enhanced. Beatrice's truth was betrayed by the rape and by the legal process. Thus her sense of security in the world was doubly wounded.

> but there can be little doubt that the love of truth is often motivated by the search for security. The 'Eureka' experience of having arrived at a new and truthful insight into some aspect of reality is accompanied by an increase in the feeling of personal security, since it implies a corresponding increase in mastery over the external world. Increments in understanding are generally felt as increments in power, even when the latter is not actual, but imagined.
>
> (Storr 1972:240)

In her art therapy sessions Beatrice began to get in touch with her reality beyond the legalistic and institutionalised handling of her affairs, to express and to be seen naming, drawing and making visible her truth. Passivity, terror and shock can be wrongly interpreted as consentual compliance. Rape, abuse and all that they entail can damage immeasurably the abused person's future building of trust in loving relationships and trust in their own capacity to distinguish between not just subtle tones of feeling within themselves, but in their experience and perception of others. Whilst it may be mature and healthy to recognise in one's self the possibility of loving and hateful feelings toward the same person, it is not good for the rapist to kill a context for love with hate.

Beatrice has to build love for herself which rape hatred has sought to mock and undermine. The rapist does not love himself: he violates himself also by rape. The biblical saying 'Love thy neighbour as thyself' is reversed, becoming 'Hate thy neighbour as thyself'. Rape destroys the most fundamental form of love, brotherly love, the love of humanity upon which all other love needs must rest.

Beatrice has just begun to reclaim this love and I hope that humanity within and without brings enough to help her heal and expand. Art therapy enabled Beatrice to get in touch with and express her thoughts, feelings and sensations about being raped and going to court. She named her anguish and began to reintegrate the 'good' and bad' of life and pivotally reclaim love and trust. Of this love Erich Fromm writes:

> The most fundamental kind of love, which underlies all types of love, is brotherly love. By this I mean the sense of responsibility, care, respect, knowledge of any other human being, the wish to further his life. This is the kind of love the bible speaks of when it says: love thy neighbour as thy self. Brotherly love is love for all human beings; it is characterised by its very lack of exclusiveness. If I have developed the capacity for love, then I cannot help loving my brother. In brotherly love there is the experience of unison of all men, of human solidarity, of human at one-ment. Brotherly love is based on the experience that we are all one. The differences in talents, intelligence, knowledge are negligible in comparison with the identity of the human core common to all men. In order to experience this identity it is necessary to penetrate from the periphery to the core. If I perceive in another person mainly

the surface, I perceive mainly the differences, that which separates us. If I penetrate to the core, I perceive one's identity, the fact of one brotherhood. This relatedness from centre to centre – is 'central relatedness'.

(Fromm 1995:37)

As I close, Beatrice's 'singing session' comes to mind, in particular these words which correspond beautifully with Fromm's words:

Edelweiss, Edelweiss, every morning you greet me. Small and white, clean and bright, you look happy to meet me. Blossom of snow, may you bloom and grow, bloom and grow for ever. Edelweiss, Edelweiss, bless my homeland for ever . . .'

BIBLIOGRAPHY

Brown, D. and Pedder, J. (1979) *Introduction to Psychotherapy: An Outline of Psychodynamic Principles and Practice*, London: Tavistock.
English, J. and Card, R. (1994) *Butterworths' Police Law* (fourth edition), London: Butterworths.
Fromm, E. (1995) *The Art of Loving*, London: Harper Collins.
Hill, A. (1945) *Art Versus Illness*, London: George Allen and Unwin.
Mann, J. (1973) *Time-limited Psychotherapy*, Boston, Mass.: Harvard University Press.
Storr, A. (1988) *Solitude*, London: Harper Collins.
Storr, A. (1960) *The Integrity of the Personality*, Harmondsworth: Pelican.
Storr, A. (1972) *The Dynamics of Creation*, Harmondsworth: Penguin.
Wolfe, T. (1952) *Look Homeward Angel*, London: Charles Scribner's Sons.

Chapter 8

Is art therapy?

Some issues arising in working with children with severe learning difficulties

Sigrid Räbiger

Central themes
- Reflections on my experiences as an art therapist working within educational settings with children who have severe learning difficulties.

Key points
- The essential differences between learning difficulties and severe learning difficulties.
- Knowing when art is a therapy and when it is not. In particular, emphasis on correct assessment and familiarity with other therapeutic approaches.
- How the manner in which art therapy is both introduced and structured may require modification in order to meet the needs of children who are largely without boundaries.

I came to art therapy by a curious route. I originally trained as an art teacher, and taught in Grammar schools to 'O' and 'A' Level standard, but it became apparent to me that I was far more interested in the 'Please Miss, I can't draw' pupils than the able sixth-formers, who seemed self-sufficient. I began to sort out the 'can't draw' from an expectation of exact replication, and tried to introduce the idea that *any* mark made was valid, that we all saw things differently and that there were various ways of representing or expressing – that nobody was expected to produce a 'photograph'!

Then I started my family, and gradually came back to work via arts and crafts in Day Centres and Homes for the Elderly or Disabled. I became more interested in problems and special needs, and noticed just how similar was the work of the elderly to that of young children, in clay-work especially. At the same time, I offered myself as a home tutor for my local borough, and moved to a unit for school-phobic children as 'art teacher'. On picking up a copy of *Inscape* one day, I remarked to my boss that I thought I was an 'art therapist'! She supportively replied: ' I never thought you were anything *else*!' I was still not in a position to do the art therapy training, however, but later in 1980 began to work at Family Tree, a private school for autistic children of potential and intelligence (six children to six teachers and a pair of video technicians – we were on video all the time, for record, review and discussion). I shared teaching and art therapy with the part-time art therapist, under whose encouragement I enrolled at St Albans on the part-time course of two years, one day per week.

We integrated the children at Family Tree into mainstream primary schools and eventually most moved on to mainstream education with minimal support. It was an enormously important learning experience for me, with strong director-ship and staff meetings every day, twice a day, before and after school. After a while I did feel critical that we seemed to be 'making a case' for each child, rather than honestly observing their nuances of behaviour. The children were aged from two to ten, and we worked one-to-one for half-hour sessions. This experience led me to believe totally in the efficacy of one-to-one therapy and teaching, so that one could pace oneself to that child's own needs, moods and abilities. We were occasionally supervised by Frances Tustin, the first person to use psychotherapy with autistic children. She would watch a video of a particularly problematic child and with amazing insight, somehow put her finger on the bits we were missing, or unconsciously reinforcing. I became passionate about the waste of potential ability of autistic children with high IQs, the need to help free them from their perverse and bizarre expressions which kept them encapsulated from devel-opment. I also became aware of just how different autistic children could be from each other. Frances later divided these into two main groups: the entangled (who could not separate from their mothers and close adults) and the encapsulated (who could not bear touch, physical contact of any kind or any closeness). She described the latter as 'shell-like' (Tustin 1981).

Once I had qualified as an art therapist I was lucky enough to be employed as such at a school for children with severe learning difficulties (originally called educationally subnormal – ESN – divided into 'M' for 'Moderate' and 'S' for 'Severe'). These children were from two years to nineteen years old and I began to realise the best training for severe learning difficulties is an Infant or Primary school teacher's training. Luckily I had my experience at Family Tree and that of my own children to help me make appropriate comparisons with the normal stages and deviations. (At one time it was compulsory for teachers in special schools to have had at least five years experience in mainstream schools first. I think this is still valid, and I am rather critical of what I have seen of attempts at Special Needs education training, though I would hope these are improving.) I am a firm believer in the need for the specific rather than generalised academic conclusions. In my own work I have come to see as an essential the need to begin from the stage the child is actually at, and work from there, rather than make assumptions due to age, size, outward appearance and so on.

Anyone with experience of such a school can see the children are functioning on an unconscious level most of the time, mindless and at times apparently deliberately destructive, but the *intention* is not always destructive though the effect is. It is born out of panic, fear, confusion and often a total unawareness of the meaning of their surroundings, with no expectations or understanding of required response. Unless one has spent at least a day in such a school it is impossible to convey the utter incomprehensibility of many of the children, who can be ambulant and of teen-aged size but have no more idea of what or who they are than does a baby of a few months old. All such observations are my own and stem from my own experience of eleven years in special education, but I think most colleagues would agree. One teacher, who took a 19-year-old to buy shoes, commented that her own 2-year-old daughter was 'further on' than he. It is this need to be ruthless in one's understanding and observation rather than senti-mentally assume and hope more is there than at first appears that holds back the work with this client group. It was on this point that the educational psychologist and I came to work so closely together – possibly because we both worked from an understanding of developmental levels, and more perhaps because we each had the opportunity to assess such children individually.

It may seem startling to question the efficacy of art therapy with any client group, but it is important to make a distinction between learning difficulties and *severe* learning difficulties. This is not a case of 'worse' or 'less' but is a funda-mentally different condition, often involving a degree of mental illness. It is my opinion that many – most – children with severe learning difficulties are lacking in boundaries and, to a large extent, lacking in control. They are functioning on an unconscious level most of the time, so that the major contribution of art therapy – to help get in touch with the unconscious – is inappropriate and any therapy provided needs to offer structure and boundaries rather than 'release'. Most of the children, except for the withdrawn and traumatised, seem permanently 'released' which makes their management problematical, especially in groups, however small. Using art therapy with these children can produce unexpected problems, mostly due to the severe developmental delay. I have tried to stress before (Räbiger 1990) how unaware we seem to be that the same cognitive level is required for the use of art as is required to learn to read and write. Above all, most of these children are unable to play, are at a pre-play stage, which in itself impedes their ability to learn. Certainly one needs to be able to play in order to use art materials meaningfully. For children with severe learning difficulties, art therapy and art materials can be perceived as an intrusion, a threat, or to be completely meaningless.

DEFINITION OF CLIENT GROUP

In the special school for children with severe learning difficulties aged from two years to nineteen years where I worked the population can be roughly divided into three or four main categories, with very many shades in between. First, and least able to use art on *any* level are the special care group who have brain damage, either from birth, or from a negative reaction to vaccination for early childhood illnesses, such as measles or whooping cough, or from contracting meningitis. Some of the nursing staff often comment that for a child to have such a devastating reaction to normal vaccination there must have been some initial frailty already in existence; I don't think there is a medical verification of this. A few children are similarly said to have become autistic as a result of such vaccinations but, again, I do not know of any categorical medical confirmation. However, when I first joined the school, I was surprised to see how many children did seem to have similar mannerisms to the autistic children with high IQs with whom I had previously worked, or had 'autistic features', to use the preferred terminology. It is possible to be autistic *and* have brain damage or some other complications, whereas it is equally possible to be autistic and have a high degree of intelligence, impaired by the limitations of the autistic concrete-thinking, which I shall describe in more detail in another section of this chapter.

The children in this special care group may reach adolescence in physical size, and traverse puberty normally, but remain at only a few weeks or months in mental and emotional developmental level. They are unaware of their surroundings to a large extent, do not use their eyes to focus, have no speech, hardly move their limbs and often also have a physical impairment as a result of their brain damage. The priority for this group seems to be quiet nursing care, with emphasis on successful feeding and, where possible, encouragement of any form of self-feeding if there is any use of an arm or hand. To offer art materials to these children is like approaching a baby in a pram with a paintbrush, yet there does seem to be a tendency – in my opinion, misguided – to introduce 'stimulation' in the form of noises and colours, as if bombarding the inert will activate them. Since there is not only no language but no language comprehension, this seems to me like some kind of assault.

The children in the next group are very similar but are ambulant and known as special needs (although *all* children in this school have special needs). These children also do not make any eye contact, or else stare fixedly at the adult, but rarely use their hands and eyes in unison. They are still at the stage of needing to mouth everything in exploration and so view all the art materials as edible! One *can* offer water 'play' but even this usually fails to arouse any interest or invite any kind of focus, with a few exceptions. One meningitis survivor was deaf and blind, yet he loathed any experience of touch, so it was very difficult to try to engage with him. In fact, most of this group had either a sort of manic, unaware destructiveness – arms swinging wildly, knocking objects off surfaces – or were passive and inert and automated in their responses. There is an over-riding sentimental idea that it is 'not fair' to deprive such children of art therapy but to me it seems a kindness to recognise its inappropriateness. It is so important to realise what point these children had or had not reached in their developmental level and to respect what is not happening as well as to observe what is, or might be. I *was* required to work with this group, however. Possibly the most therapeutic part of the work was the journey to and from the art room itself and, for several, the mastering of the stairs as well, perhaps also being taken out of the classroom for a brief while as a diversion, although for some even this was upsetting and added to their confusion and bewilderment.

AUTISTIC FEATURES

This 'group' of children with autistic features cannot be called one as such as they were not in a group together, unfortunately, but were scattered among the other groups, so that their needs were often in severe conflict with those of the rest of their class.

These individuals have some mental illness intermingled with their learning difficulty and show degrees of traumatisation, either in a 'shell-shocked' fashion, seeming dazed and confused, or with a more excitable and panic-struck manifestation. Frances Tustin (1972, 1981) who worked in depth with autistic children as a psychotherapist, and Sheila Spensley (1995) who has written her biography, describe very vividly the autistic state. There is a need to rely on their own compulsive objects or mannerisms, such as twiddling or flicking fingers or rocking to keep the outside world from impinging on their awareness. They have attachment to bodily sensations, the preoccupations with which take the place of feelings and acknowledgement of the outside world: a depth of fear and terror which is held at bay by these 'magical' obsessions all mean that the severely autistic child is not likely to be interested in any activity offered to him or her. The materials are denied, misused, ignored. One needs to be aware of the underlying terror behind apparent apathy or perverse behaviour. Frances Tustin describes how these children need a firm containment and stricter boundaries than usual to help make them feel more secure. She also advises that the therapist should not allow him or herself to be used as an 'object' as autistic children are wont to do – using one's hands to open doors and ignoring the actual presence of the therapist as a whole person rather than an assembly of sometimes useful 'bits'. Sheila Spensley (1995:89) devotes an entire chapter to 'Mental Handicap and Mental Illness'. She discusses how one of the main features of autism – and of many children with severe learning difficulties – is their concrete thinking, their inability to symbolise, their literal interpretation of the world and hence their inability to play, which also impedes their cognitive development. Children who cannot play cannot learn.

In his collection of essays entitled 'Churchill's Black Dog' Anthony Storr describes how, in schizophrenia and other mental illness, the symbolic function fails and reality is turned away from as bringing no satisfaction: thus the inner world becomes increasingly incomprehensible to others (Storr 1965:323). He describes how cohesion becomes so impaired that there is no longer an entity of personality but a state of being governed by the emotion of the moment. This excellently describes the condition of so many of our children. As a colleague in Bettelheim's Orthogenic School has remarked, to be seen as mad is to be seen as bad, and this is certainly true of children with severe learning difficulties, where mental illness and mental handicap are inextricably mixed.

Sheila Spensley (1995) reminds us that the failure to learn is inevitably accompanied by failure to comprehend personal relationships, which makes therapy of a psychotherapeutic nature problematic. Frances Tustin (1972, 1981) says we must be cautious about transposing therapeutic techniques suitable for neurotic or borderline clients to the treatment of autism or psychosis. I therefore feel exactly the same applies to the use of art therapy techniques and even materials. Sheila Spensley concludes that we must be equally cautious about the suitability of treatment approaches to those with mental impairment, whose conditions include psychotic impairments in their incapacity to comprehend mental space.

The extreme panic and fear among those children with psychotic and autistic features can produce a reaction which is often seen as aggressive or violent. If one can understand that this is a hitting out in terror, rather than an attacking of something or someone specific, it is possible to offer reassurance rather than reprimand. Sheila Spensley points out how the wrong reaction to supposed violence can heighten tension and persecutory fears. She says terrorisers are always terrified people and that nothing increases the risk of violence more than the sensing of fear in those who are expected to be in charge. The head of Shenley Psychiatric Hospital in Boreham Wood, Hertfordshire was once showing a group of visitors over the grounds when a patient rushed towards them, brandishing a gun. The Senior Consultant put out his hand and said 'Don't be afraid!', whereupon the patient let go of the gun. A salutary reminder.

For all these reasons, art therapy can seem like an intrusion and an assault to some of these children. Of course, many autistic children can be extremely gifted at art and can make good use of art therapy, but I am talking about what it is *not*, when it does *not* work, and the need to try to understand why. When they are non-verbal, art therapy can be an important outlet for any child to be able to express their needs and emotions but, where there is minimal brain damage or other factors, the art materials can present a threat or be perceived as an irrelevance. I have found that offering *non*-art activities can be extremely helpful as a container, and can also encourage greater hand–eye contact (although many intricate tasks are performed with an averted head!). This use of a more practical task seems to provide a concentration and focus which is in itself extremely relaxing. To concentrate is to relax: to avoid the present and to be unable to settle into the moment is to be anxious and tense. The sorts of activities I present are buttoning, lacing, popping and unpopping press-studs, dressing and undressing dolls – although the latter is not usually perceived at all as symbolic or 'play' but a merely mechanical activity.

The more apathetic autistic child will merely twiddle the pencil or felt-tip, or make desultory swipes with a paintbrush, not looking at what he or she is doing and often becoming perversely obsessed with some tiny mark on the table or his or her own hands. Offering clay or playdough will sometimes encourage a half-hearted jab at the material but will also often seem to elicit a scream or moan of anguish and an occasional throwing onto the floor. I have observed many autistic children colour in their own fingernails rather than use the paper provided. Offering non-art activities can be a way through to establishing some sort of relationship with the therapist and can also provide an important period of concentrated attention. It is also an extremely good cognitive assessment, as many do not even have to be shown how to do these tasks. These non-art alternatives can lead to use of paint and graphic media and clay eventually, especially if there has been the opportunity to work on a daily basis, which builds up continuity.

The autistic manifestation of art expression is interesting, as is the observation of a gradually increased relaxation through the use of art materials. There are two kinds of autistic response in the art room. The most difficult is the apathy, the *misuse* of the materials, the indifference, the faintness of marks made, the avoidance of eye-contact with either hand or the surface being worked on. But the second kind of autistic child covers his work as he covers his eyes (it is a typical autistic gesture to hold the hand over the face as if to protect oneself from being seen, even from being *there*). One adolescent, Karl, spent hours quietly in the art room, making detailed squares and circles and then filling-in with complicated grids in fine lines – only to obliterate all this detailed work by colouring in with the identical colour, or with black, so they completely disappeared. As he became gradually more at ease and more trusting, Karl began to allow the grids to show through and to fill them in with different and lighter colours, or sometimes not at all. He would also do stripes as so many autistic children and people are wont to do, in true autistic fashion, in a stereotyped and apparently mindless, compulsive fashion, or cover one piece of paper with a single colour but, in general, his art work became more intricate and delicate. I am sure this opening-up of his art work, and allowing more of it to be seen, could be symbolically related to his psychological willingness to open up to the outside world more and to let himself be more seen.

Karl would hold the felt-tip in one hand, and with his other, place a finger on the hand which was drawing, as if to guide it the better. It did seem therapeutic for this greatly misunderstood boy to sit in the art room calmly drawing, totally absorbed, whereas outside the art room he was seen as disruptive and unpredictable. It is so important to understand autistic 'violence' as fear and panic. One day, another adolescent, who had much language, a great deal of creativity, was volatile, gifted, verbal, and with a tremendous behaviour problem (until he moved to a special needs college where he never had another outburst!) – threw a broom through my one-way mirror. Karl sat calmly drawing, oblivious of the noise and furore outside. Later, I noticed his image did indeed resemble shattered glass, although he had never been figurative in any way before.

The last group in the school are those who often do have some language and language comprehension – in fact, many of the Asian children are actually bilingual; even when non-verbal, they understand both their parents' language and English to a remarkable degree – something we often seemed to overlook.

This group is not traumatised, and has a level of sociability and can often draw figuratively, albeit with fluctuating perceptual inconsistencies. It is possible that some of these children have been wrongly placed in this school and could have started off in a school for moderate learning difficulties. However, when the school was established it was decided by the authorities to try to spread the intake a little to achieve a wider cross-section, including those released at early adolescence from hospital where they had been most of their lives until the new Education Act (1992) which entitled *all* children to receive 'education'. I have written about this group of children before (Räbiger 1990) and they were certainly too damaged by their intense lack of any emotional 'holding' to have received much help from anyone, and they caused severe mayhem and confusion to the environment by reason of their manic outbursts and expression of their non-comprehension of their surroundings.

The more able, small group have suffered greatly from this administrative decision, and have undoubtedly not reached their full potential. The most patently able is the 'infant class' (aged 9–13!). Some of these show a marked readiness for pre-reading and pre-writing skills and will possibly move on to a school for moderate learning difficulties, although not enough attention is paid to this potential and opportunities are often missed. This is also due to the fact that what might suit one or two of the children will cause one or two others confusion bordering on distress – there is not enough credence given to the need for individual sessions, even of a cognitive nature. These children's cognitive potential is often shown in the art room either by the ability to make figurative or pre-figurative drawings or simply by the way the materials are handled and the general way they conduct themselves. It is interesting, though, how many children will make quite detailed faces eventually but do not show any inclination to add body or limbs. This is indicative of the very uneven development of children with severe learning difficulties.

ASSESSMENT

It is possible in the art room to ascertain a child's cognitive potential by their ability to figurate and their lack of stereotypical behaviour. Even the ability to find the right brush for the right pot and to become aware of 'sets' – groups of like objects – such as putting crayons in one container and felt-tips in another can be indicators. One boy, who was obviously deaf-only, rather than having severe learning difficulties, began to paint his first figure and to *paint numbers* up to ten! This was unusual also in that most children develop furthest through their drawings rather than in paint. Luckily, he was soon transferred to a school for the hearing-impaired, where he thrives. His clutching of his hearing-aid box on his chest was in marked contrast to the many autistic children, presumed deaf by their lack of speech and apparent indifference to words, who repeatedly threw their hearing aids down the lavatory. So strong is the autistic mechanism that these children can defy even the most sophisticated of medical hearing tests and still be wrongly diagnosed. The school social worker agreed with me that an autistic adolescent designated deaf, was *not*, when he saw him turn his head as my noisy flip-flops approached the art room door. Yet this boy was packed with hearing aids however many times he threw them away.

I have developed through close observation and over several years an ability to assess which children are autistic in the art room, by reason of their consistent use of stripes in every situation, whether in paint, pastel or clay, even when they are also able to draw figuratively. One boy made a complicated striped structure out of corrugated cardboard! However, the best assessment tool, especially for the multiply handicapped, seems to me to be music therapy. I saw on video a small group of young, multiply handicapped children who had each been given their own tune. Most were typically apathetic and unaware, but one little girl became so visibly excited when she realised her tune was being played, her eyes positively lit up, showing that she obviously did have intelligence.

The importance of correct assessment of the multiply handicapped was illustrated by a boy with severe athetosis who was obviously bright, as could be deduced by the alert expression in his eyes. He showed a degree of language comprehension by his response to adult jokes but he had no speech nor any use of his limbs, which shot out in all directions at unexpected moments, impeding any co-ordination. He struggled manfully with clay and paint but I am not sure how 'therapeutic' this was for him, as sweat would pour down his face with the effort and presumable frustration. My own frustration would be increased by well-meaning staff walking through the classroom and asking him what he was supposed to be making, while I had been content for him simply to manipulate the materials as best he could without any expectation for any attempt at figuration, which would have been impossible anyway for such a child, both conceptually and technically. This boy, who could not even feed himself, should never have been placed in a school for learning difficulties but in a school for the physically disabled where they might have been better able to understand his medical condition and have had better means to help him. The *Oxford Medical Dictionary* states that in athetosis, intelligence is often unaffected.

Another advantage of music therapy I witnessed was in a video of a boy with whom I also worked. He had autistic features as well as physical disabilities, including a shunt to counter-act hydrocephalus and a pronounced limp. This extremely resistant child, who had been abused by his family and was fostered, was eventually persuaded to beat the three drums in their required sequence so that he learned the joy of co-operation whilst being rewarded by the sounds produced. (As few children make eye contact at all, few are ever rewarded by *seeing* anything they have produced in the art room!). One of the advantages of music therapy, at least in the Nordoff-Robbins method, is to have the use of two workers. One miraculously adapts any noise the child makes into some recognisable tune (at the piano) while the other supports the child where necessary and guides him or her into activity where appropriate. This seems to me to provide a symbolic parenting and thus a 'holding' of importance. 'Daphne', whose case I have described elsewhere (Räbiger 1990) also had music therapy in my last year at the school, and her roars and screams were transformed into an extremely moving 'tune', to which she contributed in a clear musical voice whenever the piano paused for her to do so. Daphne happened to be very musical and could sing many words she could not say, so this experience was doubly meaningful for her but, I believe, as with art therapy, one does not have to be musical (or artistic) for the therapy to be beneficial.

Sheila Spensley (1995) puts a strong case for a more psychodynamic approach to working with children – and people – with severe learning difficulties. With such stressed, often under-prepared staff, many of the children's actions are seen as 'deliberate', and as sabotaging and adding to the general frustration of the work. In my experience, there is a poor understanding or a lack of understanding of the effect on these children of the day-to-day aspects of our world, such as festivals and supermarkets, visits to which can only lead to greater agitation – due to little comprehension – and thus more aggressive behaviour. Such outbursts can have a negative effect on everybody: the child concerned, the staff involved and the more sensitive, passive witnesses among the already more fearful of the children. There needs to be far more specific attention to details like this or much good work can be negated. Bettleheim echoed this plea for attention to detail when he told his staff at a meeting that according to their detailed notes, none of the children had been to the toilet for at least two weeks! (Sutton 1995). The attention to specifics is vital. One must observe and think about each child individually and not apply 'blanket' theories. It is essential to think what might be suitable for *that* child in *that* situation. Furthermore, and so often overlooked, if a solution is seen to work or to be helpful, then it is important to realise when this particular approach may become outgrown and needs to shift. One must allow for change, especially for those with autistic features, as routines can so easily become established, so it is very important, within a safe framework, to try to desensitise the fixed need for sameness and to vary one's own expectations subtly. Similarly, age should never be taken into account: developmental stage is all. One very violent, overweight, aggressive and psychotic adolescent, who had failed to breathe for minutes at birth, showed a great need for a transitional object to help anchor him. On reading his notes I saw that the cloth he had been used to carrying everywhere with him had been removed as 'age-inappropriate'. This was well before my joining the school but I would hazard that this very removal may have exacerbated his totally unsocial aggressive behaviour, which used to frighten staff and children alike. This boy was very difficult to work with in art therapy as he had a fetish about hands, any use of which would set him off into manic masturbation. (It is very difficult not to use one's hands in the art room!).

USES OF ART IN THERAPY

I have described before (Räbiger 1990) the various ways that art materials can be used to soothe or to encourage violent or apathetic children and have also noted the recognition of the value of scribble as a developmental starting point. Fordham (1994) discusses the relation between the discovery of the circle and the discovery of 'I', which seems to prepare the ground for the emergence of a sense of self, so markedly lacking in most of our children. He says the circle seems to express the feeling of 'I', of completeness, of momentary recognition of individual status and a boundary between self and others – also lacking in the children in our school. Fordham (1957: 134) observed that children used circles both as containers which could include even bad experiences and as a protective barrier against intra-psychic dangers. (He also likens the use of circles to Jung's Mandalas.) In our children, the confusion over language comprehension can reveal itself in interesting ways, as in the drawing of a fish done by an extremely able adolescent, Abba, who would probably be able move on to some kind of independent living. She drew a fish, putting in the eye (quite a sophisticated achievement in itself) and then got confused between 'eye' and 'I' and ended up drawing herself *inside* the fish! (Figure 8.1).

It is also possible to see in early scribbles where the use of a circle (as opposed to latitudinal scribble) is an awareness of pre-figuration, on an unconscious level, so this can often lead to a 'face' (unconsciously) and dots for 'eyes'.

The inability to generalise is universal in a school like ours, even amongst the more able of the children. This was illustrated by Daniel, a very verbal, very able, socially adept adolescent who had decided to draw the visit of a mounted policeman to the school. Seeing he was in some difficulty, and trying to get him to think a little about what he was doing, I asked him how many legs did a horse have. His slightly shamed reply was, 'I don't know – I forgot to look!', as if only *that* particular horse had a specific number of legs. (See Figure 8.2.)

I have described elsewhere (Räbiger 1990) how beneficial can be the use of water play in art therapy and how it can sometimes lead on to further development

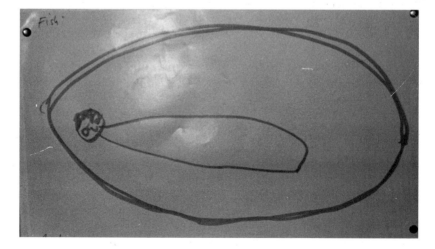

Figure 8.1 Abba: A fish, containing an 'eye' and an 'I'

Figure 8.2 Daniel: A horse

and involvement with art materials; at least it can be safely drunk by those still at the oral stage! The success in the case of Daphne may be due to the fact that her ego was strong enough to produce appalling behaviour, so she was assigned art therapy daily (more by reason of needing to be removed from the classroom than by any acknowledgment of the benefits of art therapy *per se*, I suspect). Work with this child was extremely rewarding in the end, although at the beginning I despaired as the behaviour was so very destructive.

Clay is another very important medium as it can be used completely non-figuratively, simply as a tactile experience on a primitive level. It can encourage autonomy in that it offers the child the ability to make shapes or produce indentations and then eliminate them at will – such an important experience for our children who have very little autonomy throughout their lives. 'Dangerous' tools, such as blunt knives and sharply pointed objects, can be used to stab and make holes, thus providing an outlet for latent – or overt! – aggressive feelings. One adolescent made extremely good use of these possibilities and developed rather ritualistic pattern-making and later began to make coiled pots. Handling clay can also promote language, as food is often represented and sometimes a form of 'sharing' play ensues. From conversations with the speech therapist I came to understand that hands are connected to speech, so that both the non-art activities described earlier and the use of clay and playdough can all facilitate language development. For those with figurative awareness, clay can offer an

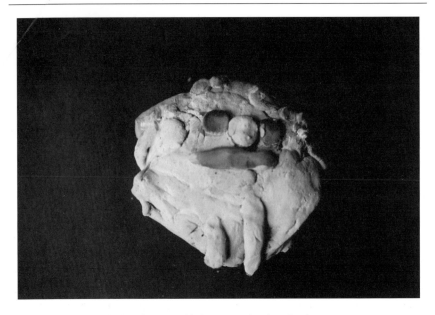

Figure 8.3 Roger: A clay figure, with legs attached to the face

easier way to build up features and limbs than can be done with two-dimensional techniques. However, there are still those who continue to put legs on the face itself, as did Roger, unable to incorporate the concept of a body (Figure 8.3).

Finger paint has a similarly autonomous effect but it is important to be careful that the child is ready for this medium and not still stuck at a too-faeces-stage, as Lowenfeld (Räbiger 1990) points out. The wiping-away of all marks and then bringing them back, or not, is the child's choice. There is also a certain scope for an awareness of colour-mixing and a possible realisation of colour changes. When the child is actually able to *look* at the print taken, this is a landmark indeed. Even helping to wipe down the table afterwards can be a developmental and therapeutic experience as well as a reassurance that chaotic mess can be contained rather than contaminate. Language is another factor again, and another developmental stage is reached when the child can lift their hands in the air to enable a print to be made. Daphne became able to communicate when she was ready for a print by spontaneously raising her hands – real communication!

Soft and hard pencils, chalk, conté crayons, pencil-crayons and felt-tips of various thickness all provide different opportunities for different mood and expression. Primary and secondary colours are ready-mixed in pots, with a brush for each, on trays at the easels. Older children often become able to use water-colours and to learn the art of washing the brush in between, so that many of the art materials can also encourage cognitive development and thought and an increase of control. However, there are still many automated children who will wash the brush, rather over-enthusiastically, take some colour; and *wash the brush again* – without ever actually putting brush to paper, until shown or reminded. Monoprints can be made; paint blown through straws; paint squeezed directly from bottles – all techniques can be chosen for each individual child's need and stage at the time.

BODY IMAGE

This medium is a prime example of damage that can be caused by introducing it before the child is ready to comprehend the task or to execute it. The method involves drawing around the person, who stands against a door or a wall or lies on the floor according to space available and preference shown. Later, the features are filled in.

Without language comprehension to understand *why* she was lying down on the landing at all, one adolescent with Down's Syndrome became outraged by a well-meaning teacher-training student's attempt to do a body image with her. This girl was still at the scribble stage and could have no concept of 'filling in' an outline, nor of features themselves. When I tried to discuss this with the student, he told me that his tutor would be furious if he did not apply the techniques taught at college! This demonstrated that there was a considerable lack in those training people to work with severe learning difficulties of a proper understanding of the client group, their needs and developmental level.

It never ceases to amaze me, however, that merely outlining a person's body could produce a likeness, even before the features are added. This seems to show how our very personality is expressed in our physical stance, the way our arms hang by our sides and so on, rather than by the colour of our hair or eyes. Those able to do body images are thrilled with the life-like results, as well as their sheer size. There can be surprising therapeutic effects of a different kind, too. One 10-year-old autistic boy at Family Tree made a body image with me and we put it on the art room door. When his mother came to fetch him she was quite astonished and exclaimed, 'Why, Donald, how big you are!' which may well have helped her to treat him in a more age-appropriate way thereafter. Darren, a 6-year-old, functioning at an almost 6-year-old level in many ways, and who would soon move on to a school for Moderate learning difficulties, seemed ready to develop his increasing interest in the body by making one himself. I had worked closely with him since our first session, when he had drawn a muzzy figure and asked, 'How do you draw a skirt?', indicating an awareness and possible uncertainty or anxiety about sexual differences. When I asked him what colour we should mix for his face and arms, he replied immediately 'Black!'. I commented on his choice, holding out my own suntanned arm to show its colour and commenting how similar it was to his, though he was Jamaican and I not. He asked in amazement, 'Are you White?' thus showing racial differences are not so much about colour as about emotional closeness and emotional identification. We had worked so closely together he had completely identified with me, even though he happened to come from a very militant family.

SOME CASE EXAMPLES

Even with children who do not seem to benefit at all from using the art materials there can be encouraging and surprising responses from time to time. We are talking about severe developmental delay in all these children, so one has to be prepared for slowness of change or improvement and have faith to continue although often a feeling of hopelessness does set in.

Teresa was overweight, apathetic, non-verbal, inert and absolutely exhausting to work with by reason of endless repetitions, seeming to get us nowhere. There was little response, little acknowledgement of me, though an occasional stare, and incredible slowness of all movement, whether walking or sitting or using any of the materials. In the dining room she would continually pull out her chair in a seemingly mindless way, fail to notice where it was and let herself fall to the ground, day after day. I offered various materials to try to get her interested or even active: scratchy chalks on rough sugar paper, soft, free-flowing felt-tips to allow marks to spread themselves across slippery, shiny paper, almost of their own volition. Clay, finger paint, playdough – all were apathetically received. Even when putting the clay away in the bag, she would repeatedly miss the bag itself and drop the contents on the table or floor, over and over again. One day, after about four years of little change or development, Teresa suddenly emitted a noise and began to make vigorous circles with black and white conté crayons, with great energy, round and round (Figure 8.4). This was certainly an expression, a statement, of *something* and also very effective on paper. I cannot say this led to

Figure 8.4 Teresa: Circles in black and white

any significant breakthrough but it did at least give her a release, perhaps, and certainly made a stronger link between us. As she was epileptic (her slowness may well have been drug-related) she had many absences from school, so we lost the initial impetus.

What is interesting about this work, however, and what makes it so essential that one does not make theories or assumptions, is that almost identical marks (Figure 8.5) were made by a quite different child, who had a similarly silent, slow, passive mode. James was in his teens, with pronounced autistic features and was the boy I quoted (Räbiger 1990) as having made clay images to express his growing awareness of pubertal body changes. Yet, he too one day suddenly asserted himself in vigorous black and white circles, huge, emphatic and very, very similar to Teresa's, even though he could also be figurative and even though they were such very different children. James had some language and was excessively acquiescent but I do think through art therapy he managed, very slowly – over years! – to become able to assert himself and express himself. In fact, he later became quite difficult for his elderly parents to handle and began to have 'temper tantrums' on the dining room floor, lying down and screaming in protest at the various things to which he might be objecting. (Teresa was also capable of temper tantrums in the classroom.) This again is one of the problems of

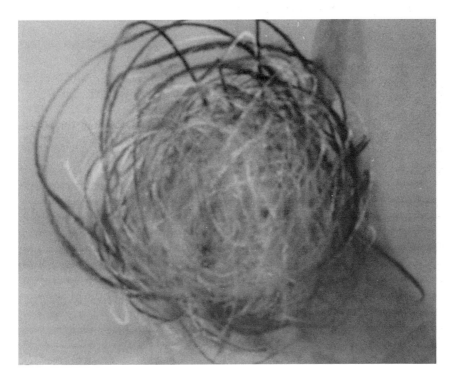

Figure 8.5 James: Circles in black and white

art therapy in such a setting: most children seem able to keep protest to within the art room but several take it outside and create a problem for their teachers and carers – as if releasing self-expression can be extremely inconvenient for social conformity. What to do? Which action is most helpful? An unanswerable question and, once again, a specific response, specific to each child, is needed in each situation. Both these children were basically amenable and their tantrums not an insuperable problem. I would hazard that their increased self-assertion could only be of benefit to them – perhaps a bit like kick-starting a motorbike! However, as art therapist in a school one does feel horribly responsible if one seems to be encouraging or even introducing a problem rather than containing it within the art room.

This again leads to the need for greater communication between staff, almost impossible to achieve in the existing school timetable structure but vital if real work is to be done with the children. One cause of outbursts is the pressure in the classroom, even with only six pupils. One has to understand what the teacher and welfare worker may be grappling with at the time, but for the art therapist it is very disheartening to hear, within minutes of a calm, positive, productive session, the familiar, distressed screaming of a child. It is difficult to know how to suggest the child might be more actively welcomed back into the classroom, given a moment's individual attention and reintegrated into the group, rather than be ignored and so reduced to screaming to gain attention and acknowledgement or a recognition of the pain of being one of several. It is difficult not to appear intrusive if one leads the child back into the room, sits her down, finds an activity she can do. Because the staff are under such pressure they can feel very sensitive to any implied criticism, rather than viewing such an action as an attempt to help the situation and the child concerned. All sorts of resentments can grow, including the 'envy' of the privilege of being allowed to work with the children individually. Indeed, one of the main causes of disruption and acting-out in the classroom is the mismatch of assorted pupils with very different needs and at very different developmental stages, even within the broad groupings described earlier, so that an activity for one or two can greatly conflict with the needs of one or two others.

Sheila Spensley (1995) describes most graphically the kinds of mis-understandings and imperceptions arising out of this work. To my mind, one of the worst aspects in such a school is the message that it needs to 'educate' because it is a 'school', and not seeing what might be truly educational in a broader sense and what is both an irrelevance and an intrusion into the developmental stage. Conversely, there is not enough opportunity for recognition of the potential of some individuals, especially in the 'infant' class, some of whom might be taken much further if there were more credence given to the justification for individual sessions, even of a cognitive, as opposed to therapeutic, nature.

An example where art therapy with severe learning difficulties *can* be much like art therapy in any other setting is the use of unconscious factors portraying themselves visually even when little or no representational expertise has been

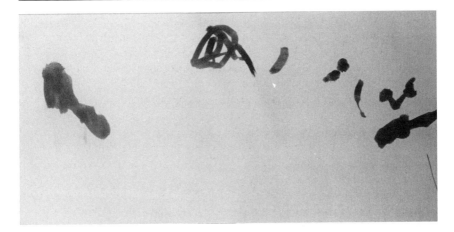

Figure 8.6 Binesh: A fretsaw

possible. Such an example was Binesh, a very bright-seeming, eager, moody, humorous Asian boy with Down's Syndrome who was brilliant at signing (that is, using the Makaton Sign Language) and who would get very frustrated and annoyed at anyone else's inability to be equally adept and to respond immediately. He would grunt a great deal as communication when I first knew him, but later came to use more intelligible speech. He was very uneven in his uses of art therapy and in his art work. In the very early days he made an astonishingly representational drawing of a fret-saw (Figure 8.6) and then very little else for several terms. He mostly used the carpentry tools but he did draw intermittently and after a few years became very articulate in his work, using much wishful thinking at times. For instance, his class teacher told me how terrified he was of swimming, yet he constantly drew the swimming pool with himself in the water, often shown performing feats of daring and confidence. He also managed to master depicting the rectangular shape of the pool, a task which necessitated the use of a ruler. He delighted in learning how to handle this and it may also have provided a symbolic boundary/container for him. However, during my last year, his family suffered great upheaval. His father left home to live with a young aunt and for many months it was uncertain where Binesh lived or from which house the school bus should fetch him or to which house he should be returned. His evident feeling of being 'dropped', of having little importance in the family context, of holding no place, was beautifully expressed in an eloquent drawing – as eloquent as in any verbal therapy in what it left out – of three tiny dots, spaced far apart, calling them 'Daddy, Binesh, Mummy'. This was a child well able to figurate by now (Figure 8.7). However, his class teacher did not agree with my interpretation and insisted 'children often draw dots'! At least in the art therapy room there was space for Binesh to convey his despair and to receive concentrated attention and support, and he later regained his former confidence and outgoing attitude.

Figure 8.7 Binesh: Daddy, Binesh, Mummy

Simply making this image in my presence may well have been the 'therapy' for him.

SUMMARY

I have tried to show that for some children with severe learning difficulties art therapy may in fact be inappropriate, an irrelevance and, at worst, an affront. It is essential to gauge the developmental level of the child before attempting to offer art as a therapy. I have also tried to show how I have found it necessary to adapt art therapy to the needs of these children and almost turn it round into a structural, containing provision rather than allowing the continuation of the chaos which generally pertained. Further, that bombarding the apparently inert with greater stimulation is often misguided: the presumption that frenetic activities will jerk the more apathetic into activity is false and indeed can have an opposite and negative effect. At the same time, art therapy *can* be helpful and therapeutic in enabling some children to develop their emotional potential, which can, of course, lead to greater cognitive potential. For children without spoken language, drawing and painting, even on a non-figurative level, and using clay similarly, can be an outlet for expression of feelings and fears though by no means always. All too often it seems a pointless, useless activity altogether. I suppose the 'therapy' is in the individual attention, the insistence on entering and leaving the art room in a more sensible, controlled way than most exits and entries throughout the school and an emphasis on normality, together with a strong expectation for all kinds of self-help on a practical level. At most, merely manipulating the materials themselves is a therapeutic exercise. To have the empathy of one adult all to themselves is for many children who are so often institutionalised or from stressed and distracted families what I consider a 'holding' and a containment, so essential for such needy children's development and sanity. I have also tried to show when art therapy can help us to see potential and sometimes glimpse things that are more commonly conveyed in most art therapy. When this does happen it is both encouraging and exciting, but mostly an art therapist working with children with severe learning difficulties has to ask the question, 'Is art therapy therapeutic for this client group and how can we make it so?', as well as to accept and recognise when it can *not* be.

BIBLIOGRAPHY

Fordham, M. (1957) *New Developments in Analytical Psychology*, London: Routledge and Kegan Paul.
Fordham, M. (1994) *Children as Individuals*, London: Free Association Books.
Lowenfeld, V. (1965) *Creative and Mental Growth*, New York: Macmillan.
Räbiger, S. (1990) *Working with Children in Art Therapy*, London: Tavistock Routledge.
Spensley, S. (1995) *Frances Tustin*, London: Routledge.
Storr, A. (1965) *Churchill's Black Dog*, London: Fontana/Collins.
Sutton, N. (1995) *Bruno Bettleheim: The Other Side of Madness*, London: Duckworth.
Tustin, F. (1972) *Autism and Childhood Psychosis*, London: Hogarth Press.
Tustin, F. (1981) *Autistic States in Children*, London: Routledge and Kegan Paul.

Chapter 9

Learning to say 'goodbye'

Loss and bereavement in learning difficulties and the role of art therapy

Ed Kuczaj

Central theme
- The experience of loss and bereavement in the lives of people with learning difficulties and their families.

Key points
- How the experience of loss may be protracted in the lives of people with learning difficulties.
- The tendency to deny people with learning difficulties' subjective experience of grief.
- How art therapy can be a fertile ground for the exploration of key themes in this area.

You cannot prevent the birds of sorrow from flying over your head, but you can prevent them from building a nest in your hair.

(Chinese Proverb)

INTRODUCTION

This chapter is based on my own work and experiences whilst working as an art therapist in a NHS Trust over the past ten years.

The various moves forward in the quality of the lives and opportunities for an individual with a learning difficulty have taken many years to come to the point we are now at, where a psychotherapeutic intervention can be thought to be a normal matter of choice alongside other services where it is felt necessary.

Individuals are usually referred to art therapy by members of community learning difficulty teams or by carers, with occasional self-referrals being made. Experiences discussed in this chapter relate to both hospital- and community-based clients. In all cases a six-week assessment period is carried out, followed by further reviews, usually on a three-monthly basis. As with other therapeutic interventions, a contract is drawn up with clients in relation to the contact being offered, with the individual having the ultimate choice and being able to withdraw from it at any stage.

In this chapter my aim is to look at the losses we all, client and therapist, experience at some point in our lives, and the need to both understand and allow for that specific experience for someone with a learning difficulty.

The key point or position that does now seem to have been reached is the acceptance that a cognitive skill does not necessarily equate to a specific emotional expressive ability or level of understanding. A concern many people have had in working or being with individuals with learning difficulties is that of understanding and being understood, where there is a notable difference in IQ and verbal ability (Bungener and McCormack 1994:369). In this context, the concept of 'emotional intelligence' (Sinason 1992:74) becomes an important consideration.

The extent to which the emotional life of an individual with a learning difficulty has been denied or simply not understood has been quite considerable, the main reason being our own lack of understanding of the individual and the many preconceptions we carry. In seeing this group of people as different in terms of need and ability we immediately separate ourselves and our common bonds as human beings, specifically in relation to our emotional and psychological lives.

Whilst we can acknowledge this emotional need, I feel more importantly that we also need to accept there are and will be many significant changes and losses of people, objects, ties and relationships that can and will influence the way an individual develops. In this context, loss is seen in a broader sense than simply that of a bereavement.

A RIGHT TO FEEL

During the course of working some years ago with a client who had a learning difficulty I had my first experience of dealing with an individual who had suffered a loss. My contact with the client, a young girl in her twenties, had existed for only two or three weeks when she came to the session and announced she had bad news. There had been a week's break in our sessions and she had been home from the hospital where she lived to see her parents.

Whilst at home her grandmother had died suddenly. 'I don't want to talk, I want to paint' she told me. So I sat with her at the table and she painted a large image of what seemed to be a grave with flowers framed in a rectangle of murky brown paint. She told me that she hadn't been at the funeral but had stayed at home to look after her baby nephew with the next-door neighbour. Her parents also thought that she might have become too upset. The next day she had visited the grave with her parents. She said little else during the session and left after her hour, choosing to leave the image on the table for me to put away when dry.

The session had felt awkward but poignant, with a sense of the pain that is suffered when something is taken away from someone. I thought I knew the feelings associated with grief, both from my own experiences of colleagues and distant relatives who had died and from textbooks. In a way I had neatly packaged her grief up until the next session.

Two months later I myself experienced a close bereavement and suddenly realised with tremendous clarity that I didn't know the feelings associated with grief but only thought I knew. I also realised how 'open' grief can feel. During the course of my own bereavement I began to consider the bereavements and losses of the clients around me. What effects did it have on them? Did they understand? Were they involved? The pain my client felt and expressed through her image and her few words made me feel as if I had just woken from a dream: I felt stupid. The stupidity I felt was for not thinking, not realising that someone with a learning difficulty might experience a bereavement, loss, in the same way as I had. I had thought that my feelings were different.

Psychotherapist Valerie Sinason describes one of her first encounters with a client and her own feelings of stupidity when facing and realising her client's sexual abuse traumas. 'We had all managed not to see something: we had gone "stupid", knocked silly by the grief we were witnessing' (Sinason 1992:7). Stupid, which historically originally meant 'numbed with grief', aptly described my position. From this position as a therapist came the question, 'What other griefs, losses had my clients experienced and what effect had they had on their lives?'

Whilst at the optician sometime after my client's bereavement, the conversation came around to my job and where I worked. On hearing of my work at the local learning difficulty hospital the middle-aged optician stopped the test and she said, 'I have a son who is mentally handicapped, he lives in a Home Farm Trust home nearby. He went into the hospital you work in when he was six. I'll never forget the day I took him there. The staff said not to worry about him, that I could forget about him now.' She had not forgotten, nor the words spoken to her.

There are two sides to each story and what becomes apparent is the need to understand both in order to see the total picture.

CLIENT AND FAMILY

Chris, a man in his forties with a moderate learning disability, was referred to me by a community nurse. He was living with his parents and was displaying behaviour problems. He had no speech or self-help skills and was cared for at home by his parents.

Chris had come to the notice of the community nurse only because the parents, both retired, had asked for financial help for incontinence pads from social services. This had led in turn to the community nurse's involvement. For forty years his parents had, with the help of their immediate family, catered for all his needs, physical and emotional.

Chris had attended school for one day. On his return home on that first day his mother had noticed marks on the back of his legs. Her brother, a nurse at the time, suggested these were probably marks from being tied to the chair in school. He never went again and his mother vowed to care for him at home.

The aim of my input was simply to offer a space to Chris, and also to his parents, whilst he attended the sessions. As no-one had worked with him, ever, we were unsure of what he could or couldn't do.

The parents' initial request was for something practical, not for direct work with their son, and this we needed to acknowledge. Both parents, but in particular his mother, were fearful of him being angry and aggressive in the session, possibly damaging the furniture. Working with the community nurse we persuaded them both that it would be all right and started sessions at a hospital close by. The sessions themselves were very slow and most of the time was spent simply 'being together' as any undue pressure or new demands simply provoked anxiety in Chris.

Unwilling to use art materials for any length of time we used a sand tray with him, allowing him and us to play in the sand and gradually build up trust together.

As the sessions progressed his concentration span and tolerance of us increased, with him also initiating some play. This seemed wonderful to us and on one specific occasion after a session we returned Chris home to tell his parents of the progress. Their reaction was one of absolute guilt. In the space of a few short weeks we had, for his parents, simply emphasised their own failings for not having requested help earlier. They had done what they thought was best, had asked for help and now they felt inadequate. It took some weeks to restore their own faith in the care they provided and in doing so we, and I, acknowledged the depth and complexities involved in that parent/child relationship.

There was though a need for Chris's parents to keep him as a child. He was their only child and would never be anything else. He would never have a job, get married, produce grandchildren or be able to look after his parents when they were old. This was emphasised by his mother saying, 'I worry about us both dying and then what would happen to Chris? I really would be happier if he died first and then at least I would know he was all right.' She did in fact have her wish because Chris died of kidney failure about one year later and one year after his death she herself died.

REACTIONS TO LOSS

A normal reaction to a loss follows a pattern of phases (French 1995) that the individual needs to work through in order to come to terms with that loss. The four phases are:

- Shock – when the reality of the loss is yet to be understood.
- Protest – when the person cannot accept the loss but has evidence it has happened.
- Disorganisation – when the reality of the loss is only too real.
- Reorganisation – when the person starts to rebuild their life.

It is easier to think of this 'work' as being in phases or tasks (Worden 1983) as the length of time (usually 2–3 years) and depth to which someone is involved can vary considerably. Often there can be the misconception that if the process is seen as stages (Kubler-Ross 1969), each has to be reached and gone through before the individual is able to move on to the next.

In relation to reactions to a loss, in working within the field of learning difficulties it is important to acknowledge both the effect that a learning difficulty has on the individual and also on their parents as well. For the parent there is often the feeling of the loss of the normal child and a continued reminder of disappointments as milestones fail to be achieved (Bicknell 1983:167). For the individual themselves there can be realisation of their difference, both from brothers or sisters and from the many other individuals who pass through their lives.

There are five important life-events for individuals that can affect the way they see themselves and others around them: diagnosis, separation experiences, broken friendship ties, dawning sexuality and bereavement (Bicknell 1983:175). For the therapist, what is important is the understanding of these potential life experiences for both the individual and their family and our own reaction to it.

It becomes important to consider these influences or dynamics because therapists often find themselves working with a client and then realise that the family or carer is intrinsically linked with the individual's problem.

When a parent has a 'handicapped' child they in fact have two children – the child with the learning difficulty and alongside it the normal child that should have been. As their child grows, the normal child that should have been constantly reminds the parents of that fact.

Joan Bicknell, in her paper on the psychopathology of handicap, illustrates the way some parents in their response to having a handicapped child follow closely the reactions and feelings we associate with a loss, that is, shock, panic, denial, grief, guilt, anger, bargaining and finally acceptance (Bicknell 1983: 168). As well as each parent being affected there is someone else involved, namely, the child, the person with the disability themselves: they too often have the sense of being two people, having two lives.

A LOSS CONTINUUM

In training with staff groups with whom I am involved on loss and bereavement, part of the day considers the various types of losses we face in life from birth to death for an individual. A usual list will contain:

Childhood pet	Security	Friendships
Grandparents	Possessions	Divorce
School changes	Adolescence	Personal relationships
Redundancy	Illness	Sensory impairments
Ageing	Independence	Privacy
Hope	Control	Freedom

The question is then asked, 'Would these losses be the same for someone with a learning difficulty?' The conclusion is of course mostly 'Yes', the difference being that for some individuals many of the losses come earlier and continue throughout their lives, for example, independence, friendships.

It can be easily be seen that those early losses we experience – be they the death of a pet or leaving friends when changing school – are preparations and learning experiences for the future losses we experience in life. We all as children act out lives, loves and losses through our play, burying the goldfish with religious fervour and being a part, however tenuous, in our families' own losses. Acting out in our childhood play, by ourselves or with others, is a way of coming to terms with the reality of life. But for an individual whose slow development and reduced ability might preclude full involvement in that play and involvement with others, this learning may never be fully realised.

Another important factor involved is of course the personal relationships we create within our families, in particular the bondings and attachments that develop between mother and child and that create the potential for the child's own development, as shown through the work of Winnicott (1958) and Bowlby (1969).

One of the main difficulties that often occurs is the lack of involvement the individual may have, or be allowed to have, specifically in a bereavement. Often this is seen as a necessary avoidance on the part of others. Death often feels like a disease, transmittable, and therefore avoidance or the packaging of it to maintain the minimum of discomfort becomes a way of keeping it at a healthy distance.

It is unfortunate that for some people with learning difficulties there is no directly allowed involvement in family losses, and sometimes deaths are kept from them.

This exclusion, which certainly occurred in the past in residential care but fortunately less so now, may occur for a number of reasons. Four factors may be involved:

- First, a perception that some individuals show no sign of grief after a loss.
- Second, an inability to make their feelings known.
- Third, a delay for the individual in the realisation of the implications of that loss.
- Fourth, the often presumed assumption that a limited cognitive capacity equates with a limited emotional capacity.

(Kitching 1987: 62)

What can also be seen is the fact that often one loss can quickly lead to another – a loss continuum. In changing to a different school a child may then lose schoolfriends and teachers he or she is used to, and with this loss the loss of the confidence and security they have developed in those surroundings. A loss therefore has the potential to be a catalyst for other losses, thereby adding to or sometimes confusing further the situation the individual is experiencing. This can in extreme situations lead to delays in the grief process itself.

Relating this to an individual with a learning disability we may find a scenario of someone coming into emergency care after the death of a parent, to be then moved on to a more permanent residence, and perhaps having to change their day placement and key workers all at the same time.

SPECIFIC THEMES

There are, I feel, two running themes I frequently see in work with clients – dependence and independence, and similarity and difference. Both themes are associated with loss to varying degrees, and often reoccur within an individual's life at various times. Although clients are referred for a variety of reasons, including bereavement, these two themes are often present in most referrals and I would like now to look at some specific cases where they arise together with loss issues.

As soon as a session begins, a potential contrast is revealed. Whilst we can acknowledge the many differences there are in therapy – client and therapist, the individual in need and the helper, controlled and controller – there is the aspect of intelligence or ability that is often present and rarely addressed. These two themes are often related to this.

A 14-year-old boy I worked with would continually, in the first few months, check out the difference between us by trying to make us the same. Having a physical disability which made walking, sitting at a table and holding a pen or brush difficult and awkward, there was an initial demand for me to draw for him. Attempting to work at a level that would not intimidate him but also not deny my 'ability', we worked together, taking turns at first until his confidence grew. He could be and was very verbal, with a tremendous memory.

One day he decided not to sit at the table in the classroom where we met but in a soft chair. 'Sit here,' he said, pointing to the chair beside him. 'I want you to sit by me. I'm going to draw you something, but don't look, close your eyes and don't peep. Are they shut? Say it.' 'Yes, they're shut,' I said. 'Say ready steady go; go on, say it,' he replied.

This sequence of his question/demand and my answer was repeated a number of times until he felt I was 'listening'. He then drew on a piece of paper placed on the chair beside him four images – a car, a bus, a lorry and a helicopter. Occasionally as he drew he would check and ask if my eyes were still closed. 'Are they good?' he asked when he had finished. I replied that he had worked really hard and they were good because he was pleased with them. 'Thank you for saying that,' he said, smiling. Later, looking at me expectantly, he asked, 'Am I clever? You are clever.'

My immediate thoughts were to wonder what 'clever' meant. In the context of being with him in school it may have had an educational reference but in the world outside of school a whole set of other values came into play. I chose (and it may have been through discomfort or avoidance on my part) to say that I felt he was clever for having done these four drawings. He smiled broadly and proceeded to say I was cool and offered me a handshake. It felt he was saying, 'We are the same' or perhaps more importantly 'I am (want to be?) the same as you.' The demand for the closing of my eyes, though a game, felt very much as though it were perhaps making it easier for him to draw without my eyes gazing upon him.

In the same session, the comparison he was making with my own ability extended from the room to a classmate who was playing outside. We both heard a boy's shout and the kick of a ball against the side of the building. 'Stop it, Tom,' he shouted, 'You're not allowed to play with the ball.' I asked if Tom was at Games because I thought I could hear other voices too. 'Yes, they're playing,' he said. I suggested perhaps he was telling Tom off because he would have liked to have been playing too but was in here with me? Indeed, he would have liked to have been able to play.

Although the art works he produced (which were usually of vehicles) were an important expression of himself, what for him was more important was the testing of his 'ability' with me. From this testing can come some understanding and acceptance of a situation, thereby using the therapist as both a container and mirror for a part of themselves.

In all situations though, for the client to have a real understanding and acceptance of their situation they perhaps have to let go part of the hope they have of being the same as everyone else – everyone that is not 'handicapped'.

In a more direct and specific way this was illustrated to me whilst working with a young man who had been in care from sixteen years of age. John had spent his early years at home with his parents and brother. A number of times, due to medical problems related to his hydrocephalus, he had had spells in hospital. When John was four years old, his father died and the family then moved. As he grew up his behaviour began to cause concern at home, until a point was reached where residential care was needed. This situation continued with occasional spells at home until finally he moved to permanent hospital care. His mother had later remarried. He was referred to art therapy because of his problematic behaviour, both inside and outside the ward, which sometimes resulted in behavioural approaches being used as a control method. The weekly sessions took place on the ward because of his reluctance to meet outside that situation.

John could be extremely verbal at times and had a powerful voice when he chose to use it. Although he could be aggressive, more often than not it was his verbal approach and manner that caused most problems. He did though know where to take his problems and knew that the consultant, or medics, were very useful authority figures who often had ultimate control.

During the first few sessions, the issues of control, independence and intelligence were of paramount importance to John. As with all clients, at the start of the input I had explained the nature of the sessions, the boundaries, and agreed on a contract with him. At the first session, feeling a little nervous, he drew quickly on a piece of paper a few lines that he said was a river with a barge on it. After talking about the image for a very short time he then spoke to me about the people around him who he felt were out to get him or who had been unfair to him recently.

As each subsequent session neared he would often catch me somewhere in the hospital to cancel the session, blaming his busy life. But each session took place, with him choosing to forget what the reason for cancellation had been. One time this became even more direct with him complaining of a migraine on my arrival at the ward. 'Fine,' I told him, that was no problem, I would go to the room and he could come up if he felt better but I would wait the hour. Ten minutes later he arrived, minus the headache. As with most individuals who have challenging behaviour, control and more importantly who has that control is of vital importance.

The images in the next few sessions all revolved around himself, drawn very quickly with him 'talking' to me for the remaining part of the session. It often felt hard to be with him at the sessions because of the control he obviously needed to exert during them. This came through in his continual references to individuals who hadn't done what they should have done, or with people he thought were getting away with 'things'. What was impossible was for him to talk specifically about one issue or stay on one point. For me the image, however minimal, became an anchor to the session because it was the one point of contact that I had with him which I could bring him, and myself, back to. Issues related to home and his visits were almost non-starters and always became stuck with an outpouring of hostility, usually towards his stepfather.

John's need for control hid, I think, a need for security and understanding and also importantly for trust in a relationship. At one session he asked about showing the images to others. I replied that that was up to him and reaffirmed my role in being the keeper of them, referring also to my contact with the staff in relation to the sessions.

'Can anyone hear what we are talking about?' he asked. I replied I thought not, but we could do a test if he wished. This we then did, with him standing outside the room to see if he could hear me talking inside. He came back in the room reassured.

John tested out his own life possibilities in the sessions by bringing ideas for approval or checking. This happened on two occasions. On the first he came to a session clutching some human biology textbooks. 'I'm going to do an 'A' level in human biology,' he proudly said. Quite independently he had borrowed the books from a library, telling all the staff on the ward of his intentions. I said I was interested in his ambition and wondered what he might do with the 'A' level once he had got it. He paused and then suggested he might like to become a doctor. This fitted in very well with his belief in the power doctors had, certainly over his own life, but it was also about making a statement about himself and his own ability.

On the second occasion he looked at the images he had produced so far and then said he had an idea. 'I think these pictures are quite good. I'm going to have a book printed of my pictures to raise money for Mencap.' With this in mind he then asked if he could take the pictures away to do this. I suggested it might be an interesting idea but that it might be a shame to lose the pictures from the sessions we had had because I thought they were quite important pictures. In response to this he came up with the suggestion of copying each image and duly set to work. As with the proposed 'A' level, the following week nothing was mentioned until I asked. The books had been returned and the images were in his locker.

Gradually it became easier for John to talk within the session about matters particularly related to his family. He remembered dad dying of a heart attack and being in hospital. Mum had later remarried and he didn't like his stepfather because of the way he controlled things at home. This was brought into the open over a short period of time.

He had been on a trip into town and had called into the building society to withdraw some cash. Whilst there the cashier had called him by his original surname, which was written on his cash book. He told me only certain people he knew well were allowed to call him by this name and he had become very angry. I asked what he had done when he had become angry. 'I just came out,' he said. I suggested he had probably been very wise and that it was a positive step that he had not shown that anger. I wondered what it had been like – could he draw this anger? He drew an image (Figure 9.1) of his stomach. Inside he said were fluids which were good and bad. In the image, the stomach contained blue and black lines, blue representing good fluids and black bad. It was the black fluids that had made him angry. Had he felt anything else I wondered. He said only a headache.

The following week he came to the session very angry: he had just come back from being at home. He told me that on the day he was due to go home his parents had phoned to say that they had had a puncture in the car and would be late coming

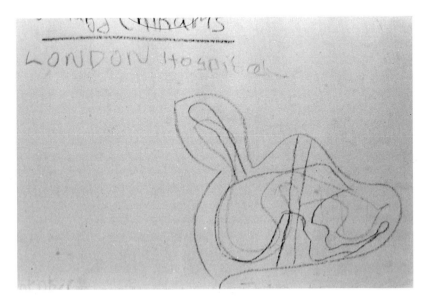

Figure 9.1 John: First feeling

Figure 9.2 John: Step-dad

Figure 9.3 John: Step-dad and mum

to pick him up. The real reason, he said, was that they 'didn't want him to come home'. But they had come, I pointed out, and he had gone home. Was he angry there? He had felt angry but again as before had chosen not to show it. He readily produced an image (Figure 9.2) of an angry step-dad, with his head and arms swirling with energy. I suggested John was now showing the anger he had felt at the time and that was OK. What was positive was his understanding of being able to bring that emotion to the session, actually holding on to it in the mean time.

A week later he produced another image of step-dad (Figure 9.3) but this time his mother is included as well. Step-dad appears on the left, smiling. John, for the first time, became very involved with the materials, concentrating on step-dad's body and using felt-tip and crayon until a glossy finish was produced.

The preoccupation with step-dad was reflected in his conversation. He had felt sad that he (step-dad) had never had a 'relationship' with him and had not been there when he was younger, 'always at work'. At this point he started to cry but quickly held the tears back saying he wanted to pay step-dad back for being unkind to him.

Now that experiences of his life at home had been opened and were on paper their expression continued. He was eager to start the sessions and would almost snatch the paper from me as I entered the room. A subsequent session produced an image of himself and his brother having a pillow-fight at home in their bedroom. He described his brother as his 'long-lost brother' because he was in the forces and he only occasionally had a letter from him. The control that was so necessary early on in the sessions diminished but was never far from the surface. On one occasion he asked what he would have to do to make me leave the session. Together we went through the various scenarios of behaviour etc. that was acceptable for the session to continue and that which would curtail a session. His ideas were mostly of the physical kind and, admitting he had no intention of 'trying them out', he suddenly came out with 'On your bike'. This was repeated continuously for ten to fifteen minutes without a real pause whilst I sat passively wondering where it would lead to next. He then stopped, saying, 'You're not going to go, are you?' I replied no, not until the end of the session, but of course he was free to go. The conversation then changed to what had been happening during the week until the end of the session. Then as he left the room he turned, looked at me, and said, 'On your bike' and quickly shut the door.

For John, the years away from his family had forced upon him a need for independence but also made him dependent on many others. He had had to come to terms with the loss of his immediate contact with his family, the loss of his real father and a later replacement. There was also the knowledge and insight he and others had of his own limitations, that is, his learning difficulty.

Bicknell (1983) talks of the need there is for a wider view of a definition from that of an organic definition of a learning difficulty for a individual. She suggests the questions:

What does it mean, to this person, to have this handicap? At this time in his or her life? With these caretakers? In this environment? And in this peer group?

It is with these questions that we can as therapists, carers, etc. start to understand the position we find our client in at the moment we meet them and, importantly, form an understanding of the experiences they have come through.

BEREAVEMENT EXPERIENCES

The need there is to allow a person with a learning difficulty the chance of understanding is often caught up with the needs families and carers have in keeping the individual themself safe. Particularly in relation to bereavement, the person suffering it is sometimes excluded from direct involvement and, in the worst cases, even collusion takes place so that they are shielded from the reality of events.

Where families are involved, directly or indirectly, an understanding of their own relationship with the individual is important. How many times have therapists wondered during therapy whether it is the client who has the problem or someone else? Carers, concerned with the grief that an individual may be experiencing after a bereavement, will often seek outside support in the belief that the individual needs help now. The fact that the normal bereavement process will take two to three years does not hide the fact that in witnessing someone else's grief we often reawaken our own responses and the helplessness that so often accompanies a loss.

This, I feel, is particularly prevalent in this field of work and sometimes undermines the confidence of carers in their own ability to offer support. There is the problem therefore of creating a need for bereavement counselling where it does not exist – 'a new technology' (McKnight 1984).

Support therefore sometimes needs to be extended to both the client and the carer, particularly where there are difficulties over the extent to which an individual is experiencing or understanding a loss. Concerned with the opportunities there were for individuals to share their own grief experiences I ran, with a colleague, a two-day experiential workshop for individuals who had suffered a bereavement. Individuals came, supported by carers where they wished, and bringing a range of personal experiences. All had suffered a bereavement within the last year or more. The overall aim was to help those individuals explore some of the feelings encountered after a loss and also to look at ways of giving and gaining support with each other.

Being concerned at tackling a very personal subject over just two days we became cautious in our planning, not wanting to expose anyone to their own specific experiences until it felt safe to do so. With this in mind we thought it might be better to leave those experiences and the sharing of them until we were well into the workshop.

After some simple ice-breaking exercises we invited the individuals and their supporters to draw a body image of themselves and indicate the different types of feelings they felt and where they felt them in their body.

As each image progressed it became apparent that each person was responding

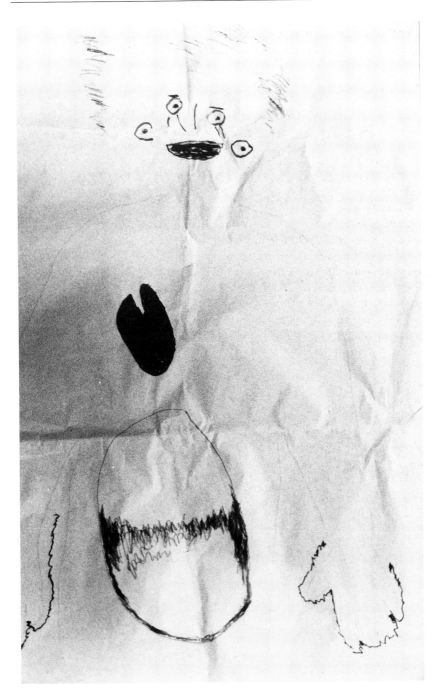

Figure 9.4 Robert: Body image

to the feelings they had experienced following their own bereavement. One image in particular explored so simply the range of feelings felt. Robert drew around himself and then filled his body with a huge hole that represented his stomach (Figure 9.4). Above his stomach lay his heart, and around his head and his hands he drew wavering lines. What we had not anticipated was everyone's readiness, indeed eagerness, to talk about their personal experiences.

Robert remembered well the day his mother had died. Shortly after, he became physically unwell and was admitted to hospital with suspected heart problems. He had begun to shake in his hands and was convinced that his hair was falling out: his stomach felt completely empty. All his problems were diagnosed as psychosomatic.

People's eagerness (or our reluctance) to look at their specific experiences led us to changing the day to respond specifically what their own needs were. Desiring to talk about their loved ones led to people bringing in the next day photographs and personal belongings that they valued. Time was also given to looking at their personal experiences. Robert drew the day he and his father had found his mother (Figure 9.5) when she had died. He chose only to talk of the ambulance coming after they had found her – the image said enough. Sharing that grief was important for Robert, as it was for the other individuals in the group. It was a way of reliving, thereby understanding what had happened. The importance of reliving and sharing a grief in therapy is described by Caroline Case in her work with a child (Dalley *et al.* 1987:47). She describes the child's use of a sand

Figure 9.5 Robert: The death of his mother

tray as being 'like spring-cleaning of the head, a necessary clearing out'. The remainder of the workshop centred around the support people had received and whether this had been appropriate or sufficient. This in turn led to thinking around support they had now or wished for in the future.

In evaluating the workshop we realised the importance that the creative component had played in it, because 'a record of progress, thoughts and feelings could be made by each person on their own terms' (French and Kuczaj 1992:111). What was apparent from the images produced was the absolute strength an image can have in containing the emotional content of a personal experience, and the lack of need there is sometimes to accompany this with words. Patsy Nowell Hall describes in her work with clients how they felt the images and the creating of them were the agents of change, and that interpretation and talking was like 'continually pulling up a plant to inspect the roots' (Nowell Hall *et al.* 1987:182).

Working with individuals who sometimes have limited verbal skills often presents difficult transference and counter-transference feelings, in terms of wanting to fill the void with words or being too directive. In being left with 'only' the image there is sometimes the feeling that this is not enough and does not adequately justify the reason for the individual being there. We do however need to trust the image, and so the session, because in doing so we give trust and possibility to the client.

WORKING WITH LOSS

In beginning a relationship with a client we automatically begin the ending of it. So many individuals who are, or have been in care, have had dozens of people pass through their lives, so it is no wonder that often relating to or trusting others proves so difficult for them.

Through art therapy, individuals can and will test out the meaning of relationships and the complexities involved in them. Inevitably, because of this, sessions/inputs may mirror past relationship experiences; the simple establishment of a relationship with a therapist in itself becomes a learning possibility in the trusting and understanding of another human being, and ultimately of themselves.

One of the most difficult lessons to learn for the therapist is that of 'being with the client', that is, understanding one's own needs as well as those of the individual and working with that potential unknown. But that unknown is often the position clients find themselves in. In working with the theme of loss, be it in a therapy session or outside of it, in relation to person with a learning difficulty what I feel we need to offer and to understand we are offering are four particular components: *Honesty*; *continuity*; *consistency*; *possibility*. In offering these, we can achieve both for our clients and ourselves an awareness of the position in which we find ourselves. They may seem basic rights for any individual and, indeed, they are but they are important for the individuals we work with simply because they are often neglected. Understanding the effects of loss, both for the individual and the people around them including ourselves as therapists is, I feel, a way of starting to understand someone who has a learning difficulty as a person in their own right.

BIBLIOGRAPHY

Bicknell, J. (1983) *British Journal of Medical Psychology*, 56.

Bowlby, J. (1969) *Attachment and Loss*, London: Hogarth Press.

Bungener, J. and McCormack, B. (1994) *The Handbook of Psychotherapy*, London: Routledge.

Clarkson, P. and Pokorny, M. (1994) *The Handbook of Psychotherapy*, London: Routledge.

Dalley, T., Case, C., Schaverien, J., Weir, F., Nowell Hall, P., Halliday, D. and Waller, D. (1987) *Images of Art Therapy*, London: Tavistock.

French, J. (1995) *Bereavement and Loss: Training Information*, Bristol: Phoenix Trust.

French, J. and Kuczaj, E.(1992) 'Working Through Loss and Change with People with Learning Disabilities', *Mental Handicap*, 20.

Kitching, N. (1987) 'Helping People with Mental Handicaps Cope with Bereavement', *Mental Handicap*, 15.

Kubler-Ross, E. (1969) *On Death and Dying*, New York: Macmillan.

McKnight, J. (1984) *John Deere and the Bereavement Counsellor*. Annual E.F. Schumacher Lecture, in *An Introduction to the Whole Community Catalog*, New Haven, Conn.

Nowell Hall, P. (1987) [Author: please complete.]

Sinason, V. (1992) *Mental Handicap and the Human Condition*, London: Free Association Books.

Winnicott, D.W. (1958) *Through Paediatrics to Psychoanalysis*, London: Tavistock.

Worden, J. (1983) *Grief Counselling, Grief Therapy*, London: Tavistock Publications.

Part 3

Allied approaches

Chapter 10

Journey in joint working

Some reflections on an experience of arts therapies collaboration

Chris Gale and Rachel Matthews

Central theme
- Description of a collaborative venture, namely a combined assessment group involving an art therapist, dramatherapist and music therapist.

Key points
- The nature of assessment; what do we assess and how do we assess, particularly where clients are non-verbal?
- The anxieties and benefits elicited by collaborative working – what it can tell us about the scope and limitation of our particular professional skills.
- The relative merits of different professional approaches in meeting varying perceived clients' needs.

INTRODUCTION

This chapter describes a short-term project involving co-operative working in sessions between an art therapist, a dramatherapist and a music therapist. The idea was discussed by therapists in the TAITH[1] Arts Therapies Service for some time before it became a reality. Whilst such joint working has taken place elsewhere, it was the first time such an approach had been adopted within TAITH. As the idea developed, it took on a particular importance to team members. Thoughts were prompted not only about the needs of clients, but also about the nature of the media used by practitioners within the different arts therapies professions. The history of this Assessment Group project is described below, from its inception to the culmination of the first group which actually met.

THE IDEA OF AN 'ASSESSMENT GROUP'

In December 1994 the five therapists in TAITH began to think about something which was new for the department. An afternoon was set aside to discuss the idea of an assessment group which would involve all three media. It was a year since the new team of therapists had been completed by the appointment of a drama-therapist, and we had experience over that time of receiving and considering referrals.

There had been several considerations behind this idea. The number of referrals, especially those from the community, had far exceeded the amount of session time available, which meant that many clients had the prospect of a long wait. At the same time, before actually starting work with someone it was not always clear whether a client would wish to take part in therapy, or whether it would actually turn out to be useful.

More specifically relevant to an arts therapies service was the question of which medium to identify for therapy for particular clients. Sometimes this was difficult to determine, and even where it seemed clear, we were not sure that our decisions had a very methodical basis. It was noticed that within the referrals meetings there was a tendency to make assumptions that clients who expressed themselves in one way or another might find a certain medium more useful in therapy. The assessment group offered an opportunity to explore this with the same clients, using different media.

When the service was being developed it had been felt especially important to emphasise ways of working which gave focus and containment to the sessions. Maintaining a consistent relationship with a particular therapist was one of the main principles and, whilst the art therapists (of whom there were three) had sometimes worked in pairs, the prospect of combined working across the media potentially raised a greater number of issues. Might there be different expec-tations between disciplines about the nature of the relationship between therapist and client?

The knowledge which team members had of each other's disciplines had been gained largely from hearing descriptions of the work, most notably in regular clinical supervision sessions with an external supervisor. These took place on a group basis, which meant that as well as providing an opportunity for each therapist to reflect on his or her own work, an impression was gained of the approaches and ways of working of others in the team. Further opportunities to share in using various media came through participation in All-Wales profes-sional meetings[2] which included one-off experiential sessions on particular themes. These sessions were not intended as therapy.

We were aware that there was some variety of approach to therapy within the team. It was likely that some of this stemmed from individual differences, as there are a number of perspectives in each profession. However, it also seemed that the qualities of the different media had an influence on this. As colleagues we had co-operated a great deal outside the therapy rooms; the idea of working together within therapy sessions was a prospect which was both challenging and exciting.

THE IDEA DEVELOPS

Over the next few months the team of therapists met several times to take the idea forward, and to think how best the practical tasks might be approached. Initially the group was envisaged as starting in March 1995, but as more elements came to be included, it was proposed instead for June of that year.

Assessment was seen as a process by which certain questions might be considered, both for clients and therapists. These questions were implicit in the existing assessment, but needed to be clarified in relation to the proposed group. The team drew up a list of questions (see Table 10.1) and discussed how answers could be ascertained and recorded.

Discussion then turned to designing a workable format for the group. On three successive mornings, the group would experience each of the arts therapies media in turn. Throughout the preparations, clients and their supporters would be kept informed by letter and through meetings. Sessions giving information on the arts therapies would be run for support staff in parallel to the actual therapy sessions. We wanted to identify a venue for the work away from our hospital accommodation, where clients who lived in the community would be more likely to feel comfortable. It was also felt that, following the sessions, it would be useful for the therapists to discuss the experience with the assistance of an outside facilitator. A group of clients was identified, and a specific week in June chosen for the group to take place. The therapists in the team began working on the various practical tasks which would be necessary.

THE GROUP DEFERRED

Each stage of the process which had been arrived at during discussion seemed very logical, but it gradually became apparent that the logistics were rather complicated. It had felt important that everything should be 'just right', as if this group would somehow answer all the outstanding questions about the work of the department. Further queries arose the more thought was given to the process, particularly whether such a group could be regarded as being therapy, and about what exactly would be useful about the group for the clients.

As time moved on, it became clear that it would not be possible to undertake everything which had been planned within the time available. The group was postponed, initially for four months and later, when further changes seemed likely to the work setting, the postponement became indefinite.

THE IDEA REVIVED

The early planning for the group had been quite elaborate, but as a result a number of complex issues presented themselves. Despite the postponement, however, the idea of an assessment group continued to be important to the team of therapists, and was referred to periodically.

Table 10.1 Original review questions for the assessment group

THE CLIENT'S QUESTIONS
1 *Therapy or not?*
(a) Does the client want therapy?
(b) Does the client understand the nature of therapy?

2 *Choosing the therapy*
(a) Does the client have a preference for medium?
(b) Does the client have a preference for group or individual therapy?
(c) Does the client have a preference for a particular combination of a) and b)?

3 *Choosing the therapist*
(a) Does the client have a preference or need for particular considerations, for example,
> male or female therapist
> Welsh/English/other language/signing
> ethnicity/race/class

(b) Does the client have a particular response to an individual therapist?

4 *Conditions for therapy*
(No client questions currently indicated here)

5 *Aims and points to note*
(a) What are the client's aims for being in therapy?

THE THERAPIST'S QUESTIONS
1 *Therapy or not?*
(a) What level of engagement has the client given
> with the therapist(s)?
> with the group?
> with the medium?

2 *Choosing the therapy*
(a) What is the therapist's assessment of the client's response to each medium?
(b) What do the therapists see as appropriate media for each client, and should therapy be on a group or individual basis?

3 *Choosing the therapist*
(a) What was the response of each therapist to the clients?

4 *Conditions for therapy*
(a) What is the therapists' assessment of the following issues:
> How long will the client choose to remain in the room?
> Is there any risk that the client may hurt people or damage objects?
> What location for therapy would be suitable for this client? (room, setting, area, facility)
> Would the client need to be escorted to the session, and would this be possible?
> What support may be needed during the session, either inside or outside the room?
> What level of information-sharing is appropriate, and with whom?

Table 10.1 continued

(b) What financial considerations are there, and can they be met?
(c) Is the network of carers of a kind conducive to sustaining what has been
gained through therapy?

5   *Aims and points to note*
(a) What are the therapist's impressions of the client's agenda?
(b) What are the therapist's impressions of the referrer or key carer's agendas?
(c) What is the match between a) and b), and are there potential points of
conflict?
(d) What interpersonal dynamics in the group may have affected the client in
some way (for instance, pre-existing relationships)?

In early 1996 the idea was once again raised, this time against a slightly different background. Whilst the community waiting-list was shorter, it had been noticed increasingly that when referrals were received for clients living in the hospital, it was especially difficult to make decisions about whether therapy would be useful. Visits were often made in which clients would be rather uncommunicative, and it would be far from clear whether this was because of an intrinsic difficulty or was due to a habitual response brought on by many years of living in an institutional setting.

It was decided to run an assessment group within a rather less ambitious format; the group would be specifically for clients living in the hospital, and would be run within the arts therapies department there. There would be six one-hour sessions once weekly, focusing in a rotating format on each of the three media. Sessions 1 and 4 would be for dramatherapy, sessions 2 and 5 music therapy and sessions 3 and 6 art therapy.

One further element from the original plan was retained – that of approaching an outside facilitator to lead a discussion among the therapists. This time, however, there would be a day-long session for the whole team of therapists, a week before the assessment group began.

TRANSITION

The discussion day was a turning-point in the development of the assessment group. It gave time for the therapists to talk explicitly about their own approaches to the work. This included each of us talking about our training, and how our subsequent practice had led us to reflect on this, and develop our initial learning. We also considered our ideas about how the other two therapies were practised; in what way they were effective; and how this differed from – or perhaps even contradicted – our own theory and practice.

The issue of working alongside colleagues inspired some anxiety. Our work as therapists normally takes place in a private space. There was a difference for each of us between discussing something in a supervision and having work with clients observed by other therapists in the room. This was welcomed in principle but we felt wary about it in practice. In particular, we needed to consider the roles we would play in relation to one another. One person would be leading the session, the others supporting. These roles would change from week to week. Although we could not really predict how this would work until we actually began the group, we had to discuss what we expected from one another.

SPECIFIC PLANNING

Questions of joint working would affect the group at a very practical level. In early discussions of the group, one of the art therapists had wondered how we would present the different media. Would we put the various materials – art materials, instruments, props – into a room along with an art therapist, a music therapist and a dramatherapist, let a group of clients come into the room, and see what each individual responded to? The dramatherapist had envisaged something much more structured, with the whole group participating in one medium at one time.

In the second part of the discussion day, the three therapists running the group, Hilary (art therapy), Chris (music therapy) and Rachel (dramatherapy) considered ways to bring together their respective approaches. As the group was considered, a structure emerged which seemed appropriate but would differ from each of our usual ways of working.

In this discussion, it was decided that the music therapy room would be used for all the sessions. The room would be set up with easy chairs in a circle, and spaces for those in wheelchairs. For the art therapy sessions, several low tables would be available to work on. Art materials, musical instruments and props were available in the room every week.

It seemed important to have some things which were constant throughout the six weeks. Rachel would lead an opening exercise which would help clients to feel they had arrived in the session, recognise each individual and develop group cohesion. Each session would end through Chris initiating a song which would acknowledge each person who had been present, and mark the end of the group time.

The group had been designed specifically as an assessment group, and there was no intention of it having a long-term life. We had therefore not taken the kind of care in considering (or guessing at) compatibility between clients which we would normally exercise in setting up therapy groups. This was one of the areas which interested us in approaching assessment for therapy in a different way. Although each client had met at least one of the therapists, and detailed information had been gathered from the referrer, the therapists had very little idea how people would respond to the therapeutic setting. It held all the usual uncertainties for clients and therapists of a new situation, with the extra fillip of a new way of working for the therapists.

The team of therapists had been working together and in group supervision for just over two years, but this would be the first experience the team had had of joint working with clients across the media. There was a significant process taking place within the team as well as in the assessment group itself.

INTRODUCTION TO THE CLIENTS

Seven clients were invited to the group who will be referred to by the names given below.

Maud

A woman in her sixties, who generally likes to keep moving, and will often be seen walking around the ward where she lives. Maud uses her voice in a variety of ways, but does not use spoken language. She often approaches people working on the ward to indicate her wishes.

Wilfred

A man in his seventies who is able to stand and walk short distances, but uses a wheelchair for longer trips. Wilfred does not use spoken language, but occasionally makes sounds in a regular rhythm with his voice or his hands.

Paul

A man in his forties, who is very friendly and eager to communicate. Paul tends to make large movements of his limbs, and sometimes may take hold of other people or just touch them. He does not use spoken sentences, but at times uses single words. He often is heard reciting clearly structured melodies, some of them familiar nursery-rhyme tunes.

Margaret

Also in her forties, makes her own way around the hospital, communicating through gesture and some single words. She likes to spend time with particular individuals, and has very clear ideas about her own preferences.

Kath

A woman in her forties who uses occasional spoken words, and sometimes sings. Kath takes a lively interest in a variety of activities but finds it hard to continue being in the same place for a very long, sometimes becoming anxious.

Edith

A woman in her eighties, who converses fluently, but finds unfamiliar situations difficult.

Michael

A young man in his twenties who also also enjoys conversation, and makes his own way around the hospital.

Four of these were people who had been referred to TAITH and were on the waiting list (Maud, Wilfred, Paul and Margaret). The other three (Kath, Michael and Edith) had been specifically referred for this assessment group. Four clients attended most or all of the sessions, with a fifth, Margaret, attending somewhat erratically. Two clients, Michael and Edith, only came to session 1.

REFLECTIONS ON THE CONTENT

Dramatherapy – sessions 1 and 4

The opening part of session 1 felt very chaotic. Michael had arrived early, Margaret and Kath were reluctant to enter the room, Kath arriving ten minutes late. Paul arrived crying out and waving his arms, apparently excited. Edith was extremely anxious when she arrived and left the session after half an hour. Wilfred and Maud did not attend.

The session began with introductions, a name and movement exercise, a gentle physical warm-up and a brief introduction to the 'rules' of the group. There was a lot of noise going on for much of this period, in particular from Paul and Edith. It was hard for the group to concentrate together on anything.

The group were then given an opportunity to move within the room, exploring the space and the materials from the different media. The clients actually did not show a lot of interest in the contents of the room but seemed to welcome moving. They appreciated the opportunity to do something on their own, and for individual interaction with the therapists. There was a marked change in the atmosphere at this point. Attention moved from the general to the specific, and both clients and therapists became more comfortable. The exploration of the room was followed by movement with music – in the group, individually and in pairs.

Everyone sat down and a soft ball was passed around the group. As the ball was rolled across the floor, Rachel would speak the names of both the passer and the receiver. Those clients who could speak were encouraged to say the name of the person they were passing to. Group members became much quieter and more focused than before, and everyone took part. This was the moment when, in the simplest sense, those in the room began to function as a group. The ball exercise was subsequently used to open each session. Over the weeks, it was developed and used in different ways by the clients.

The session concluded with Chris singing a phrase which the group then repeated. The main part of this was the singing of 'Thank you, thank you, see you next time' then to thank individual members of the group. Within this structure, there would sometimes be improvisation which responded to what individuals were doing. This song grew very directly out of the atmosphere and character of the group; it would have been hard to devise it in advance. The group ended in a very still and quiet way – very different from its opening moments.

Common group traits and themes were apparent even in this opening session. Relationships between clients and therapists were in their very early stages. In the ball exercise, in session 1 clients only passed to Rachel. As this developed through the weeks, clients expanded the activity to include the other therapists, and later, some clients were able to pass to each other.

The therapists learnt a lot in this first session about the range and means of communication of the clients. In the chaotic opening, we really had very little idea about the capabilities of the clients in the group, and of how they would express themselves. However, we felt that in a variety of ways, all the clients had communicated a great deal about themselves.

The session showed a clear progression in group involvement. The opening part of the session was chaotic; each person had their own anxieties, often clearly demonstrated. This was followed by a period where the freedom to explore and not be part of a group increased each person's feeling of safety, allowing them to come back together slowly, through pair work, into a whole group activity – the ball exercise – where a remarkable degree of concentration emerged.

The therapists were surprised by the lack of interest the clients showed in the objects and furniture in the room, although they seemed pleased to move about in it. This was a consistent response throughout the life of the group. It is hard to judge whether this was about individual preferences, or related more to the effects of institutionalisation, which tends to stifle curiosity, creativity and imagination.

Session 4 began late. Wilfred, John, Kath and Maud were present. Kath had again been reluctant to enter the room.

Kath started the session, picking up the ball and passing it to Rachel. She also ended this exercise by going to the piano and playing it. After attempting to get the group standing in a circle, which was not taken up, Rachel then began to copy and describe, in turn, how each person in the room was sitting. This focused the attention of everyone in the room. The clients did not copy one other, but attended to what Rachel was doing and saying.

Rachel went to each person in turn, touching hands. The nature of the touch, and how it was received varied a great deal but the group stayed well focused. Rachel sat on the floor, mirroring a rocking movement of Maud's. Kath in particular was fascinated by this, coming to sit by Rachel on the floor and copying the movement. As this was happening, Hilary commented on how others in the room were reflecting this movement in some way, whether intentionally or not. The rocking and mirroring developed into a process where Rachel noticed movements and sounds from different people, reflecting and developing them. In copying Maud wiping her eyes, a movement and sound sequence emerged which included yawning and stretching. A small mime of going to sleep, using the ball as a pillow, was then acted by each person in the room, before moving on to the closing song.

At this stage in the development of the group, most clients were not willing to be proactive. The passivity demonstrated is common in clients who have become institutionalised and who are not used to having much freedom or choice. Rachel responded to this by using herself as the actor, becoming a vehicle of communication through which attention could be focused on each client in turn. Everyone in the group welcomed the personal attention of having their posture or sound copied, and seemed able to consider what Rachel was commenting on, through movement and voice, about others in the room.

By session 4 roles in the group had become more clearly defined. This was especially noticeable with Kath, who was very much the group 'doer'. In this session, she started and ended the ball exercise by her actions and joined Rachel in mirroring posture. In this and other sessions, she would fetch the ball if she thought another member was not picking it up or passing it on soon enough. This was a role which was apparent in both the music therapy and art therapy sessions, especially the final session, where Kath was the only person to use the art materials.

This fourth session was a time of consolidation. The people who attended were now the group, with the possible addition of Margaret, and a sense of cohesion was apparent through the work.

Music therapy – sessions 2 and 5

Four clients attended the second session, Paul, Kath, Maud and Margaret. Maud was hesitant about coming in, but seemed reassured by the presence of Rachel, who she may have remembered from a visit made to the ward some time before. She soon became quite settled in one particular chair, and this was helped by a more comfortable feeling in the group, as the session opened with the ball activity which was familiar to the other group members from the previous week.

Chris tends to approach sessions with a generalised format in mind, allowing a structure to emerge from the improvised musical exchanges. This session was prepared in rather more detail, partly to follow on from the relatively structured pattern of the previous week's dramatherapy. However, once the focus turned towards music it was clear that a more flexible approach would be appropriate this week. Chris used a small electronic piano rather than the upright piano he was accustomed to playing, as this preserved the seating plan where everyone was included in a circle.

Paul and Maud both used spontaneous vocal sounds, whereas Kath and Margaret were both interested at various times in initiating work on the instruments. Paul's vocal sounds tended to be in a rocking rhythm, moving at times into recognisable songs. Although intensely interested in others in the room, he was not very willing to engage in musical interplay with anyone. He would either initiate musical phrases himself or repeat phrases sung by Chris – some time later. Although he had tapped a thimble against a table in the initial dramatherapy session, he was reluctant to play the percussion instruments now offered to him.

This changed to some extent later in the session when others had played and he did some playing along similar lines to them.

Maud's vocal sounds were sustained and repetitive. Chris found it quite hard to engage with these sounds, as Maud appeared to move out of any given musical key as soon as he sang to her in that tonality – something which is somewhat difficult to do, and rather unusual. Maud was unambiguous in her attitude to the instruments, pushing away any which were offered to her.

Kath and Margaret developed a degree of kinship during the course of this session, as both used the instruments clearly and with determination. Kath's playing always came in bursts which she initiated herself, often on the electronic piano. On other instruments she tended to use a similar pounding motion, but was willing to imitate other techniques of playing, such as the stroking motion necessary to play the small zither which was offered at one point.

Margaret's use of unpitched percussion instruments consisted of strong and uniform beating, most notably on the snare-drum, which she played for a long stretch, only at the end showing some signs of flexibility of tempo. This had been uncomfortable for some other group members to experience; Maud in particular showed signs of discomfort, although it did seem to be bearable for her.

The metallophone, a pitched percussion instrument not unlike a xylophone, was at different times offered to both Kath and Margaret. This instrument, with its range of pitches and mellow tone, evinced a response from both of these clients which contrasted to their customary assertive ways of playing. Kath used it in rather an exploratory way, whereas Margaret's usual heavy beating was replaced by a light and delicate flurry of notes.

At the end of the session Kath chose to sing the verse of a hymn, after which Chris vocalised in response on the word 'thank you' before starting the closing song in the same key as she had been using for the hymn. Kath gave a look of recognition at this, as if this acknowledgement of her contribution to the group had been appreciated.

In the fifth session, Wilfred, Paul, Kath and Maud were present. Wilfred and Paul both made repeated vocal sounds in a rather similar lilting rhythm, but the degree of communicativeness of the two clients was strongly contrasting. Wilfred's sounds were very introspective with little discernible connection to anything else happening in the group. Although Paul was again reluctant to engage directly, his sounds were varied in order to attract attention and gain a response from others.

This session marked a particular stage in the development of a group interaction. At one point Paul was sitting next to Kath and began touching the edge of her chair in a repeated pattern, watching closely for her reaction. Kath tolerated this for a time, then stood, becoming unsettled for a time and moving from one chair to another. This in turn influenced Maud, who herself became restless, and for a moment was on the point of leaving the session.

Before and after this interaction, there were times when the medium allowed a sense of connection between members of the group who were responding in markedly different ways. Kath's use of the electronic piano settled into a pattern in which she would go away from the instrument and then return. Each time she came back, Chris would move his playing into the key of F sharp major. This provided a focus for Kath, giving a structure over which she had control with a clear shape and involving a predictable response. Interestingly, Maud's vocalisations showed a noticeable change each time Kath began using the instrument; her sounds became milder in tone and were at these times within the tonality of Chris's improvisation.

Art therapy – sessions 3 and 6

Paul, Maud and Wilfred attended session 3. It was Wilfred's first session. The session began with the ball exercise. Hilary then brought the small tables in to the circle, with a variety of art materials on them. She introduced the materials, and gave people an opportunity to use them if they wished. This brought no response, so the therapists worked together to bring materials to each client and offer them specifically. Each therapist worked with one client following where the client seemed to be leading. The session concluded with the group song.

No-one was interested in using the art materials, either when they were initially made available or later. Paul and Maud pushed the offered materials away – a frequent response for both of them. Paul would generally take first, then push away. This was typical of many of his interactions, in particular with the ball in the opening exercise. With the art materials, he wanted the attention and contact in the interaction, but did not appear interested in what might be achieved with the materials themselves.

Maud responded in a similar way, seeking out physical contact in order to then push the person away. She also sought out and strove to maintain strong eye contact. In this session she moved to sit nearer Rachel, and also pushed Rachel off a chair she herself wished to sit on. Hilary sometimes commented on her movements, and Maud seemed to respond with interest to this.

The 1:1 ratio of therapists and clients in this session gave an opportunity for individual interaction between clients and therapists in pairs. Contact developed in a more intuitive way when the materials were not taken up and used for their usual purpose. Wilfred used his hand to beat out rhythms on his body or his chair. Chris mirrored these, using his own hand to make rhythmic patterns on a piece of plasticine. A kind of dance developed between Paul and Rachel growing out of brushes or crayons being offered. This gradually developed to include Rachel making brushstrokes on paper in response to sounds made by Paul.

This session was quite surprising, as such a marked lack of interest in the art materials had not been expected. However, the small group which was present responded in ways consistent with previous weeks. Paul and Maud seemed generally more settled in the room, and more attentive and responsive to what others were doing, even when their main focus of attention seemed to be on one person.

Session 6 was attended by the four regular members of the group, Paul, Kath, Maud and Wilfred, and for the first 15 minutes by Margaret. Margaret was a formidable presence, being clear that she did not wish to be in the room, and certainly had no interest in doing anything involving the art materials. Chris was not present in this session.

The group opened with the ball exercise. Hilary, reflecting on the previous art therapy session, suggested that we create an ending picture for the group. She brought some large pieces of paper into the centre of the room and some paint. Kath began using these with speed and alacrity: there was little response, even with encouragement, from other group members. Kath continued to paint, whilst small interactions developed between therapists and clients, before the session ended with the group song.

Kath used the materials with great vigour. She used paints and crayons, and was obviously choosing her colours with care. Her pictures filled the paper. At times, she went and played the piano, slamming the lid down. She seemed conscious that the instruments were in some way Chris's domain, and was aware that he was not present. At the end of the session, she was the only person singing with the therapists – the whole group seemed to realise that Chris was not present and to find it uncomfortable having others lead the part that was usually his responsibility.

Paul and Maud, in this session, demonstrated a significant shift in their ability or inclination to take responsibility for themselves. In previous sessions, they had been 'done to' when therapists had approached them and offered an interaction or an object. They had also been observers, for instance when their posture and sound had been taken on by Rachel, or when sounds and movements had been translated by a therapist through the art materials. In this session, both clients used the therapist as a kind of extension of themselves, in order to achieve a desired end. The therapeutic space may provide an opportunity to experiment with this.

Paul did much less by way of grabbing, touching or reaching, but concentrated on his standing up and sitting down. He actively sought out Rachel, placing her body to support him as he stood up. He pushed materials away when they were offered but, towards the end of the session, picked up crayons, gave them to Rachel and moved her hand so that they were put away in the appropriate pot.

At one point, Maud approached Rachel, grasped her hand and led her to the door. She may have been indicating a wish to leave but needed to demonstrate this by using Rachel. She did not actually attempt to open the door.

Wilfred was apparently asleep for all but the final five minutes of this last session. This was consistent with other sessions, where there had been little engagement.

THE ASSESSMENT

Three weeks after the group finished, the therapists involved met to discuss how useful it had been in terms of assessment. Michael and Edith had chosen not to attend after the first week, but it was unclear whether this indicated a general wish not to be involved in therapy, or was to do with a response to that particular group. The reasons for Margaret's choice not to attend some sessions was also unclear; on occasion she had seemed convinced that another activity which involved going out of the hospital was about to take place. From the involvement which did take place, however, it was felt she could make use of either a dramatherapy or music therapy group. Maud and Paul had used both sound and movement to engage in the group process, and they were also identified for a future group in either music therapy or dramatherapy. Wilfred's level of engagement was so minimal that it was felt that unlikely that he would find the arts therapies useful. Kath had made use of all three media, and the flexibility of this sort of group setting seemed to suit her well. There was some question as to whether she would find work centred on just one medium as comfortable. It was felt that any of the three media might be useful, and as an art therapy group was about to start which seemed particularly suitable, she was offered a place in this, which she accepted.

GENERAL THOUGHTS

In the planning stage the approach of the therapists had been generalised and speculative. Questions about the assessment group had arisen from personal and professional approaches. When running the group itself, answers emerged to some much more specific questions relating to the clients; in this, the assessment group had been a success. We felt more relaxed as there seemed to be less need to solve the global questions, although some of the specific encounters helped us understand broader issues.

First, the issue of whether or not the group could be therapy was clearer and less problematic than it had seemed beforehand. The assessment group drew a very clear distinction between assessment and therapy, although the principles of working in therapy very much underlay it. In our usual way of working the assessment period is more of an initial contract for therapy, as it has the possibility of continuing in an uninterrupted way with the same therapist after the first review of the work. The assessment group, however, was clearly in existence for a limited time, and there would be a pause before any longer-term form of therapy began.

The use of the three media in the context of an assessment was also important for a number of reasons. In previous work, clients had sometimes been reluctant to engage with their therapist. Team members had often wondered whether one of the other media would be more useful. The assessment group offered an opportunity to make some quite direct comparisons and contrasts. Sometimes it did seem that the nature of the medium made engagement more possible for certain clients, but at other times the interpersonal issues meant that specific ways of relating were transferred from one medium to another.

Similarities and differences in the approaches of therapists provided some interesting insights. This applied to the language through which therapists described their work, and the response of other therapists to this. The drama-therapist's use of the word 'exercises' to refer to activities within the session sounded unfamiliar to the music therapist, whose own use of the word 'song' for activities he had led was hardly transferable to the other media. On the other hand, the music therapist tended to describe as 'vocal sounds' what the art therapist and dramatherapist might refer to as 'noises'.

The structure of the session also differed. The dramatherapist had based sessions on a series of planned distinct activities, whilst being flexible within that framework to actions taken by clients. The music therapist preferred to work in a more open-ended way, but prior to the group felt that a more structured approach would be appropriate in this instance. However, the pattern which emerged from the way clients used the sessions completely supplanted the intended sequence of activities. In the sessions led by the art therapist no specific activities were planned, the purpose of the group being exploratory. The therapist relied on the distinct phases of the group – beginning, middle and end – and on the therapist's stance or focus to provide the structure of the group.

Elements of the different media were present at all sessions, but the focus of the therapist determined the shape of the session. When art therapy and drama-therapy were the predominant media, sounds the clients were making continued without necessarily influencing the pattern of activities. In sessions led by the music therapist, however, they became a central focus of communication between clients and therapist; each change had an influence on the texture of the musical fabric.

The way physical objects were used was also of key importance, and had varying meaning in terms of the relationship with the therapist and with the medium. In developing a relationship with clients in therapy, objects used in the room may be seen to a greater or lesser extent as the property of the therapist. Art therapists may offer art materials to clients but often do not choose to use the materials themselves. This has implications for the particular ways in which interactions develop. The objects used in dramatherapy may include everyday ones which might be familiar to clients in other settings, giving a particular level of accessibility and sense of shared ownership. There is also a focus on movement and body posture in dramatherapy, which can involve those who reject objects, as happened with Maud. Music therapy may focus on the one hand on physical movements and vocal sounds, and on the other on work with instruments. Whilst instrumental exploration may apparently introduce a divide in the group between those who do and do not play, it is also possible for individuals to relate to one another musically using very differing resources. Musical instruments have a clear, specific purpose, and are likely to be seen in some way as the therapist's property. Then there is the additional choice of making musical use of portions of instruments not traditionally associated with producing sound, and this can have a particular meaning in terms of ownership within the therapy relationship.

CLOSING REMARKS

The assessment group was an important experience for the TAITH arts therapies service. In the planning, a number of areas were highlighted where the team's ways of working were unclear. This stimulated questions about aspects of therapy, and how the assessment group might assist us in developing the service. In moving from general issues to the specific business of running a group, the process became much more focused. The observations which flowed from the work related to the particular individuals, so it was important not to draw rigid conclusions. Relationships in the group were at the heart of the work; it was in concentrating on these that the contributions of the different arts therapies media were seen in a clearer light.

NOTES

1   TAITH is a Welsh word meaning 'journey', related to the verb 'teithio', to travel.
2   The *All-Wales Network Committee for Arts Therapies Professions* was formed in 1989 to promote communication between arts therapists in Wales, and to encourage a wider understanding of their work. The shared use of the arts media has often been included as one component of the meetings between therapists.

Chapter 11

Chances for change
Counselling people with learning difficulties

Lillie Fennell and Enfys Jones

Central theme
- An exploration of the value of counselling for people with learning difficulties, both individually and in groups.

Key points
- Factors which may influence the effective practice of counselling with people with learning difficulties.
- The specific counselling needs of people with learning difficulties, both practical and thematic.
- A guide to some approaches and techniques which may be useful in this field.

INTRODUCTION

The value of counselling has been recognised for many years both in a one-to-one and group situation. This has meant that a bank of knowledge and expertise has been built up in many specialist areas, for example, for survivors of sexual abuse, those suffering bereavement, people who have eating disorders, etc, but only in comparatively recent times has it been recognised that people with learning difficulties have counselling needs.

Even the term 'learning difficulty' can be a problem, as people who carry this label can have marked variations in all areas of ability. Many of the problems which are encountered by people with learning difficulties are made up of the emotional reactions to the disability by others (Rieser 1994:40,41). This is then compounded by the way they are unnecessarily isolated and excluded as a group from full participation in society.

When people are regarded as a group, they can be treated as a race apart and differently to the norm, resulting in them not being appropriately supported (Oswin 1991:26) and any counselling needs that they may have not being met at crucial periods in their lives.

If the counsellor thinks of the term learning difficulty as a continuum, they will find that at one point there is no difference between counselling someone with or without this label. At another point, counselling may have a qualitatively different feel, with the counsellor needing to develop the additional communication skills of sign language and interpretation in order to understand the unique communication of some clients. At yet another point, clients benefit from the use of counselling skills but it is not counselling *per se*.

Counselling skills exist on the continuum between counselling and listening skills. The British Association of Counselling (1989: B1.1–B1.2) makes the point that the distinction is not always a clear one. It means that the client may not identify the professional as a counsellor and may expect this person to work in a more directive than facilitative way.

INDIVIDUAL COUNSELLING

Counselling occurs when the two people concerned explicitly agree to enter into a counselling relationship. The counsellor will then facilitate the client's work in addressing and resolving specific problems, making decisions, coping with crisis, developing personal insight and knowledge, etc. in ways which respect the client's values, personal resources and capacity for self-determination (British Association of Counselling 1996:3.1–3.3).

Establishing a contract for counselling

Right from the beginning, the counsellor needs to be clear in their own mind about the boundaries of confidentiality, for example, with whom will information be shared, under what circumstances, etc. This must then be communicated to the client, just as it would be if the client did not have a learning difficulty.

Counsellors may find it appropriate to explain they will seek help from others if:

• The client may harm themself or someone else.
• If anyone has harmed the client, either recently or in the past. If there was a peripatetic abuser, it may be necessary to know where that person is now and where that person has been in the intervening period.

The role of a supervisor may be explained as the counsellor needing help and support from a more experienced counsellor, whose concern is that the clients are helped to look at their thoughts, wishes and feelings in the best ways possible for them. If the counsellor is independent, clients can be told that they will not share any information with family, support workers or team members. If the counsellor will be sharing information with others, these people should be named and the reasons for doing so explained. The counsellor may wish to add that if information is to be shared, it will only be done when the client is present. If the counsellor feels uncomfortable at the thought of these requirements, exploring the situation with a supervisor may be helpful in providing new insights.

It is worth remembering that many people with learning difficulties may have no notion of privacy because they have been used to carers, family members and so on, interpreting and conveying their speech and communications to others. This may be the first time they will have encountered the concept of confidentiality. It may be necessary to return to this part of the contract several times.

The counselling environment needs to be clarified in the contract. The duration of a counselling session traditionally takes place in a quiet room with comfortable seating for two people. However, this may not answer the counselling needs of all people with learning difficulties. As well as the comfortably furnished counselling room, I find some clients need access to a table where they can draw, model with clay or construct models of the issues which they are communicating, with whatever materials they think necessary. They may require a sink in order to use water as a means of expression. It may only be possible to provide these additional requirements outside the traditional counselling room.

The counsellor needs to clarify exactly where the boundaries of confidentiality apply – only in the comfortably furnished counselling room, or for the entire session regardless of where it takes place? If the boundaries of confidentiality apply for the entire session, how will the counsellor ensure uninterrupted privacy? There are many more facets to the counselling contract than first appears.

Issues relating to counselling

The counsellor will find it useful to have an understanding of the life experience of people who have learning difficulties. They may have been subject to a powerful devaluing process by society, either by those considering them to be lesser beings, or by those providing well-meaning over-protection. Some may have lived their lives on segregated wards in special hospitals, in a regime which suppressed individuality and denied them the opportunity of normal life-styles and relationships (Barron 1989a:17, 1989b:121–4; Blunden 1989:180; Stevens 1990:191). Others may have lived at home but will have experienced segregated education and restricted social lives (Gaukrodger 1990:197–208; Thomas 1990:33). Such segregation inevitably leads to a relative paucity of experiences, restricting the opportunities with which most of us experiment and which bring joy and sadness into our emotional lives.

Segregation in its various forms can lead us to believe that someone with a learning difficulty is different. This perceived differentness can easily blind others to the whole person, for example, seeing a Down's Syndrome man, instead of seeing someone aged twenty-six, with dark hair, who enjoyed swimming and going to pottery classes with his girlfriend, worked part-time at a supermarket, disliked loud music and happened to have Down's Syndrome.

As others become blind to the whole person, the individual – because of the reactions of others – perceives themself as different. This perception may be generalised and can permeate the whole sense of self, creating a persistent feeling of powerlessness, characterised by lack of motivation, depression and interference with learning. Swain (1989:109) reminds us this collective condition is termed 'learned helplessness', and that the text most frequently referred to on this topic is 'Helplessness: On Depression, Development and Death' by Seligman (1975). Counsellors frequently see learned helplessness resulting in low self-esteem and anxious compliance, with accompanying lack of assertiveness and self-advocacy.

It is at this point that a client may be introduced to counselling. Providing the counsellor is practising in an area which enables the client to access the service without help, this may be by self-referral; otherwise it may be by assisted referral. Most of my clients self-refer, due to the fact that I established a counselling service at an evening leisure club for people with learning difficulties, because I was concerned not only about the lack of counselling provision for this client group but also with the lack of facilities for these people to refer themselves to services. I now find that some clients, having used counselling as and when they thought appropriate, are now self-referring to the local advocacy agency and housing association for assistance, as well as joining activities at the local community centre.

Beginning counselling

After explaining the contract in an understandable way, the counsellor who is beginning to work with people who have learning difficulties may initially find themselves using speech and language, whether verbalising, sign language or gesture, in a simpler form than usual. This may not be a bad thing providing they are not afraid to extend their vocabulary and language in accordance with the clients' needs and comprehension. The counsellor would naturally ensure that they use a tone of voice that is appropriate when speaking to any adult. The counsellor may find that clients have no experience of counselling as well as very little experience of the duality of conversation. Clients may expect the counsellor to ask questions which require monosyllabic answers. It may take some time for them to realise not only is it acceptable but, indeed, desirable to initiate and take a full part in conversation. Therefore during the initial sessions, when the relationship is being built, counselling as such may not be taking place. However, this foundation work of sharing information is often vital to the counselling relationship.

It is important to remember that many people with learning difficulties live with high levels of intrusion into all aspects of their lives. They may have little sense of the boundaries of self. I have seen this show itself in various ways. At one point the client does not recognise where the appropriate concern one person can have for another ends and where inappropriate intrusion begins. I have known a client subjected to sexual abuse who needed assistance with intimate personal hygiene. Because the abuser had access to their body to help with these tasks, they thought their abuser was allowed such access whenever it was demanded, to be used in any way the abuser wished. One way clients may have developed to cope with this invasion of boundaries is to withdraw, communicating very little. It clearly requires the use of care and understanding when dealing with this. Again, returning to the contract in order to repeat or clarity confidentiality may be required.

Counselling approaches

When it is time for counselling *per se* to begin, it is often appropriate to consider using a person-centred approach, which again concentrates on building the relationship. Many of my clients experience a rise in self-esteem by being offered the core conditions of empathy, congruence and unconditional positive regard (Rogers 1980:115–17).

The act of being listened to properly conveys the message 'You are worth listening to'. This rise in self-esteem is in itself empowering. However, a cautionary note is necessary regarding one element of unconditional positive regard, namely, warmth. While it is important to offer the client warmth, if overdone I have found it can have a stifling, disempowering effect – the precise opposite of what the counsellor is hoping will be achieved.

Some clients urgently seek change and action, for example they want to have a boyfriend or girlfriend. Here it may be appropriate to consider using a more structured method such as Solution Focused Brief Therapy (de Shazer 1985; Cade and O'Hanlon 1993), or a cognitive approach (Beck *et al* 1987) while still maintaining the relationship with the core conditions (Rogers 1980:115–17). While a counsellor will not be fully acquainted with every theoretical approach, they do need to be aware of a variety of theories in order to address the needs of each individual client.

Alternative communication

In addition to being familiar with a number of theories, the counsellor also needs to be familiar with alternative means of communication. Unless a counsellor can use Makaton (Walker 1977), the sign language used by people with learning difficulties, they may be restricting themselves to counselling a small proportion of this client group, or restricting the channels of communication between themselves and the client.

Counsellors using communication based on speech, body language or facial and eye expression, realise that inarticulacy does not create a bar to forming a relationship with the clients, or to therapeutic movement within that relationship, even though the client may have little expressive or facilitative language. I find these people are often brimming over with feelings which begin to be expressed once trust has developed in the relationship.

While the counsellor is building the therapeutic relationship, they may find that some clients feel uncomfortable with or are unable to make use of a counselling approach that is based initially or primarily on the direct forms of communication such as speech or sign language. They require means of expression that are more practical. In fact, taking the emphasis off the struggle to speak can help reduce any anxieties of the client, which in itself can facilitate spontaneous verbal expression.

If pens and paper are available, some clients are able to draw their thoughts and feelings in ways that become vividly obvious. They may do this pictorially, with the picture showing what the client is conveying. The counsellor and client can look at the picture together and communication will often proceed on a more direct level. The client may choose to draw their thoughts, wishes and feelings symbolically, requiring the counsellor to tentatively feed back what their own impressions are. In this situation, the counsellor is not attempting to use art therapy to assist the counselling process; instead, art materials are used as an adjunct to enable clients to communicate their thoughts and feelings more fully. The use of cards upon which are simply drawn happy, sad and neutral faces, may help clients to begin communicating their feelings. The introduction of clay can be another useful medium to express thoughts, wishes and feelings, sometimes by modelling the actual concerns, at other times modelling family members and carers in various activities. Clay is also a medium that can be pounded, squashed, ripped apart, etc, to help release anger safely. The use of clay may arise quite naturally such as during a pottery class, or it may be introduced intentionally. Pastry may be used in similar ways to clay and the opportunity may arise naturally during cookery or, again, it may be introduced intentionally.

Water provides similar opportunities, with the client possibly naming objects and using them in the water to communicate their thoughts and feelings, or perhaps 'washing the feelings down the drain'. This can also arise naturally, as when washing up, or it can be introduced.

It must be stressed that the use of any tangible means of expression should be provided in an age-appropriate way, otherwise the experience could be infantilising or patronising for clients.

If the counsellor is going to interpret anything from the client's use of expressive materials to aid communication, they need to check tentatively that they are on the right track, in the same way that, by using reflection and paraphrasing, any counsellor checks while empathising with any client. If there is a trusting relationship between them both, the client will be able to correct any inaccuracies held by the counsellor, enabling them both to proceed with the therapeutic work.

Some clients come to counselling with the intention of achieving an urgent goal. For example, in the time following a bereavement, family members may expect that someone with a learning difficulty will not attend the funeral and may subsequently be going into care. The person may, however, want to mourn with the rest of the family. The counsellor may then use one of the more structured approaches such as Solution Focused Brief Therapy (de Shazer 1985; Cade and O'Hanlon 1993). This may need to be offered to the client in an appropriate and accessible manner while still adhering to the general tenets of that theory. For example, in Solution Focused Brief Therapy, it may not be appropriate to ask the client to rate their difficulty on a scale 1–10. Instead, if clients have a simple auditory comprehension of scale, they could be asked to rate the issue on a scale of (a) Bad–Medium–Good; or on slightly more complex scale of (b) Very bad–Bad–Medium–Good–Very good.

I have found it best to begin with a simple scale, then the client will prompt me into using something more complicated, such as saying, 'It's in between bad and medium'. If I begin with a more complex scale, there is a risk that the client will not succeed at using it, adding failure to the original difficulty.

If clients need visual aids as well they could be offered, for example, a long piece of paper upon which a series of squares are drawn with a pictorial representation of the scale. The clients could either point to the appropriate square, or draw their own particular difficulty and place it on the appropriate square. Some clients like to work with a more three-dimensional type of representation – for example, clients may choose to make a model of the difficulty and place it on one of a series of boxes used to represent a scale. In subsequent sessions, the model could be moved into a different box to demonstrate the degree of improvement, or the model could be altered to show how the difficulty has changed. Clients may also alter the model to communicate how they would like the situation to be, then decide what they would like to do in order to achieve this.

Working with any counselling theory just requires a counsellor to be adaptable, creative and flexible in their approach with clients. If the counsellor is working with a mainly person-centred, non-directive approach, clients may find this quite challenging. Clients who have been encourage to suppress their feelings and told what to think and do all their lives are unaccustomed to being given opportunities to explore these hitherto unknown areas and may find this a new experience. This can be refreshingly stimulating, providing them with opportunities to explore and carry out their thoughts, wishes and feelings.

Many of my clients show a marked rise in self-esteem and self-empowerment as a result. It is possible this rapid progress may be due to the client's comparative absence of experience in encountering such things as the problem pages in magazines, help-lines, etc. It means I have been able to offer counselling in an appropriate and accessible form, if I have seen movement taking place quickly.

However, the stimulating effect of the non-directive approach needs to be balanced with the occasional need to share advice and information with the client. If a client is 'floundering' and experiencing distress because of being stuck, to insist on continuing with a non-directive approach can hold its own form of tyranny and seem punitive. In some cases may even seem negligent (Burnard 1995). Balancing the need for a non-directive approach, with the occasional need to share information with the client, will help to deepen the relationship. When this happens, I have found that some clients express themselves more directly and less inhibitedly than those who do not have learning difficulties.

There are people who have not yet acquired the nuances in vocabulary, whether verbalised or signed, which most of us use all the time. This can produce an immediacy of communication unmediated by language, giving a rawness to the feelings that are expressed. Counsellors who have been trained to work primarily with adults without learning difficulties, while sensitive to non-verbal communications, work mainly through the medium of words and may therefore feel de-skilled when first facing this perspective of counselling. Counsellors with experience of working with young children may have encountered this already.

I am fortunate in receiving feedback from carers, staff and others as well as from the clients themselves and, to date, I have found that all clients with learning difficulties who refer themselves to counselling have shown a rise in self-esteem and self-empowerment, as well as ability in defining and obtaining goals, that is visible to others.

Clients who have come for counselling through assisted referrals have shown more varied results. If the assisted referral consisted of a simple explanation of counselling, helping clients to make a telephone call or providing any necessary transport, clients have shown results similar to those who self-refer. If the assisted referrals contained any elements of the clients being told that counselling would be a good thing which they should receive, I have seen only limited success with subsequent relapse. It would appear that the client is reluctant, although seemingly complying with myself and whoever is assisting with the referral at the time.

My experience is similar to that of any community counselling agency, in that if the facility is available, people will want to use it. I can see no reason why counselling should not be available to anyone who requests it, with or without learning difficulties. If the counsellor is adaptable enough to be able to respond to the client, with whatever flexibility and creativity is required, the ambition of many people with learning difficulties to be ordinary people living ordinary lives may be facilitated.

> Counselling people with learning difficulties can be the full flowering of human ordinariness. It can help devalued and marginalised people feel much more human, valued and worthwhile, able to cope with the ordinary sufferings and joys of life.
>
> (Brandon 1989:13)

For many, even though it is likely that earlier they could not conceive ever feeling differently, the dream of having control in their own lives may begin to be realised in the counselling relationship.

Other people may choose to begin this exploration in the group setting.

COUNSELLING IN GROUPS

'Part of the experience of being a person with a learning difficulty is to be constantly invalidated as a full human being. That means not to feel important, that you count.' (Brandon1990:21). 'Statistics show that people with learning

difficulties are more likely to experience emotional distress than other groups'
.... 'Figures range from 8 per cent to 15 per cent when personality disorders and
psychoses are considered, but rise to be over 50 per cent when less serious
emotional disorders are included' (Nadirshaw 1996:104).

Among explanations for this rise, Nadirshaw cites: 'Repeated loss/separations.
Low self-esteem from repeated failures/unattractive appearance/rejection from
family and significant "others". Family difficulties and problems accorded to lack
of adult role and status' (Nadirshaw 1996:104).

Group work offers an alternative path from individual counselling along which
to explore such issues. Learning from each other about what is possible is a
powerful and validating process. There can be enormous value in creating
'opportunities to make links and share experiences and activities with others who
have survived the system' (Brown and Smith 1992:156).

The issue of power and the concept of the counsellor as the expert are
important considerations in any counselling setting, whether individual or group:
'all too many of those who seek the help of counsellors have spent much of their
lives surrounded by people who ... have appointed themselves experts in the
conduct of other people's lives' (Mearns and Thorne 1988:6).

Such an experience of being told 'what is best' is continually present in the
lives of people with learning difficulties. They have rarely been encouraged to
feel that they have any control over what happens to their lives. Nadirshaw (1996)
includes the idea of 'learned helplessness' as one of the factors contributing to the
high instance of emotional problems in women with learning difficulties. Swain
(1989) explains this theory.

> The learned helplessness hypothesis states that if people are frequently
> in situations over which they have no control they can learn 'helplessness', that
> is the expectation and belief that they can do nothing to effect or change
> events.
>
> (Swain 1989:109)

He goes on to describe the impact that the opportunities for choice at
various levels can have on such feelings of powerlessness. He ends by saying,
'Possibilities for overcoming helplessness essentially involve change in social
relationships with a transfer of control to disempowered people.' (Swain 1989:
116).

Providing a space for people to reflect on what they want for themselves and to
offer that support to others can also begin to contradict feelings of helplessness. In
a group setting, the opportunity to learn from each other can be of more value than
looking to the counsellor(s) for that experience. 'The ability to use therapy does
not rest exclusively with the "experts". Each of us has within us the power to
change ourselves and to help each other' (Ernst and Goodison 1981:4).

The social context of the group can complement the emotional and psychological benefits by offering a friendship network that is set within an atmosphere
of validation of self and others. Women, black people, lesbians and gay men may

want to explore themes that relate to this particular aspect of their lives in groups where other members and counsellor(s) share similar experiences. It is not always recognised that people with learning difficulties face issues other than those connected with their disability: 'the majority of services operate in a way that is gender and culture blind' (Nadirshaw 1996:105).

Ignoring the impact of gender, race, sexuality, etc. denies some of the reality of people's lives: '[disabled] women are doubly at a disadvantage because as disabled women they have to live within the confines of two sets of devaluing expectations' (Brown and Smith 1992:162). Describing her experiences as a black woman with learning difficulties, Jackie Downer writes:

> As I was the only black pupil who was also having difficulties with my learning, I felt very isolated. I had a long hard struggle to get where I am now. The struggle goes on daily for black people, especially those with different kinds of learning difficulties.
>
> (Downer 1994:206)

Addressing such issues in a group can empower people to own and value all aspects of their identity.

As a counsellor, I work within a humanistic framework. Humanistic philosophy takes an optimistic view of human nature and believes that people can take responsibility for their own lives. Carl Rogers developed this thinking further into what became known as 'client-centred' or ' person-centred' therapy: 'the person-centred point of view places high value on the experience of the individual human being. . . . It also challenges each person to accept responsibility for his or her own life' (Mearns and Thorne 1988:5). Mearns and Thorne point out that such a philosophy is 'strikingly out of alignment with much that characterises the current culture of the western world' (Mearns and Thorne 1988:5). It is also at odds with much of society's view of people with learning difficulties. Traditional views have ranged from likening people with learning difficulties to innocent children unable to take care of themselves to seeing them as a threat because of a supposedly high sexual drive and an inability to understand and act on more moral concepts (Philpot 1995). In his opinion, whatever the view is, it is likely to be a negative one. Working from a person-centred perspective offers the space to begin exploring a more positive self-image.

Rogers described three main conditions that need to be present in a therapeutic relationship in order that the client can 'begin to flourish as the unique individual he or she actually is' (Mearns and Thorne 1988:14). These conditions are congruence, unconditional positive regard and empathy.

Congruence or genuineness demands that the counsellor is real and open both to him/herself and to the client. In an article describing his work with a group of men who had been sexually abused, Steve Morris observed:

> The group needed to know that I too knew the experience of being without power. I started to talk about my vulnerability and the times I had been

vulnerable in my life. Being all-powerful can be interpreted as being able to make everything all right. In reality we cannot make things right or better.

(Morris 1994:11–13)

Unconditional positive regard is Rogers' term for acceptance of and respect for the client. The experience of being consistently valued as an important human being is in itself challenging to people who see themselves as insignificant or powerless.

The final main condition – empathy – is the ability to explore and understand another person's world and to be able to convey that understanding. Such an experience of feeling understood by another human being can increase a person's sense of self worth and significance (Mearns and Thorne 1988). Working in a group creates the possibility of both giving and receiving empathy.

Beginning a group

People come to the groups mainly through referral from agencies but occasionally people refer themselves. Clearly written and pictorial information about the group made available directly to people with learning difficulties may make it possible to achieve a more open-access groups. Groups need to be small enough for people to feel that there is space for them. Two counsellors working with a small number of clients, maybe six, may offer this. In group situations I usually work with people who can communicate verbally. Using counselling skills with people with more limited spoken language is a challenging and possible process and has been described earlier in the chapter. I believe that group work can be effective in this situation but a small number of clients would be even more essential.

The groups begin by drawing up ground rules. These include agreeing a contract of how we want to relate to each other as group members. Statements such as the following affirm the idea of valuing oneself and others:

'We will listen to each other and not interrupt someone when they are speaking.'
'Everyone has the right to say what they think even though others may not agree with it.'
'Everything we talk about is private.'

Establishing ground rules can also help to create an environment where Rogers' conditions are present.

Working with feelings

many people with learning disabilities have an impoverished emotional vocabulary. . . . This often means that, before much in the way of counselling, active listening or therapy can be done, many people need to learn a vocabulary to describe their feelings.

(Conboy-Hill 1992:157)

Group exercises that focus on 'feeling words' can enable people to extend their emotional vocabulary by learning from each other as well as from the counsellor. For example, we brainstormed names of feelings and recorded them on flipchart paper. Collage exercises – looking through magazines and identifying particular emotions in photographs and pictures – allow time for reflection before discussion. The pictures are then cut out and made into a collage which is used as a focus for the discussion. We look at what the people might be feeling, what might have happened to trigger off this emotion and the possible ways of dealing with it. This can provide a safer structure for group members to discuss feelings from more distant perspective before owning them for themselves. It may be easier, for example, to say 'She feels lonely' rather than 'I feel lonely'. The collage can also stimulate discussion around shades and degrees of feeling, examining the difference between angry and upset, angry and irritated, etc.

Discussing body sensations, facial expressions and body postures that might be linked with emotions give people valuable information about how they and others might be feeling. Exercises round the group such as 'Today I'm feeling . . .' and 'I feel sad when . . . ' encourage people to discuss feelings more personally. Space can be made for group members to work individually on what triggers different feelings in them, using exercises involving drawing or writing.

Active listening skills – an open body posture, minimal prompts, head nods – and the use of open questions can encourage people to continue and expand on what they are saying. Paraphrasing and summarising while checking for understanding can give clarity to both clients and counsellors. Reflection of feelings, picking up on 'feeling' words that clients have used and echoing them back helps to explore the emotion in more depth. If the reflection is accurate, the client is likely to feel understood and safer to continue exploration.

Working with thoughts

'The cognitive approach to counselling takes the view that what we think about ourselves affects the way we feel about ourselves' (Burnard 1989:28). This approach was developed as Cognitive Psychotherapy by Aaron Beck and as Rational Emotional Behaviour Therapy by Albert Ellis in the 1960s. One of the tasks of both client and counsellor is to identify false beliefs and negative thoughts about oneself and the world and adopt more realistic ones. An example of a false belief would be 'I'm never able to cope with things'. A negative thought about a specific situation might be 'I can't cope with this'. Replacing such a thought with something like, 'Things are very difficult at the moment but I am doing the best I can', may reduce feelings of anxiety and depression.

Burnard considers this way of working

> almost diametrically opposed to the style of counselling advocated by Carl Rogers. In the latter the aim is to fully accept whatever the client says as a valid point of view of how that person views the world at that time.
>
> (Burnard 1989:29)

But, as a counsellor, if I feel discomfort at the harshness of a client's view of her/himself and share that, I believe that this is in keeping with Rogers' concept of congruence. In my experience, if a person recognises that the way she/he looks at things is causing distress, it can be empowering to work to change that view in a way that is real to that person.

Work can be done in groups and individually to help people build up a more positive image of themselves and provide a balance to negative thinking. Magazines are useful as a preparation for thinking about skills and abilities. Choosing pictures of activities relevant to their own lives can enable clients make affirmations about themselves – 'I can swim', 'I am good at talking to people'. The counsellor(s) and other clients can remind an individual of qualities and abilities that have been displayed during the session.

Someone I worked with identified the negative thought 'There must be something wrong with me', as an underlying thought when she felt depressed. We made a list of her strengths and skills and she copied them into a book. This was then used as a basis for contradicting her negative thoughts when she felt depressed. Together we drew up sheets.

There must be something wrong with me   I'm OK
                                          I can. . . . .
                                          I can. . . . .
                                          I can. . . . .

This particular client could read but the format could be adopted for use with pictures that could remind people of their strengths.

Another exercise worked on developing people's abilities to verbalise qualities they value in themselves and others. We brainstormed words that we felt were good or validating. We then took it in turns to use these words to describe ourselves and our neighbour in the circle. Having the words available avoids the person being 'put on the spot' and unable to think of a complimentary word for self or others. Care does need to be taken with the words used and this exercise can be very uncomfortable for people, bringing up strong feelings of denial of the validation. However, the contradiction that it can bring negative perceptions of ourselves can be a first step to owning the positive. Space needs to be allowed in the group for people to express their feelings about praising themselves.

Clients who use a lot of negatives in their talk, such as, 'I can't cope with anything', can be encouraged to find exceptions. People can be helped to think of the times present and past when they have coped. Solution focused therapy can be useful here to encourage people to identify and build on their strengths.

Body image

Body image is often a focus for exploration in the groups. Stereotyped ideas of attractiveness present a source on conflict for many of us and this is even more likely to be the case for people with learning difficulties (Brown and Smith 1992). The media also presents images of perfect bodies, healthy and active, which might be difficult for people to identify with.

In the groups time is spent developing awareness and appreciation of our bodies. Some exercises concentrate on physical appearance – describing our hair or eye colour, sharing with others something we like about our bodies. Other exercises focus on what our bodies can do. We brainstormed words like 'kick', 'touch' 'run' and cut out pictures of people using their bodies in different ways. We then developed this into work exploring our senses – what we liked or didn't like to taste, smell, touch, etc. These exercises can trigger painful feelings and care needs to be taken to allow time to work through these and offer clients the opportunity to own both the negatives and positives of themselves.

Chances for change

In her book *Feminist Counselling in Action*, Jocelyn Chaplin describes the concept of a 'rhythm model of life': 'the path of the rhythm could be seen as the path taken by a person who experienced first joy and then sorrow, first strength and then vulnerability at different times of one day or one lifetime' (Chaplin 1988:6).

Each individual person will create their own balance of strength and vulnerability. Part of the work of a counselling group would be to enable people to feel safe enough to express such different shades of themselves. 'Love and acceptance in the group can help you to feel that you have the potential to change' (Ernst and Goodison 1982:8).

CONCLUSION

People with learning difficulties have the same need for good counselling services as the rest of the population. Improving access for them both to agencies and individual counsellors would be a step towards providing them with the counselling support to which they should be entitled.

BIBLIOGRAPHY

Barron, D. (1989a) 'Slings and Arrows' in Brandon, D. (ed.) *Mutual Respect*, Hexagon Publishing.

Barron, D. (1989b) 'Locked Away: Like in an Institution' in Brechin, A. and Walmsley, J. (eds) *Making Connections*, London: Hodder and Stoughton.

Beck, A., Rush, A., Shaw, B. and Emery, G. (1987) *Cognitive Therapy of Depression*, Guildford Press.

Blunden, R. (1989) 'Robert Griffiths' in Brechin, A. and Walmsley, J. (eds) *Making Connections*, London: Hodder and Stoughton.

Brandon, D. (1989) *Mutual Respect*, Hexagon Publishing.

Brandon, D. (1990) *Ordinary Magic. Counselling People with Learning Difficulties*, Tao.

British Association for Counselling (1989) *Code of Ethics and Practice for Counselling Skills*, Rugby.

British Association for Counselling (1996) *Code of Ethics and Practice for Counselling Skills*, Rugby.

Brown, H. and Smith, H. (1992) 'Assertion not Assimilation: A Feminist Perspective on the Normalisation Principle' in Brown, H. and Smith, H. (eds), *Normalisation*, London: Tavistock/Routledge.

Burnard, P. (1989) *Counselling Skills for Health Professionals*, London: Chapman and Hall.

Burnard, P. (1995) 'Implications of Client-Centred Counselling for Nursing Practice', *Nursing Times*, 91:26.

Cade, B. and O'Hanlon, W. (1993) *A Brief Guide to Brief Therapy*, Norton.

Chaplin, J. (1988) *Feminist Counselling in Action*, London: Sage.

Conboy-Hill, S. (1992) 'Grief, Loss and People with Learning Disabilities' in *Psychotherapy and Mental Handicap*, London: Sage.

Downer, J. (1994) 'Black Self Advocacy – My Experience of Being Black and Having a Learning Difficulty' in Martin, R. and Whitehead. C. (eds) *Speaking Out*, London: Health Education Authority.

Dryden, W. (1989) *Rational Emotive Counselling in Action*, London: Sage.

Ernst, S. and Goodison, L. (1981) *In Our Own Hands*, London: The Women's Press.

Gaukrodger, R. (1990) 'Life History' in Atkinson, D. and Williams, F. (eds) *Know Me as I Am*, London: Hodder and Stoughton.

Mearns, D. and Thorne, B. (1988) *Person Centred Counselling in Action*, London: Sage.

Morris, S. (1994) 'Healing for Men' *Llais* 31 (Winter).

Nadirshaw, Z. (1996) 'Learning Disabilities: Mental Health Issues' in Perkins, R., Nadirshaw, Z., Copperman, J. and Andrews, C., *Women in Context*, Good Practices in Mental Health.

Oswin, M. (1991) *Am I Allowed to Cry?*, London: Souvenir Press.

Philpot, T. (1995) 'What the Papers Say: Medial Images of People with Learning Difficulties' in Philpot, T. and Ward, L. (eds) *Values and Visions*, London: Butterworth Heinemann.

Reiser, R. (1994) *The Social Model of Disability, New Learning Together Magazine*, 1.

Rogers, C. (1980) *A Way of Being*, Houghton Mifflin Co.

Seligman, M. (1975) *Helplessness: On Depression, Development and Death*, Freeman.

de Shazer, S. (1985) *Keys to Solution in Brief Therapy*, Norton.

Stevens, P. (1990) 'About Myself' in Atkinson, D. and Williams, F. (eds.) *Know Me as I Am*, London: Hodder and Stoughton.

Swain, J. (1989) 'Learned Helplessness Theory and People with Learning Difficulties: the Psychological Price of Powerlessness', in Brechin, A. and Walmsley, J. (eds) *Making Connections*, Milton Keynes: Open University Press.

Thomas, M. (1990) 'They Said I was Unteachable' in Atkinson, D. and Williams, F., (eds.) *Know Me as I Am*, London: Hodder and Stoughton.

Walker, M. (1977) *Makaton Vocabulary*, Royal Association of the Deaf and Dumb, Action, London.

Part 4

Professional issues

Chapter 12

There is light at the end of the tunnel
Ways to good 'clinical effectiveness research'

Sandie Taylor

Central theme
- To introduce the concept of clinical effectiveness research within an art therapy context.

Key points
- A review of standard research methodology and explanation of common research terminology.
- A consideration of current clinical effectiveness initiatives.
- How the issue of clinical effectiveness is being tackled within a specific arts therapies service for people with learning difficulties.

When I was asked if I would like to contribute a chapter for this book, my initial reaction was one of apprehension. My primary concern was that I am not an art therapist and my academic background contrasts quite sharply with the arts therapies. My qualifications and experience lie mainly in the fields of psychology and criminology. However, I am currently employed as a Research Support Worker within a combined arts therapies team in a service for people with learning difficulties. On reflection, it seems that many of my core research skills have transferred quite smoothly into the arts therapies arena. My key areas of responsibility are that of service evaluation, clinical effectiveness research and obtaining user feedback. Some of my specific tasks are as follows:

1   Administration of questionnaires and undertaking informal interviews with clients and carers to establish both their level of satisfaction with the service and the outcomes of therapy
2   Data collection and analysis
3   Upkeep of databases
4   Production of reports and presentations
5   Exploring new ways of engaging service-users in service planning and evaluation.

The intention of this chapter is to address the importance of research and in particular the investigation of clinical effectiveness, that is, 'Does it work?' But it is more than just this: it must surely be about our quest for furthering our knowledge. Epistemology, the theory of knowledge itself, can be a useful ally for it specifies what can be known about different phenomena and how best to investigate them.

From my vantage point outside of the profession, it seems to me that art therapists have historically been very wary of studies founded on scientific principles. Perhaps there is a feeling that the magic at the heart of the creative process will be lost if subjected to rigorous scrutiny and the spell will be broken. However, if art therapists are well informed about the process of research, then can they not use their skills to weave enchantment into the very fabric of research design?

To be confident about taking such risks and exploring new possibilities, we must first ensure that we are well informed, that we have a full palette of colours at our disposal. Hence, this chapter will review different research methods and explain important concepts commonly used in research. This will tie in with clinical effectiveness initiatives currently in vogue throughout Britain. TAITH, the arts therapies service for people with learning difficulties in Cardiff I currently work for, will be used as a special example of how the Clinical Effectiveness Initiative for Wales is being approached and research operationalised.

INTRODUCTION TO CLINICAL EFFECTIVENESS AND RESEARCH

The term 'clinical effectiveness' has been looked upon in a sceptical way by some art therapists and yet welcomed by others. It is not surprising that some art therapists are sceptical, as the whole issue of clinical effectiveness is not very easily defined and explained. Furthermore, there is some evidence to suggest that art therapists have tended to avoid outcome-based research in favour of 'softer' qualitative descriptions of their work. The historical antecedents of why this is so will be addressed later.

Clinical effectiveness conjures up images of accountability and justification of your area of work, when in fact it is about adopting a methodical way of looking at whether a clinical approach to client care is working and how it can be improved. What better way is there of knowing whether your clinical approach is doing some good than by looking at the effects or the results of your labours in a controlled manner? Research enables us to do this.

The term 'research' refers not only to quantitative, scientific regimes, but in fact also encompasses a wide range of methods and depths of analysis. It could range from a short interview to an experimental set-up in a laboratory. Analyses might involve the use of text transcription, percentages or sophisticated statistical interpretation. Whatever the method and depth of analyses adopted, the important thing to remember at all times is the appropriateness of your strategy used. In other words – does this type of research help me answer my question?

This appears to be a simple thing to remember and yet the number of people who get bogged down with complicated information and reams of statistics is quite high. Art therapists have not only stayed clear from quantitative research methods for fear of the analyses involved but for other reasons which are historically rooted. Although art and music therapy evolved at about the same time, their attitude towards outcomes research is very different. I use music therapy as a comparison with art therapy because the contrast in their research history is markedly opposite. Even their respective associations had a different slant. The British Society for Music Therapy was founded as a charity and it was not until the birth of the Association of Professional music therapists that they took on a trade union role. The British Association of Arts Therapists had a learned society and a trade union role, albeit limited, as soon as it was formed.

This must to some degree have contributed towards the differences in what was considered to be priority research by the two disciplines. In the case of music therapy, outcome research using quantitative methodologies was commonly undertaken. Art therapy, on the other hand, was more concerned with professional issues and how other professionals working in multi-disciplinary teams perceived the discipline.

Art therapists opted for the 'softer' research approaches. They were very much into survey-based studies which questioned issues about art therapy in private practice, standards of practice and conditions of service. Music therapists, on the other hand, aimed to show the efficiency of their practice using outcome measures. In fact, music therapy has an established recent history of process and outcome studies. Observation techniques and videotape analysis have been used to help increase therapists' understanding of client behaviour. Much research with different client groups has been undertaken – for instance, outcome protocols and process-oriented research have been considered for people with learning difficulties (Bunt 1986), autism (Muller and Warwick 1993) and schizophrenia (Pavlicevic 1988). Careful study has also been devoted to what is known as critical moments in music therapy and to analysis of musical and therapeutic components in improvisations.

So why hasn't art therapy lent itself to process and outcome research in the same way? First, using clients' art work as a measuring tool of change has been vehemently opposed by art therapists. This is partly because they find it difficult to compromise their clients' work outside the therapy room. Second, in art therapy, interpretations of meaning are drawn from the client's socio-cultural and symbolic references rather than just the quantity and quality of element representation within the image.[1] This is not the case for music therapy where it is the behaviour embracing the musical act that is evaluated. The music itself is not open to the same concrete evaluation is as a piece of art work.

In this chapter I hope to leave you with a clearer understanding of what the clinical effectiveness initiative entails and ways of going about research. I will address some of the pitfalls to avoid and issues to consider before carrying out your research. First, however, I will address what we mean by 'clinical effectiveness initiatives', referring in particular to that for Wales, and how this influences the nature of research endeavoured.

THE CLINICAL EFFECTIVENESS INITIATIVES

The ideology behind clinical effectiveness initiatives is essentially to ensure that clients are receiving appropriate and effective health care. By effective health care we mean useful and helpful. Therefore different treatments within health care should be useful and helpful in treating problems considered to be within their domain. The problem, however, lies with the fact that not all health care treatments have undergone rigorous research to ascertain their effectiveness. This can have four major repercussions.

- First, there will be very little information documented, so that any in-depth literature review would be very difficult.
- Second, a lack of documentation might create an air of suspicion about what the aims of the treatment in question are and whether any claims of success are substantiated.
- Third, by having no or little documentation, the snowball for generating further research is reduced.
- Fourth, we learn about our mistakes and successes through objective research. When research findings are documented in a recognised journal, it is easier to see how aspects of treatments can be improved. Hence by not having a system of reporting objective research findings, the feedback process, which is so important for developing improved methods of working, will not happen.

Throughout Britain there have been clinical effectiveness initiatives for therapy services as well as other health service provisions – that is, nursing, chemical and physical treatments. Admittedly, the number of evaluation projects for therapy services working with people who have learning difficulties is low. Nevertheless, there are signs of progress on this front. Large-scale evaluation projects have been underway at Wessex locally based hospital units, in Sheffield (Sheffield Development Project) and in Aberdeen (Research Highlights No.2 Normalisation). As TAITH is under the jurisdiction of the Clinical Effectiveness Initiative for Wales, I will use it as an example to illustrate the merits of considering clinical effectiveness research.

One of the questions addressed by the Clinical Effectiveness Initiative for Wales is: 'Is sound evidence available showing what effective care is for a patient with this problem?' Essentially, if the answer is 'no', then it is important to generate evidence showing the effectiveness of the health care available. If the answer is 'yes' then ways of incorporating this information into the system must be found and, further, the effects of putting this information into practice monitored.

Obtaining evidence to show health care effectiveness can be done through research. It is therefore important to know what the aims of the health care in question are and how successfully these have been achieved. We need evidence of their accomplishment, not only in terms of client satisfaction – although the importance of this should not be under-estimated – but in terms of satisfying performance measures.

Establishing performance measures is not always easy to do and if done inappropriately can do more harm than good. Inappropriate performance measures can bias outcomes and give a misleading picture of the situation. For example, if one performance measure for a therapy service is success at getting clients with learning difficulties to communicate their feelings verbally, then presumably the more clients who achieve this the better it will look for the service. But, is this a realistic aim? It may well be for some clients who need to increase their confidence and belief in themselves. On this basis, it is a realistic aim and a performance level that might be satisfied. This situation can change when a person with profound learning difficulties is considered. Communicating verbally might not be dependent on confidence and belief but instead confounded by other factors. At the end of the day, counting the number of people with learning difficulties who have satisfied this performance level may be low. Does this mean that the service is ineffective? Of course it doesn't, but the danger is that figures such as these might be interpreted that way.

Getting back to my point about inappropriate performance measures biasing results and offering misleading scenarios, it is also true that they might lead to a panic situation whereby importance is given to non-prioritised tasks for the sake of getting the numbers to fit the performance measures. By doing this, a glowing report is certain but do we compromise our ethics? So we have to be careful how we establish performance measures and analyse the aims of different health care branches. Having said this, there is no reason why some aims and performance measures cannot be established.

In Briefing Paper 1 *Improving Access to Evidence and Information* issued by the Welsh Office (August 1995), the information needs of the public, patients and carers, health professionals, trusts, commissioning authorities and GP fund-holders is addressed. The paper strongly supports the need for these groups to have access to the type of information they want to know. Any practice should be based on objective evidence of its effectiveness and the client's perspective should be seriously considered. Research should support the cycle of investigating effectiveness and considering client views. This contributes towards the setting of aims, performance measures and their assessment. The Briefing Paper 2 *Helping Practitioners Use the Evidence* (Welsh Office 1996) is more concerned with how changes will occur as the evidence becomes available. There is expressed concern in this Briefing Paper that new research findings are not incorporated quickly enough into practice and that perhaps awareness of clinical effectiveness needs boosting and that health care practitioners need to work together to change practice. Furthermore, there needs to be a change in attitude towards the valuable information that clients can offer. All this ties up with many other factors like understanding research, grasping information technology, and knowing how to monitor and objectively review one's practice and patient-communication skills.

It would appear that these papers are very much in favour of health care workers carrying out their own research – clinical effectiveness research – as long as it is objective. The other important message is the realisation that research is an ongoing process.[2] The outcomes of your research can be fed back into the system and they themselves become the scrutiny of research. After all, any changes added to a practice need to be monitored. In the Briefing Paper 2, this process has been labelled 'The clinical effectiveness cycle'.

WHAT IS RESEARCH?

According to the *Shorter Oxford English Dictionary* (1986) it is

- the act of closely or carefully searching for or after a specified thing or person
- an investigation directed to the discovery of some fact by careful study of a subject
- a course of critical or scientific enquiry

People interpret the meaning of research in different ways, which is why research is undertaken using many different methods and models. This also accounts for why there is good research and research which needs justification for its existence! In the traditional sense of the word, research involves a researcher, an object of study and a method to follow. The researcher is an objective observer, totally detached – emotionally and physically from the object under study – and follows a set pattern of instruction.

This procedure is fine when your object of study is inanimate or even beyond human means of communication as is the case of bacteria, viruses and lower forms of invertebrates not easily visible to the naked eye. This is not always possible when your object of study is people. Nevertheless, various procedures have been introduced to research thus ensuring us of a scientific method of approach. Whether these are totally successful and can be applied easily to clinical effectiveness research, in particular to services offering therapy, is an open debate. I will address this in the section below on 'clinical effectiveness research within an art therapy service for people with learning difficulties'.
There are many ways of conducting research which broadly fall into the following categories:

- documentary – archival, referenced, historical
- experimental – controlled trials/conditions, covariant studies, quasi-experimental design, survey
- descriptive – ethnographic, longitudinal/developmental
- interactive – action research, collaborative enquiry.

You could use the survey method for instance, where you send questionnaires to people in your population sample. This method enables you to find out people's opinions about almost anything. Your questionnaire could comprise a series of questions with a selection of answers provided. Or you could leave people to think up their own answers. The problem with sending questionnaires is that the return rate is low so, instead, you could interview people – ask them questions in the street or have a set time to see them at an agreed location. There are two ways to conduct an interview. You could have a standard set of questions ready to ask with standard answers from which to choose (structured) or you could be flexible and ask questions that follow naturally from the current topic of conversation (unstructured). Both, questionnaire and interview, are part of what is known as the survey method.

Another method often used for research is the experiment. An experiment is a controlled way of observing the effects of one or more events on another. You, as the experimenter, can define what events should be introduced to a situation and which resulting effects to observe, record and document. Events are normally referred to as variables. Some variables are easy to control, such as when tea is served or when 'client A' is in the same room as 'client B'. Other variables, however, are less easy to define, let alone control – for example, individual differences like personality or ability to remember information.

If, for example, you are interested in what helps client A to remember information, you could perform an experiment. You may already suspect a few factors are instrumental, such as having a good supply of magazines to read or getting staff to repeat information more than three times, but this may only be a hunch. By doing an experiment, you may find evidence for your hunch. You could simply define which information is going to be repeated and which information isn't. The level of difficulty and importance would obviously have to be the same, so that any comparisons made will be on an equal footing. If the information which is repeated is remembered and acted upon whereas the non-repeated information isn't, then you could conclude that repetition is a good aid to improving recall. Of course, this is a simplistic design and other things have to be taken into consideration, like making sure the same person gives the information and that the manner of delivery is the same. This is just an example of how an experiment might operate in this case.

The survey method is easier to administer, especially in an institutional setting. It is often favoured in preference to the experiment for its simplicity and for the diversity of information it can generate. Information attained can be general or specific which may then lend itself to qualitative or quantitative analysis.

In the case of qualitative analysis, the findings generated cannot easily be generalised to the population under study, as much of the data collected can only be transcribed or invite mere speculation. So this means that if you conduct an unstructured interview with a person who has a learning difficulty, the topics chosen by the person to discuss and therefore the resulting significance and meaning of the content, will be different from that of someone else with a learning difficulty. In other words, the experiences and the meanings of these experiences to the interviewees concerned will be difficult to quantify in any numerical sense.

Furthermore, the differences between those interviewed may be too vast to draw any consensus findings, thus rendering generalisation to all people with learning difficulties a fruitless task. A similar problem arises from research based on case studies.

On the other hand, quantitative analysis enables you to generalise about your population under study. Hence, if you conduct a structured interview, the information obtained can be graded. The pre-set questions would have pre-set answers that are graded numerically. So if your interviewee gave the answer 'sometimes' instead of 'never', to a question, then the answer is given the pre-set value of '3' instead of '1'.

To complicate matters further, quantitative analysis can vary in its exactness. Taking measurements that are numerical, like someone's height and weight or the number of words remembered, is an interval level of measurement. Unlike 'yes' or 'no' answers or 'sometimes' or 'never' answers, this level of measurement has a true scale. In other words, if you measure the height of five children, you end up with five separate measures which are what they are. There is no other way of interpreting their values except to say that John is taller than Mary by three centimetres or that Jane is taller than Mary by five centimetres and than John by two centimetres. The difference between one centimetre and two centimetres is the same as the difference between four centimetres and five centimetres. The incremental scale is the same. However, the incremental scale between the answers on a questionnaire like 'sometimes' and 'infrequently' or 'infrequently' and 'never' is not equal and has different interpretations. How do you quantify 'sometimes' – does this mean four times out of ten or five times out of ten? And where do you draw the line between what constitutes 'infrequently' and 'sometimes'?

By analysing data quantitatively on the other hand, we are provided with results that do not need an arbitrary measurement of interpretation. The researcher does not need to guess how often something must happen to label it as 'sometimes'. With quantitative analysis the answer is plain to see – the person pressed the letter 't' on the computer keyboard fifty-six times in one minute, or fifteen words were remembered from a list of twenty, or seventeen people crossed at the pelican crossing in one hour.

BASIC RESEARCH CONCEPTS TO GET YOU STARTED

If we accept that the clinical effectiveness initiative is a good one, then we need to consider ways of implementing our research projects. This can only be achieved by having an understanding of the criteria that good research must aspire to – namely that it shows reliability, validity, standardization and generalisability.

Reliability

It is important to know that our findings are not just a fluke and can be replicated using the same research tool (that is, a questionnaire), under the same conditions (that is, send to client's home) to the same people (that is, people with learning difficulties). Finding(s) which can be repeated are said to be reliable. In other words, if we want to know people's opinions towards drug-taking, the questions we ask need to be relevant but, more to the point, the answers we receive should be more or less the same a week, two weeks or even three weeks later. This is known as external reliability.

Of course, it is possible that a previously held opinion towards an issue may have changed by the time you enquire again. Changes of opinion may have occurred due to intervening life events. For instance, the experience of having a close friend who dies suddenly from a drug overdose might be enough to evoke a shift in attitude from a positive to a negative one. Such events are a fact of life so you need to be prepared for such inconsistencies. Nevertheless, in the majority of cases, results will remain fairly consistent. By obtaining people's opinions about the same issues on more than one occasion, using the same questions, we are seeing how reliable our findings are. This strategy is known as the test–retest method.

Another way of testing for reliability is by having more than one independent observer. Let us look at an example where this method can be applied. Imagine a dance competition where there are three competitors, one of whom is trained by the only adjudicator present. Could there not be any bias here? Is there a likely chance that the adjudicator will mark his/her pupil ahead of the others, wittingly or unwittingly? Given this situation, would it be fairer to have more than one adjudicator, preferably neutral ones? Of course it would, for the following reasons:

- any bias shown by the one adjudicator will be outweighed by the others
- marks given are collated and the modal mark is used
- given that all adjudicators are fair-minded, the marks awarded should be similar and show a pattern of consistency.

Although an example unrelated to health professionals, this nevertheless illuminates the problems that can arise. In areas where there is a strong emphasis on behavioural modification for instance, observation of behaviour is very important for the design of future client behavioural schedules. Thus, instead of evaluating behaviour using a questionnaire, feedback from observations is used in the therapeutic process. But how accurate are these observations? Is it possible that observers might have their own interpretations of what the behaviours communicated signify? Or, more of a common problem to observers, is he or she, due to the nature of involvement, subjective rather than objective? One way of getting around this problem is to use a content analysis strategy whereby a previously agreed list of behaviours for consideration is given to more than one observer. The task of the observers is to indicate, by way of a tick, which behaviours were observed within a set time duration. Thus, for example, for every occasion that 'client A' shows aggressive behaviour towards 'client B' on a Thursday morning between the hours of nine and ten, a tick is given.

A good or bad strategy? In an ideal world where there is no under-staffing, annual or sick leave, this would be a good way of testing for reliability. Working in a health organisation, however, may prove this to be too time-consuming and a non-priority of one's work-load. Therefore, the first method of test–retest may operate more efficiently under such conditions.

We can also examine whether our research tool is consistent within itself. In other words, we do not want our questionnaire, for example, to contradict itself in any way. It's a bit like making a statement to the police – you don't want to say one thing only to contradict yourself later in your statement. A research tool that causes you to contradict yourself by way of answers given to set questions is clearly not a well-designed one. It is not always obvious that this the case. Therefore by using a method called split-half, it is possible to see if your research tool shows internal reliability. This is done by dividing the questionnaire into two parts (first and second half or all odd-numbered questions against all even-numbered ones) and then comparing the two halves. The scores for each half should be about the same. In other words, for each half there should be roughly the same number of 'yes' or 'no' responses.

Validity

If you want to know the answer to a question, you resort to reliable sources of information. Similarly, if you want to find out whether music therapy is helping a client to communicate, you ask questions appropriate to your enquiry. You may find that a questionnaire is a good research tool for finding this out. You may instead be interested in observing communicative ability as it happens. Whatever research tool you use, it has to measure what it is intended for.

In the case of a questionnaire there are usually about twenty-four questions. Sometimes the answers are already provided and the respondent selects the most appropriate. In some cases there are no answers provided – just a space for a response. Whatever the format, the common factor separating a good questionnaire from a bad one is the relevance of each question to the area of enquiry. A question about breakfast is not going to help us discover whether art therapy helps to initiate or improve communication skills. The questions therefore must address areas where art therapy is expected to help. For example, we might be interested to know whether clients with learning difficulties have shown any improvement in their ability to communicate and be understood. Questions relevant to this area of enquiry might include,

Can she/he communicate verbally?
Does she/he use non-verbal means of communication, like signing or making certain noises?
How persistent is she/he at making herself/himself understood?

There are many aspects of communication that we could perceivably concentrate on. We must ask ourselves, however, what are the communicative parameters of our population in question. If our clients have very limited verbal ability, we may decide that asking questions about grammatical competence is inappropriate at this stage.

Colleagues can be very helpful for this. They can offer their professional knowledge about the kind of questions that should be asked and, by evaluating the content of your testing tool in this way, they can help ensure that it is representative of the area. This is known as content validity. Another way of checking for validity is to compare the results of your research tool with an existing one (that is known to be reliable and valid) using a correlation analysis. This method is known as concurrent validity. Finally, your research tool could be used to test for predictive validity. In this case, the validity of your tool would be borne out if certain expectations from your results come to light several years later. For instance, if a client scores high on ability to understand then one assumption you may have is that she will get on well in a job that requires listening to other people. The prediction is supported, if she attains such a job.

Standardisation

There are many standard tests and questionnaires available to researchers, such as the CAPE (Clifton Assessment Procedures for the Elderly) which is used to assess dementia in the elderly or the WAIS (Wechsler Adult Intelligence Scale) which measures intelligence. These tests have not only satisfied rigorous reliability and validity criteria, but have also been standardised. In other words, these tests have been calibrated so that a standard scale of measurement is derived.

Standardising a test or questionnaire is done by administering it to a large random sample of people (hundreds), who we hope will be representative of the general population. Due to the process of random selection, people should vary on a number of characteristics like age, sex, social status, intelligence, personality and education. It is not possible however, to have a population sample that represents everyone – for instance, the Germans or Mongolians. In fact, sometimes it is difficult to have a sample that represents the British population. The best we can do is try to be as representative as possible, which is why some researchers focus on people who have characteristics of interest to their research project. For example, it is possible to devise a standardised assessment for people with learning difficulties and so in this case the random sample would have to be drawn from a population of people with learning difficulties.

By standardising a test or questionnaire we hope to obtain a pattern of performance conforming to what is known as a normal distribution. A normal distribution occurs when you have some people performing at the extreme low and high ends of a scale, but the majority performing somewhere in the middle. So, for example, you would expect there to be people who perform very low or very high on a memory test, but most people to be somewhere in the middle. The average might be 50 out of 100. A normal distribution curve is expected for most tests and questionnaires.

When we standardise a test we also obtain a set of norms which can be used as reference scores. These norms are standard and are what we would expect people to perform at. For instance, if most adults get question 10 correct then it can be assumed that the norm is for adults to successfully solve this problem. Any adult who gets the answer incorrect is assumed to be extraordinary. Likewise if most people get this question incorrect, then someone who gets it correct is equally extraordinary. Sets of norms can help us evaluate someone's performance on the test in question. But these evaluations only make sense if the test or questionnaire has been standardised and has proven to be valid and reliable.

You can see the importance of standardising a test that you have devised if you want it to be used throughout the country as a standard test. Not all tests or questionnaires have to be standardised however. If your intention is to use your test, questionnaire or assessment within the hospital on people with learning difficulties for instance, then your making sure it is reliable and valid may be all you need to do. But be careful not to make too many assumptions about how a person with learning difficulties should perform on your test because your test is not standardised! Nor is it wise to generalise your findings beyond what they represent and who they represent. This leads to another important concept called generalisation.

Generalisation

It is unfair and biased to assume that all people, for instance those with learning difficulties, are unable to communicate simply because your sample of people with learning difficulties were unable to communicate verbally. To make such a claim means that you are reading more into your findings than is there. For one thing, you are assuming that communication is only verbal. Furthermore, you are assuming that your test looks at all types of communication. Further still, you may not have taken into the equation the profoundness of learning difficulty in your sample and how this compares with the general level of learning difficulty shown in the population.

In other words, without your knowing it, your random sample may have been derived from people with learning difficulties at the lowest end, in terms of ability, of the normal distribution curve. This can happen if you take a random sample of people with learning difficulties from an institution which accepts only those with profound difficulties.

Problem task – test your knowledge

The research problem is: What situations cause 'client A' to become agitated? Your task is to ascertain why Methods 1 and 2 cause problems and why Methods 3 and 4 offer better solutions.

Method 1   A questionnaire is sent to the ward manager. The questions look at all sorts of areas, including client interests, favourite food and radio programme. The questionnaire drafted by a researcher from the university is the first draft and has not been seen by any other professional. It has not been piloted.

Method 2   The mother of a client is asked to monitor her son's behaviour for one day at the hospital. She is asked to write down what her son does during the day and when he becomes agitated. She is asked to pay particular attention to what sets off his agitated behaviour and the time it occurred.

Method 3   A questionnaire devised by a researcher who has been working in close proximity with health-related workers, has been sent to client A's key worker. The key worker knows this client on a daily basis and has been working with him for many years. The questionnaire has been altered many times to take on board suggestions made by health-related professionals. Questions address the situational, individual and social factors that might precipitate agitated behaviour. The questionnaire has been compared with other assessments that look at mood swings and has been piloted on a sample of twenty clients known to show aggressive behaviour.

Method 4   Two independent observers who do not know client A have been asked to monitor his behaviour every day for one week. They are given seven sheets of paper, one for each day of the week. Each day is divided into 30-minute time slots where they record the behaviour shown by this client. They are provided with a list of previously agreed behavioural verbs such as hit, shouted, shrugged and kicked. The observers, independently of each other, write down the behaviour shown in the correct time slot. They also record who else was involved and what the client did prior to and after the behaviour. Notes are later compared and checked for obvious patterns of behaviour leading to agitation.

CLINICAL EFFECTIVENESS RESEARCH WITHIN AN ART THERAPY SERVICE FOR PEOPLE WITH LEARNING DIFFICULTIES

TAITH, Arts Therapies Services based in Cardiff, commenced a clinical effectiveness project in September 1995. An evaluation questionnaire, adapted from the one devised by Peter Toolan, a music therapist, based at Northgate and Prudhoe NHT was piloted. Comments received from the pilot sample were taken on board and any necessary modifications were made.

As TAITH offers art, music or dramatherapy to people with learning difficulties of varying profundity, the questions asked were directly relevant to their needs. Questions were put into the following categories:

Demographical details   Name, referrer's name and relationship to client, therapy received, significant life events and their nature.

Communication	Thought and feeling communication, nature of communication and its longevity.
Understanding	Of own behaviour.
Self-confidence	Level of, extent that behaviour and mood has interfered with quality of life.
Relationships with others	Toleration of other people and longevity, any supportive or close relationships, reaction to strangers/new situations, behaviour towards the familiar, problems due to behaviour.
Feelings	Temperament, expression of feelings, awareness of disability.
Choice and Decision	Perseverance at making choices, clarity of choice.
Feelings about therapy	Has it helped and how?

There are a total of twenty-six questions. For most questions there is a five-point answer scale: 'never', 'once', 'two or three times', 'at least once a week' and 'every day'. For some questions the responses are 'yes', 'no' or 'don't know'. Other questions relating to client reactions, behaviour and temperament have a list of traits from which to choose.

In order to ascertain whether art, music or dramatherapy is having the desired effect on their client population, it was deemed necessary to receive feedback over a number of months. It was therefore decided that five separate evaluations should be made. The first evaluation was made prior to any therapeutic intervention. This was an important evaluation as it gave a baseline level of performance ability from which future evaluations could be compared. As it is common practice by the TAITH service to give clients and residents an assessment period whereby they try a series of six sessions with a particular therapy to see how they get along, a second evaluation concluding this period was considered necessary. To avoid confusion over terms, I will refer to this as a 'taster' period. A further evaluation was made six months into the on-going therapy stage. A fourth evaluation at therapy termination and a fifth as a six-month follow up.

The reason for having these evaluations was so that we could compare progress over a period of time. It was therefore imperative that we had the cooperation of key workers, carers, case managers, primary nurses and anyone else working closely with our client/resident population. On the whole, evaluation questionnaires were sent to key workers and primary nurses. When these were sent depended on the outset of the taster period and on-going therapy. Hence the dates at which questionnaires were sent varied across clients/residents, but we followed our plan of assessment scheduling.

The information obtained from these assessments was then coded and put into the computer. Using a statistical package for social sciences known as SPSS, we are able to compare our client and resident progress from pre-therapeutic intervention through to taster period and on-going therapy to post-therapeutic intervention. We are still in the process of gathering information for the final assessments. Preliminary statistical findings from the first and second assessments however, reveal a high correlation. In other words, the information given for clients and residents remained similar between these two assessments – pre-therapeutic intervention and conclusion of the taster period.

This finding is very much as expected. Considering the nature of our client/ resident population, positive changes within a six-week period would, although welcomed, be too soon. We would hope to see positive changes between pre-therapeutic intervention and on-going therapy. We would further hope that these changes are permanent or semi-permanent.

In addition to having statistical information, a programme that enables the art therapists to see client and resident progress by means of graphics has been devised. Information from the evaluation questionnaires is put into the programme along with other details. Hence it is possible to obtain a progress chart for any of the questions on the evaluation questionnaire. This is a quick and obvious way of seeing progress or regression.

So far the effectiveness research outlined here has been concerned with performance measures. In other words, how effective has art, music or dramatherapy been in terms of helping clients with particular problems such as communication. In Briefing Paper 1, *Improving Access to Evidence and Information*, it was stated that the client perspective should also be taken into consideration. Because they know what their needs are and to what extent these are being satisfied, their evaluation of the situation is important. Their comments should be taken seriously and incorporated into any system of change or modification.

At TAITH, we welcome this idea and have already begun researching service-user views. I have been involved with obtaining client feedback about an art therapy group. Using a standard question list, I interviewed clients in their home and at specific community locations. The interview was semi-structured in that I followed the question list but asked other questions depending on the information received from clients. Transcriptions from these recorded interviews were made. For further details of transcriptions and their discussion refer to Chapter 3.

Are we on the right track with our clinical effectiveness research?

Current research methods can be improved. For instance, tighter controls can be made to ensure that evaluation questionnaires are completed and sent back as soon as possible so that the dates of assessment tally with our set dates. This can only succeed with the help of other professionals and a clearer understanding on their part of why we are doing this and what we hope to achieve.

Setting this problem aside, there is a more fundamental problem which is harder to control for and this is due to the way the system operates. It is inevitable that professionals working with clients and residents will change from time to time. Consequently, the person who completed the first assessment will not necessarily be the person completing the second and so on. It is common knowledge that different rapports are made between different people – some we get on with and some we don't. Furthermore, we understand and communicate more with some than others. People with learning difficulties are no different. This is why it is important that the same person completes all evaluation questionnaires. If the same person does the assessments, the information is likely to be more coherent. Any changes in behaviour noted by the person completing the evaluation questionnaire are more likely to reflect a real change in behaviour – hopefully resulting from therapeutic intervention. This conclusion would be less clear-cut if more than one person completed all questionnaires.

This is a difficult problem to resolve, if it is at all possible. It is one major drawback for adopting this method. Having said this, it is very difficult to adopt a better way of getting such information. One could argue that there is a case for using therapist evaluations, as they see the client on a one-to-one basis over a long period of time. This however, defeats the object of having a non-subjective study. Also, being objective of your own work and performance is difficult to do.

Doing observational studies of residents in a hospital setting is possible. A researcher could, in theory, spend time on the wards and make notes about the behaviour of the resident in question. This is too time-consuming and can be confounded by the presence of other residents on the ward. You could further ask, 'Is this ethical?' And what about clients who live in the community – how can such an exercise be easily coordinated?

Another way might be to go through the evaluation questionnaire with the key worker or primary nurse. This would help to solve the problem of receiving replies on time, but again would be very time-consuming on everyone's part. It appears that until a better method can be found, the sending of evaluation questionnaires to key workers and primary nurses is the easiest, least expensive and time-consuming strategy. You also have the advantage of the information coming from someone who has worked with the client.

We have far to go when it comes to obtaining service-user views. We have begun interviewing health-related professionals who make referrals to the TAITH service. These interviews are structured but allow for open-ended answers. Questions are divided into four sections: contact (details about TAITH accessibility, referral forms, phone conversations, response time); feedback (information about client progress, key worker involvement, contracts); practice (cancellation information, client evaluation forms); and understanding of what we do (understanding of therapies and resources used, areas in which we best can help, understanding of client suitability or non-suitability for service). There are plans to obtain client feedback about the TAITH service. Our current method of semi-structured interviewing for clients appears to be the most fitting, as there are differences between people – their experiences, profundity of learning difficulty and level of disclosure and elaboration – which will inevitably influence the direction of questioning.

Finally, in answer to the question 'Are we on the right track?' with our clinical effectiveness research – the answer is 'Yes'. We have used a research tool to help us obtain progress information about our clients. Careful examination of what the aims of art, music and dramatherapy are has led to a compilation of sensible performance measures. Our evaluation questionnaire is helping us to see whether we are making any headway with fulfilling these measures.

Furthermore, efforts have been made to record information on computer, in a simple visual form. The building up of information and presenting it in a form which can be shared and learned from was one issue discussed in the Briefing Paper 2 *Helping Practitioners Use the Evidence*.

For some art therapists the idea of research goes against their philosophy about what it is they do. How can we put our work into neat scientific packages when our therapeutic ideology is coming from an arts background? Furthermore, the very nature of our client–therapist centred relationship makes it difficult to quantify what we do. Meekums and Payne summarised these feelings succinctly.

> In traditional research the researcher is divorced from the individual (subject), and the real world of the study environment; the effects of the research on both subjects and researcher are rarely reported. Matching groups of patients/clients are difficult to obtain and this process is even more difficult when those clients present with complex special needs. Equally, not all individuals in a group respond in the same way to arts therapy, and the therapy is not a repeatable experience as is required in this type of research.
>
> (Meekums and Payne 1993:43)

These are valid points and should not be ignored. They should instead be taken on board when evaluating aims and performance measures. It should be remembered that not everything can be reduced to simple equations and coded in numbers. Researchers should also keep in mind what the effects of reducing therapy to outcome measures may have on quality of therapy.

Recently, alternative treatment evaluation strategies that could be successfully adopted by services offering therapy have been introduced. One such strategy is the treatment package where the question asked is, 'Does treatment produce therapeutic change?' The way to find out is by comparing treatment with a no-treatment group or a group who are on a waiting list. Table 12.1 below shows the different research strategies that therapists can adopt.

These strategies outline the different methodologies of approach but, ultimately, there needs to be a research tool for enquiring about the differences between the groups – how do we know the ways in which they differ? Do we need to use an evaluation questionnaire to find out? The following quote from Gilroy and Lee (1995:8), in my mind summarises the importance of clinical effectiveness research: 'Outcome studies are essential if we are to demonstrate that our work is effective, or to explore the appropriateness of one model of work compared to another with a particular client group.'

Table 12.1 Alternative treatment evaluation strategies to develop and identify effective interventions

Treatment strategy	Questions asked	Basic requirements
Treatment package	Does treatment produce therapeutic change?	Treatment vs no-treatment or waiting-list control
Dismantling strategy	What components are necessary, sufficient and facilitative of therapeutic change?	Two or more treatment groups that vary in the components of treatment that are provided
Constructive strategy	What components or other treatments can be added to enhance therapeutic change?	Two or more treatment groups that vary in components that are provided
Parametric strategy	What changes can be made in the specific treatment to increase its effectiveness?	Two or more treatment groups that differ in one or more facets of the treatment
Comparative outcome strategy	Which treatment is the more or most effective for a particular population?	Two or more different treatments for a given problem
Client and therapist variation strategy	Upon what patient, family or therapist characteristic does treatment depend for it to be effective?	Treatment as applied separately to different types of cases, therapists and so on
Process strategy	What processes occur in treatment that affect within-session performance and may contribute to treatment outcome?	Treatment groups in which patient and therapist interactions are evaluated within the sessions

Source: Garfield and Bergen (1994). Reproduced by permission of John Wiley and Sons, Inc.

NOTES

1 It is inevitable that therapists will bring their understanding to the therapeutic situation, this being influenced by their own socio-cultural and symbolic references.
2 This understanding is already inherent within the way art therapy functions – the therapeutic process is dynamic and requires constant monitoring of any change. Change requires understanding and the establishment of new and modified goals. The therapeutic process is constantly challenging the therapist.

BIBLIOGRAPHY

Bunt, L. (1986) 'Research in Great Britain into the Effects of Music Therapy with Particular Reference to the Child with a Handicap' in E. Rudd (ed.) *Music and Health.* J. Chester: London.

Garfield, S.L. and Bergen, A.E. (1994) *Handbook of Psychotherapy and Behaviour Change.* John Wiley and Sons: New York.

Gilroy, A. and Lee, C. (1995) *Art and Music: Therapy and Research.* Routledge: London.

Green, J. and D'Oliveira, M. (1982) *Learning to Use Statistical Tests in Psychology.* Open University Press: Buckingham.

Meekums, B. and Payne, H. (1993) in H. Payne (ed.) *Handbook of Inquiry in the Arts Therapies: One River, Many Currents.* Jessica Kingsley: London.

Muller, P.A. and Warwick, A. (1993) 'The Linking of Two Disciplines in Research: Psychology and Music Therapy' in A. Gilroy and C. Lee (eds) *Art and Music: Therapy and Research.* Routledge: London.

Pavlicevic, M. (1988) 'Describing Critical Moments' in A. Gilroy and C. Lee (eds) *Art and Music: Therapy and Research.* Routledge: London.

Radford, J. and Govier, E. (1980) *A Textbook of Psychology.* Sheldon Press: London.

Shorter Oxford English Dictionary (1986). Oxford University Press.

Toolan, P. (personal communication) 'Assessment Questionnaire'. Northgate and Prudhoe National Health Trust.

Welsh Office (August 1995) Briefing Paper 1, *Improving Access to Evidence and Information.*

Welsh Office (January 1996) Briefing Paper 2, *Helping Practitioners Use the Evidence.*

Chapter 13

Clinical supervision in art therapy
Is it really 'super!'?

Mair Rees

Central theme
- Clinical supervision and its relevance to the practising art therapist.

Key points
- A review of the literature and the various models of supervision which have been proposed.
- Knowledge and assumptions of supervision within art therapy.
- Some recurring themes in the supervision of art therapists who work in the field of learning difficulties.

SETTING THE SCENE

The term 'supervision' is now commonplace, not only in the fields of art therapy, psychotherapy and counselling but throughout many of the helping professions such as nursing and social work. However, there seems to be little evidence to suggest that there is a shared understanding of the term, either between or in some cases within disciplines. Perhaps one source of confusion is the fact that supervision is not a straightforward term, and can refer to a host of approaches and arrangements.

A growing number of professional bodies now either insist (for example, The British Association for Counselling – BAC) or recommend (British Association of Art Therapists – BAAT) that practitioners have access to ongoing supervision throughout their professional life.

Much of the literature (especially that emanating from the United States) dedicates itself to the supervision of practitioners in training. However, the course of this chapter, I intend to refer almost exclusively to what Michael Carroll (1996) calls 'consultative supervision', although I shall generally refer to it as 'clinical supervision', as this is the term most commonly understood in art therapy. In general, this describes a situation where a qualified practitioner will seek ongoing review of their clinical work from another qualified practitioner, usually in the same or similar field. The exact nature of this arrangement and the relationship between supervisor and supervisee may vary enormously.

At various stages, I shall draw from the available pool of literature on supervision in its broad sense, including individual, group, peer and staff team supervision. My net will also be cast across professional boundaries in an attempt to trawl for pearls of wisdom from the oceans of art therapy, psychotherapy, psychology and counselling.

WHY SUPERVISION?

Over the past fourteen years, I have worked as an art therapist in three large hospitals for people with leaning difficulties, one in St Albans, one in Cwmbran and at present in Cardiff. When I assumed each post, none had a history of regular supervision. Consequently, I saw one of my first tasks in each of these establishments as being the need to convince my immediate manager that supervision is a good (if not essential) thing.

Being someone who enjoys the opportunity to lock horns from time to time, I took on each challenge with gusto. My own belief that supervision is a good thing was total. However, I was reasonably pragmatic in my selection of arguments with which to sway each manager, tailoring my evidence according to the particular agenda of the day. In the first hospital (being relatively newly qualified) I argued that supervision was an essential component of my continuing development as a therapist. This message was reinforced by the fact that a local college which trained art therapists was offering a supervisory module to practising art therapists. This gave the impression that supervision was a form of further training (lucky break!).

In the second hospital, I found myself arguing that I could not guarantee the safety of the work undertaken by the department unless independent clinical supervision was available. In my present place of work I waved the quality and recruitment flags, arguing that no therapist worth her salt would apply for a post which did not provide clinical supervision. It seems to me that all along I have been eager to pick up the ball and run with it without first checking whether the game was worth playing.

So what evidence do we have that supervision is fruitful, who benefits from it and is it ever fruitless? Interestingly, in reviewing the literature, it is evident that far more emphasis has been placed on the process rather than the purpose of supervision (horses and carts come to mind, though not necessarily in that order!). Correspondingly, despite advances over the past few years, there appears to be a paucity of research designed to measure the efficacy or otherwise of supervision.

Supervision is one of those areas, like counselling to a lesser degree, which is dogged by a multiplicity of definitions, which has no agreed-upon procedures for qualification and which has had little research to demonstrate its effectiveness for either supervisee or client.

(Carroll 1988:387)

Having said this, there are authors who have attempted to clarify and define the functions of supervision. Bordin (1983) identifies 8 functions of supervision:

1 Mastery of specific skills
2 Enlarging one's understanding of client
3 Enlarging one's awareness of process issues
4 Increasing one's awareness of self and impact on process
5 Overcoming personal and intellectual obstacles towards learning
6 Deepening one's understanding of concept and theory
7 Providing a stimulus to research
8 Maintenance of standard of service.

For some, the primary function of supervision is clear and unequivocal.

> our first concern should be that we do not harm those we seek to help. In addition, it is also essential that if art therapists are to acquire and develop the skills and experience necessary to help rather than harm clients, ways must be found to continually clarify and refine our practice.

(Edwards 1993:215)

Presumably, the purpose and scope of supervision will depend on the expectations and assumptions of both supervisor and supervisee and the extent to which these can be discussed freely and frankly as part of the supervisory process.

From a research project involving semi-structured interviews with BAC-recognised supervisors, Michael Carroll (1996) has identified seven 'tasks' of supervision. (It should be borne in mind that this work relates to the supervision of trainee counsellors, although I feel that much can be extrapolated to the supervision of qualified art therapists.)

1 Creation of a learning relationship

A well-boundaried professional relationship between supervisor and supervisee should be mutually agreed for example, by establishing a contract. The relationship should allow both participants the flexibility to try out different roles. It is particularly important for the supervisee that her changing needs are identified and responded to as she continues to develop as a practitioner.

2 Teaching

Teaching is often viewed as an ingredient of the supervisory relationship. The manner in which this takes place will depend on the level of experience of both supervisor and supervisee. It may also change over time with a movement towards reciprocity as the supervisee gains experience.

3 Counselling

Some exploration of the supervisee's personal issues is often viewed as pertinent within supervision. However, this differs from therapy *per se*, in so far as issues are generally only viewed as relevant within the supervisory arena if they arise directly out of a therapist's work with her clients and clearly have an impact on that work. However, as Carroll points out, the extent to which supervisors are willing to consider supervisees' personal issues may be dictated by the supervisor's guiding theoretical model.

4 Monitoring Professional/Ethical issues

Because the welfare of the client is paramount in supervision, the supervisor will usually see it as her role to challenge bad practice and to be mindful about the possible ethical consequences of actions.

5 Evaluation

This will tend to be more formal when applied to a trainee therapist or counsellor. With experienced practitioners, evaluation may take the form of a review by both supervisor and supervisee of how the relationship is developing and to identify any unmet needs.

6 Consultation

Carroll uses this term to describe what happens during the supervisory process. This usually involves the supervisor and supervisee reflecting together about the therapy. How exactly this happens will depend on the model of supervision employed.

7 Administration

This refers to consideration of issues which do not arise directly from work with clients. These include organisational and contextual issues, processes, records, and liaison.

Despite the as yet limited research in this area, my own personal experience is that supervision can be very useful, both for myself as a therapist and also for my clients. It has allowed me to work with clients I would otherwise have given up on; it has given me permission not to work with certain other clients. My overall perception is that I work more safely and effectively because I have access to supervision. I enjoyed reading Hawkins and Shohet's analogy with the work of Donald Winnicott, where they compare the role of the good-enough mother with that of the good-enough supervisor:

This concept provides a very useful analogy for supervision, where the good enough counsellor, psychotherapist or other helping profession can survive the negative attacks of the client through the strength of being held within and by the supervisory relationship.

(Hawkins and Shohet 1989:3)

There is also a level of agreement that supervision is one of the ways in which professions can guarantee the quality of the service offered.

Yet, supervision is the profession's chosen assurance of quality and ethical practice – the vehicle for counsellors being able to say 'We are accountable to each other for the service we offer to clients . . . it is important therefore that we do it well'.

(Proctor 1994:309)

To date, evidence that supervision is effective is largely personal and anecdotal. There does however seem to be some concurrence, running across schools of thought about what constitutes good and bad supervision. The summary in Table 13.1 is again extracted from the work of Brigid Proctor:

Table 13.1 Good and bad supervisory practices

Good supervisory practice
Clear establishment of a working agreement for a session
Active, respecting and empathic engaging with the supervisee by the supervisor
Holding the agreement
Communicating of support and validation
Offering of effective challenge
Communicating awareness of contextual issues
A framework for understanding the unspoken process and agendas
An ability to share ideas and experiences in a way helpful to the supervisee
An ability to balance the different possibilities within the available time
Being open to feedback as an aid to this process

Bad supervisory practice
Unaware competitiveness and telling
Inability or unwillingness to develop empathic understanding
Failure to help the counsellor explore beyond what he or she already knows
The establishment of a hierarchical interaction
The apparent avoidance of any contention or challenge

Source: Proctor 1994: 311–12

Whilst a supervisor may use some of her skills as a therapist during the course of supervision, a wise supervisor will have no doubts that her supervisee is not her client. In the words of Carroll (1996:59): In fact, the most objectionable stance taken by supervisors (as reported by supervisee) is when the supervisor becomes or tries to become their therapist.

PROCESSES WITHIN SUPERVISION

I feel that it is fair to say that as clients are sometimes ambivalent about entering into and often about remaining in a therapy or counselling relationship, so supervisees can experience the supervisory process as both attractive and repellent. This is hardly surprising when we consider that a practitioner's tools of trade are her own feelings and responses. The majority of therapeutic approaches require the therapist to be capable of empathy with their clients (whether or not this is displayed overtly). For some, it is at the core of the healing process (for example, person-centred counselling). There will always be times when the client's pain resonates with the therapist's current wounds or inflames old battle-scars. Alternatively, the client may unconsciously fill the therapist with feelings which are too awful to bear, called Projective Identification by Klein (1946).

> Therapists can and do defend themselves from such uncomfortable feelings by distancing themselves emotionally from contact with patients or clients or by investing enormous effort in attempting to become the all-knowing, all-seeing ever-effective professional they imagine they could or should be.
>
> (Edwards 1993:215)

Whilst transference phenomena (Freud 1895) may not be an inherent part of the therapeutic process (depending on the favoured theoretical model), there seems to be some general agreement that it is important to explore such occurrences as part of the supervisory relationship. One term which is often employed with regard to some of the unconscious dynamics at play in supervision is that of 'parallel process':

> An interesting additional factor in this area of counter-transference is that the supervisor–supervisee relationship mirrors, as a parallel process, the student (supervisee) – patient relationship. . . . Therefore, what gets played out in the supervisory process may be mirroring what takes place in the actual clinical situation. The supervisor can be helpful in interpreting what s/he feels is going on in the supervisory process. This will, hopefully, help both the supervisor and the supervisee better understand the clinical situation.
>
> (Schneider 1992:77)

I have always felt that counter-transference and parallel process refer to very similar if not identical phenomena. However, Schneider goes on to make a distinction between counter-transference in the supervisory context as the supervisor directly experiencing feelings which are in fact emanating from the supervisee, and parallel process as (usually) the supervisor's emotional awareness of a replication of the therapeutic process within the supervision dyad.

> It is our feeling that *both* counter-transference (the gauging and sensing feelings brought on by the supervisor feeling certain emotions being given off by the supervisee), as well as the reflection process – the supervisor's feeling that what is going on with the patient of the supervisee, can occur in the supervisory process.
>
> (Schneider 1992:77)

Clearly, there are strong currents which run under the surface of supervisory relationships. These can either be harnessed as sources of energy with which to power further development and insight or can gather as forceful eddies dragging the supervisory process into the muddy depths of stagnation. I can think of no more compelling argument for supervisors themselves to be in receipt of regular supervision.

WHO SHOULD SUPERVISE?

To date, very little has been published about the supervision of art therapists, for example Case and Dalley 1992; Edwards 1993.

> What as art therapists we know about supervision has been drawn largely from and influenced by the supervision we ourselves have received, typically and traditionally provided by more experienced colleagues belonging to professions other than art therapy, or by the much more substantial body of literature and research concerned with the supervision of psychoanalysts, psychotherapists, counsellors and members of other helping professions such as social work and nursing.
>
> (Edwards 1993:216)

Despite the vicissitudes of the political climate, art therapy continues to be a developing profession. Whilst not in its infancy, there are still many issues which are unresolved or require further consideration. One of these areas is supervision. In its document 'Principles of Professional Practice', BAAT (1985:1) states: 'It is in the interests of art therapists to seek regular clinical supervision, ideally within the workplace.'

Unlike counsellors, art therapists are not obliged to receive supervision in order to practice. I would imagine that expectations about provision of supervision would be very different between counsellors and art therapists. Art therapy has grown up largely within the health service and tends to align itself with other health service professions. Most art therapists I know who work within the health service believe that it is the employer's responsibility to provide clinical supervision in the workplace. Although comparison figures are not available, it would seem likely that more counsellors work on a freelance or private basis and consequently expect to seek and fund supervision for themselves.

Also, at the time of writing, art therapists are not as yet state registered like their colleagues in occupational therapy and clinical psychology. Until state registration is achieved, it is difficult to make supervision obligatory. As BAAT's statement on supervision amounts only to a recommendation by a professional body which has no legal buttress, it is very difficult for jobbing therapists to convince budget-conscious NHS managers of its necessity. BAAT are in the process of developing a voluntary register of supervisors. Interested parties who are qualified art therapists are asked to complete a questionnaire. This information will be held on a database and made available to registered members. This registration form requires details of experience and training as an art therapist and also an outline of personal supervision but does not ask specifically about training in supervision. Thus the process of becoming an art therapy supervisor is rather nebulous. In fact, the current position of the art therapy profession with regard to theories and models of supervision replicates the place that the counselling profession found themselves at a few years ago:

> The next erroneous assumption was that the theories of counselling could be easily adapted to guide the practice of supervision. This resulted in the proliferation of the counselling-bound models of supervision. It has not been until the last decade that the importance of supervision in the entire training process as a unique activity for which specialised training is required has been acknowledged.
>
> (Holloway 1994:6)

As art therapists, we seem to have been working with the assumption that experienced supervisors will automatically make good supervisors. Associated with this is the assumption that art therapists are best supervised by other art therapists in preference to any other profession. BAAT's recommendation for clinical supervision stated earlier, goes on to purport that the clinical supervision of art therapists should be 'conducted preferably by an art therapist'. I have been unable to find any explanation or reason for this assumption; consequently I feel that a little guesswork is in order.

As I have indicated, art therapy is still a relatively new profession. It is only really since the late 1970s that training has become formalised and standardised. It is not that long since trainee art therapists on practical placements in the field would be very lucky if their work was supervised by a qualified art therapist. Often, other health professionals such as psychologists and occupational therapists would take on that role. This was an important phase in the professional development of art therapists and without such support further growth would not have been possible. However, a point must have been reached where most trainee students were able to find a placement supervisor who was a qualified art therapist. I know from my brief sojourn as a tutor on an art therapy training course that this was the desired state of affairs, and it was only in extreme circumstances that a student would be placed under the guidance of supervisor who was not an art therapist.

This preference clearly served, at least partially, to reinforce the professional identity of art therapy and to make it distinct from other professions. There was also the hope that trainee art therapists would model themselves on their supervisors and learn how to be a 'real' art therapist. I would imagine that belief infiltrated the whole profession and affected the behaviour not only of tutors and students but also of qualified art therapists seeking ongoing supervision for their clinical work. By some osmotic force we had come to believe that art therapists should only really be supervised by other art therapists and that any other arrangement was bound to be second-rate.

But how can we possibly know this to be true? If we have not as a profession looked systematically at the skills required for effective supervision, how can we be sure that experienced, qualified art therapists will inherently possess the skills of a good-enough supervisor? We have not named those skills: they are floating in the ether.

In not naming those skills we leave ourselves open to making unhelpful assumptions about what it means to be a supervisor. In our role as supervisees we may be seduced into believing that, as if by magic, all supervisors have attained a uniform level of skill and wisdom: the supervisor is a super-hero. If I exchange my supervisee hat for that of a supervisor, this statement is enough to strike terror into my heart! Dearnley talks about the both alluring and alarming cloak of omniscience with which it is all too easy for supervisee and supervisor to collude.

> I have come to reflect on the all or nothing conflict many have experienced between being expected (and expecting of themselves) to wear the habit of knowledge and experience when 'on parade' in supervisory sessions, and fearing they have little to offer and will one day be found out.
>
> (Dearnley 1985:53)

As a young rookie art therapist, it was indeed very important to me that my supervisor was a qualified art therapist. I was looking for models for 'The Observer Book of how to Be an Art Therapist'. I was trying out the role, and I needed space to practice my skills without causing any great injury to myself or those around me. In fact, without the aid of a formulated question, I repeated the pattern as I moved from post to post, each time seeking the services of a qualified art therapist as a supervisor.

Most recently I have been supervised in a group of fellow arts therapies professionals. Consequently, the group is a mixed one consisting of art, music and dramatherapists. Having come to a consensus that we had enough common ground to attempt common supervision, we had to think carefully about what we wanted and didn't want from supervision. Without this process we would have been unable to appoint any supervisor. The range of experience in the group varies, although most have been qualified for several years. The group in fact chose to appoint a counsellor as its supervisor. The appointment was made after taking into consideration individual needs balanced with the needs of the group.

In particular, at this stage of the team's development it was felt by all that a prospective supervisor should have sound groupwork skills.

On reflection I now feel that at certain times in my career I could have benefited from the skills of a range of practitioners, depending on my primary need at the time. My needs both in a professional and a personal capacity are like shifting sands and it feels increasingly important that my supervision is in step with this constant movement. I can foresee a time in the future when it might be crucial to have an art therapist as a supervisor once again, but an art therapist with the particular supervisory skill I am seeking at that time.

I return to the assumption that art therapists are most appropriately supervised by other art therapists rather than, say, counsellors, psychotherapists or psychologists. The underlying message is that art therapists are a uniform body of people who have subscribed to a single theoretical position and an agreed style of working. This is blatantly untrue. For some time, as I mentioned earlier, certain practitioners have become associated with different theoretical approaches. Then, could it be some special knowledge about the image-making process *per se* which makes it necessary for art therapists to be supervised by their own kind ? After all, it has become a tradition for the client's art work to form a central role in the supervision of art therapists.

Well, perhaps, but we all, art therapists or not, have powerful reactions to and associations with visual images. In a collaborative style of supervision, where power is shared and not located in the supervisor, it should be possible to share observations and feelings in a meaningful way. Further, there is far from total agreement that it is at all necessary for an art therapist to take her clients' art work along to supervision.

> Some people argue, however, that the internal image the therapist brings with her is the important thing – counter-transference and the therapist's inner feelings about the process are the real guides to the nature of the therapeutic interaction.
>
> (Case and Dalley 1992:170)

It is usually assumed that the supervisor will be independent from the practitioner in a number of ways, as is shown in the following extracts from the BAC Code of Ethics and Practice for Supervisors of Counsellors (1996) (no such guidelines currently exist for art therapists):-

> Supervisors and supervisees should take all reasonable steps to ensure that any personal or social contact between them does not adversely influence the effectiveness of the counselling supervision.
>
> Supervisors must not have a counselling supervision and a personal counselling contract with the same supervisee over the same period of time.
>
> Supervisors must not exploit their supervisees financially, sexually, emotionally or in any other way. It is unethical for supervisors to engage in sexual activity with their supervisee.
>
> (BAC 1996:5)

It is however recognised that a supervisor may have other professional relation-ships with the supervisee concurrently. In these cases, the onus is on the supervisor to uphold the boundaries between the different facets of their professional contact.

> Supervisors are responsible for setting and maintaining the boundaries between the counselling supervision relationship and other professional rela-tionships, for example, training and management.
>
> (BAC 1996:5)

I am aware of many art therapists whose clinical work is supervised by their line manager (be they an art therapist or no). Even so, this arrangement is probably even more common in other professions such as nursing and social work. I have heard cogent arguments for the advantages of combining management and clinical supervisory functions in this way, for example, that it provides more holistic support for the supervisee and allows any necessary changes in practice to be effected smoothly without the need for any further management consultation. Whilst I respect this position, I am unable to feel comfortable with it in terms of my own practice as an art therapist. The potential for a conflict of role between manager and supervisor seems high. 'Managerial responsibility entails keeping an eye on the welfare of the agency, as well as the client, and on the career of the supervisee (Carroll 1996:152).

My fantasy is that other, more mature, skilled and competent individuals can juggle these roles effectively. I, on the other hand, have erred on the side of caution and have avoided offering clinical supervision to therapists I have managed, preferring instead to make a case for independent supervision. Perhaps it is always difficult, but some people work more comfortable and effectively with looser boundaries than others.

However, it usually the case that unless supervisors who are also managers are ever-vigilant of the boundaries between the various facets of their relationship, then the efficacy of supervision may be compromised:

> Transference feelings can be especially prevalent when some kind of managerial or assessment roles are involved in supervision. This can cause both parties much anxiety, and bring up issues of authority for both. On top of these are the very real fears about needing to appear competent in front of someone in whose hands one's future may lie.
>
> (Shohet and Wilmot 1991:91)

These sort of concerns may also be manifest when staff teams are supervised together in a group and levels of trust do not permit individuals to divest them-selves of the good therapist's cloak.

In summary, the skills necessary to become a good-enough art therapy supervisor are largely covert and unnamed. The profession seems – albeit unintentionally – to be promoting the message that the skills of the experienced art therapist are directly transferable into the supervisory role. This I feel has the danger of being a cosy subliminal message which does not encourage therapists to look purposefully at their own models and style of supervision. Neither does it encourage supervisees to think creatively or overtly about their current supervision needs.

A model of supervision which is congruent with the supervisor's belief systems can enable her to work constructively with supervisees whose training and theoretical underpinning may be very different from her own. However, it is also acknowledged that inexperienced therapists may benefit from the affirmation that working with a like-minded supervisor may bring. The same could also be true for inexperienced supervisors. A model of supervision can help the supervisor look critically at her competence, strengths and needs. However, Gaie Houston reminds us that models and methods, like supervisors, have their limitations:

> Most interestingly to me, each method not only has its own restrictions of frame in the way it views behaviour; it seems likely to attract practitioners who tend to pick up or already have in their own personality some of the advantages and disadvantages of the bias of the original theorist. Rather than now telling yourself that the system you have chosen is the bee's knees and the cat's pyjamas, and takes care of all human, even all superhuman and transcendental behaviour and motivation, I counsel you to be humble. You may well be so, and will have puzzled already over what irrational let-offs you have allowed yourself in your particular method.
>
> (Houston 1990:9)

Art therapists may well benefit greatly from supervision provided from beyond the profession itself. What seems to be most important is that supervisors are clear about whether their skills are supervision-specific or theory-specific. A supervisor hell-bent on maintaining the mantle of guru might find it difficult to work with therapists from very different theoretical perspectives as this could undermine their power base and cause unproductive conflict and competitiveness within the supervisory relationship. Perhaps the more insidious implication is that good enough is *not* good enough and only perfect will do.

MODELS OF SUPERVISION

We are left with the question of how might fallible, human supervisors ensure that the supervisory skills they do possess are exercised in a manner which can be of most benefit to each individual supervisee? In order to explore this question, I make an assumption, that is, that all supervisees are different, both in terms of their skills and experience and in their personal qualities and values. So of course are all supervisors.

Consequently, it seems eminently sensible for supervisors to work within a framework or model which allows them both to be genuine and immediate in their responses to the supervisee but also to have a systematic overview of the focus and direction of the supervisory process for each supervisee.

I have already touched on one early model of supervision which was to transfer counselling theories directly into the realms of supervision. In the mid-1960s, new approaches emerged which are usually referred to as developmental models of supervision. There are now many of these models (Page and Woskett 1994 put the figure at twenty-five). The central notion of each of these models is that counsellors pass through sequential stages of competence as their skills and experience mount. Supervisors need to be aware of the particular developmental stage of their supervisee in order to make appropriate interventions. If there is a mis-match between the supervisee's level of competence and the pitch of the supervisor's intervention then it will be less likely that learning and positive change will take place.

In recent years, one of the most widely quoted models is that proposed by Stoltenberg and Delworth (quoted in Page and Woskett 1994). They propose a four-stage model of counsellor development, progressing from anxious and dependent at level 1 through to a fully functioning master practitioner at level 4 (a stage it is said which is not achieved by all).

Most of these models focus chiefly on the development of the supervisee rather than the supervisor. This seems to be explained partially by the fact that the developmental model has firm roots in the American tradition where the supervision is largely a function of counsellor training and is not, as in Britain, a requirement by the professional association for trained counsellors. Michael Carroll warns us that some concepts may not travel well across the Atlantic.

> Some recent research has indicated a difference between counselling climates in America and Britain. We need to be careful that we do not transport theories that work well in another climate to Britain without serious investigation that they will adapt well to the changing environment. Counselling supervision may not be a good traveller.
>
> (Carroll 1988:389)

There have been some attempts to explore the developmental levels of both supervisee and supervisor and how these variables could interact to produce more or less favourable outcomes. Erdman (1994) looks at the interplay between supervisee and supervisor development in accordance with three basic parameters:

1   Self and other awareness
2   Motivation
3   Dependency/Autonomy.

In this model, it is important that the supervisor's expertise should be greater than that of the supervisee on each parameter or further development of competence will not be possible. Again, this model has trainee counsellors mainly in mind.

> It is important for all professionals in the counselling fields to be aware of the developmental process that occurs in supervision. Supervisors need to be

aware that they like supervisees progress through various stages of personal and professional growth. When the supervisor is developmentally equal to or lower than the supervisee, the student cannot achieve the kind of therapeutic competence expected in supervision.

(Erdman 1994:278)

However, both Carroll (1988) and Page and Woskett (1994) point out that there is little research evidence which provides conclusive validation for one-dimensional developmental models.

In general terms these studies find that there is some empirical support for a developmental process, but there is a complex set of factors influencing that process which does not fit neatly into a simple model.

(Page and Woskett 1994:6)

Carroll (1996) also points out that the developmental stage of a counsellor or therapist bears little relationship to the amount of experience, and that personal factors in the processing of learning are important.

One diversion from the developmental path is the process model of supervision which was proposed by Hawkins and Shohet in 1989. Rather than approach supervision from a developmental angle, they concentrate on the various foci which may be adopted in the supervisory context, of which they identify six:

1   Reflections on the content of the session
2   Exploration of the strategies and interventions used by the therapist
3   Exploration of the therapy process and relationship
4   Focus on the therapist's counter-transference
5   Focus on the here and now as a mirror of the there and then process
6   Focus on the supervisor's counter-transference.

The first three foci look directly towards the original therapy session, whilst the next three use the supervision process as a vehicle for raising and exploring issues pertinent to the therapeutic process. Most good-enough supervision would require a balance in use of all these foci over time. However, it is unlikely that any one supervision session would contain all six.

This model allows the supervisor to examine where their own personal biases lie and which foci are perhaps less comfortable for them to function in. A developmental stratum can also be superimposed onto such a process model, as the assumption is made that newly qualified counsellors or therapists will need more input in foci 1–3 than is true of more experienced practitioner. Furthermore, there is some suggestion that premature over-emphasis on transferential and parallelling issues in supervision can confuse and hinder fledgling practitioners: 'Parallel process is more effective educationally with more advanced supervisees: for beginning counsellors it can either be confusing or meaningless and sometimes interpreted as punitive' (Carroll 1996:106–7).

Further, Hawkins and Shohet (1989) point out that there are a number of other factors which indicate which foci may predominate any given supervision scenario. These are:

The theoretical orientation of supervisor/supervisee
The supervisor/supervisee's style
The personalities of the supervisor/supervisee
The degree of openness and trust which has been established in the supervisory
    relationship
The amount of personal exploration the supervisee has done for themselves.

Proctor (quoted in Hawkins and Shohet 1989) has also focused on the processes underlying the supervision of counsellors. She has identified four such threads which need to be skilfully interwoven within the supervision session; these are summarised as:

Formative Relating to the welfare of the client
Restorative The professional development of the supervisee
Normative Ethical, professional and organisational aspects of the work
Creative A space to play and explore previously unconceived possibilities.

Page and Woskett (1994) have introduced what they describe as a cyclical model of supervision (Figure 13.1). Their aim in devising such a model is summarised thus:

> The model presented in this book attempts therefore to address what we perceive as a lack of an overarching framework for the supervision process, as applies to both novice and experienced practitioners, which can encompass process, function aims and methodology.
>
> (Page and Woskett 1994:33)

I view this model as a useful pragmatic tool by which supervisor and supervisee can both contribute towards the evaluation and modification of the supervisory relationship. The *contract* underpins the supervisory process, providing shape and form. The *focus* permits issues to be dealt with realistically and systematically. The *space* is the conceptual space at the heart of the relationship where the supervisee experiences being held in her work. The *bridge* is the method by which insights from the supervision itself are reintroduced as keys to learning about the counselling or therapeutic relationship. *Review* is the method by which both parties assess the direction and development of the supervisory process.

There are therefore a growing range of options available to the supervisor who wishes to acknowledge the extent and limits of their skills and power and use these in a manner which will be of maximum benefit for the supervisee and her clients.

However, with the exception of the work of Brigid Proctor, none of the models has made an overt and named space for the metaphoric and creative possibilities of the supervisory relationship. We know that parallel process is a integral part of supervision. Unconscious wishes and desires do not always manifest themselves

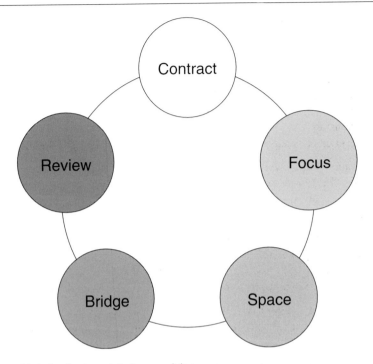

Figure 13.1 Cyclical model of supervision
Source: Page and Woskett 1994: 34

directly through language but often find more appropriate expression through more symbolic channels. This is of particular significance to the supervision of art therapists who may as a matter of course take client art work into the supervisory arena. Next to nothing has been written about the way in which client art work is used in the supervision of art therapists. Correspondingly, from a recent survey (Rees 1996) it seems that only some 32 per cent of art therapists use image-making to explore their own feelings and responses as part of the supervisory process.

At this stage I can only speculate on the reasons for this: perhaps art therapists are concerned about the blurring of boundaries between personal therapy and supervision; perhaps they feel that the physical mess of materials will make it more likely for them to become enmeshed within their clients' symbolic mess. On the other hand, it is possible that art therapy supervisees and supervisors have not always found effective ways of exploring what they need for supervision and, in the absence of this platform, have tended to repeat patterns of supervision which are familiar from their past and often borrowed from more verbal therapies.

It seems sad that the power of image-making processes harnessed so effectively in therapeutic situations are not more regularly exploited as part of the art therapy supervisory scenario. No doubt, art therapists also have skills in this area which could contribute to supervisory relationships in allied professions such as psychotherapy and counselling.

I hold a vision of a magic mirror, which is my image of what has sometimes been missing for me in my own supervision. It is to some extent a conceptualisation of Winnicott's (1979) Transitional Space within a supervisory framework. The mirror is really a triptych, holding reflections from client, supervisor and supervisee. The mirror is always available for either supervisor or supervisee to call into play, perhaps when there is a sense of stuckness, turgidity or confusion in the supervisory process.

In order to receive its nurturing reflections, the participants must be willing to stand in its gaze. To do this, they must trust their own creative processes. Sometimes the mirror will be dark and silent, at other times it will dazzle and delight. On occasion, it will cease to be a mirror, but a doorway into a magical and unexpected place. The scope of the mirror is limited only by the participants' collective imaginations, their trust in one another and belief in the power and wisdom of their own creative processes. 'The gift of supervision is the permission for the trainee to hypothesize, experiment and fantasize creative moves both with the therapeutic plan and the art expression' (Wilson, Riley and Wadeson 1984).

I would like to conclude this chapter by sharing some of the phenomena which I have noticed during the course of my own work with people who have learning difficulties and which have emerged and re-emerged within both individual and group supervision. Much of this could be labelled as counter-transference, although the resonance may have different levels of focus, for example, personal, societal or even global/universal. I have selected a few issues which seem particularly important (although not necessarily exclusive) to art therapists working in the field of learning difficulty. Some of these points may well have a commonality with the work of art therapists working with very different client groups.

UNCONSCIOUS PROCESSES AT A SOCIETAL LEVEL

From the work of individuals like Wolfenberger (1972) we may deduce that the devaluation and negation of people with learning difficulties is endemic and submerged in many societies, including our own.

I must confess that I cannot count the number of times I have under-estimated or dismissed the ability or intelligence of a person with learning difficulties, only to be drawn up sharply by an unexpected shaft of insight or wisdom. Whilst I hope that I fundamentally value and respect people who have learning difficulties, I am an integral part of a broader culture which, in general, does not. At times of stress, fear, threat or bewilderment, it is all too easy to be seduced by the *status quo* which denies the self-determining power of people with learning difficulties.

For me, supervision is a way of being ever vigilant of the values-base we are operating from and it helps us to understand where our intra-psychic maps are terra firma and where we are likely to encounter bogs and quicksand.

DENIAL OF DISABILITY

There have been a number of social and political movements which have at their core a striving for the improvement in status of people with learning difficulties (for example, All Wales Strategy, Social Role Valorisation). In the case of the examples given, both aim to encourage people with learning difficulties to enter fully in society, especially by being seen participating in activities and taking roles which are respected and revered. (How many people with learning difficulties have you seen in the audience of classical concerts or enjoying a meal at a smart restaurant ?)

Whilst I wholeheartedly endorse such drives, to some extent it can be argued that, whilst it is clearly not the intention, the effect has been to pressurise workers into under-estimating or denying the extent of disability.

For art therapists, this may manifest itself as a discomfort in tackling the fundamental issue of disability with clients. I have often experienced a strong urge to protect and deny. It somehow seems too crass or downright prosecutory to tackle the issue of disability head-on. As art therapists we may allow ourselves to be seduced by the aesthetic of the image-making process or else set ourselves up a champion of rights. We may concentrate on what appear to be the client's undamaged parts and feel indignant that their 'normality' has been so overlooked.

My sister-in-law has Down's Syndrome. One day, a small family group of us went out for an meal. The restaurant staff were obviously unused to serving people with learning difficulties and one waiter in particular stared at my sister-in-law throughout the meal. Quite naturally, she became increasingly uncomfortable and eventually blurted out, 'Why is he looking at me all time?' My immediate and overriding reaction was to protect her by saying something like 'There, there, take no notice'. I took a deep breath and somehow found the strength to say 'It's probably because you have a learning difficulty and they are not used to serving people with learning difficulties here, which is a shame.' She nodded sagely saying, 'Yes, it *is* a shame' and continued her meal.

In all my years of knowing her, neither of us had acknowledged that she has a learning difficulty. In that split second in the restaurant I was afraid that my stating the reality of this would be a crushing blow to her. In fact, she seems perfectly aware of her learning difficulty and all along we had both been playing 'Don't mention the war !'

By not naming the beast we render it more powerful. Learning difficulty becomes an unspeakable evil, too awesome or painful to acknowledge. As people who work in the 'caring profession', we may feel guilty about our wholeness or may seek to diminish the very real differences between ourselves and people with learning difficulties. I have often heard the line that no-one is 'normal' and that everyone has a disability or learning difficulty to some extent.

It is painful to acknowledge but at the same time undeniable that my experience of life has been vastly different from that of many people with a learning difficulty, particularly where the disability is severe. I have been free to live, love and make my own decisions and mistakes. I cannot really have anything but the most tenuous grasp of what it feels like to be denied even the meagrest autonomy, to be derided, humiliated, infantilised, ignored, abused and wished dead. Further, to be refused the opportunity to be heard, to rarely experience intimacy or sexual expression and for the love which is received (usually from parents) to be tinged with a sadness and regret that you are not other than what you are.

Having written this last paragraph, even now, my immediate reaction is to tone it down, to make reparation and to say 'Of course, it's not that bad for many people'. In my heart I know that *it is that bad* but the pain of acknowledgement is almost unbearable.

Supervision has an important role in enabling us as art therapists and clients to hold onto our common threads of humanity whilst witnessing and validating the trauma and pain which the label of learning difficulty may bestow. The holding power of supervision can also hopefully allow us to dispense with the defensive need to diminish our clients' experiences, or else to become totally overwhelmed by them.

INDIVIDUAL COUNTER-TRANSFERENCE

There are probably many examples which could be used here, but a couple spring immediately to mind. The first phenomenon I shall refer to has already been alluded to by Hilary Lomas and Penny Hallas (Chapter 3). A common theme I have experienced in supervision is that of disempowerment. After an initial period of working with a client, the art therapist may experience powerful doubts about her competence and a nagging feeling that she is just not good enough. Without appropriate support and supervision, such situations can progress to a point where the therapist may feel totally deskilled and disempowered. Either (or both) therapist and client may experience the work as pointless. In fact, this is often a telling insight into the client's self-perception and the therapist herself becomes disempowered by the same forces of inadequacy and self-doubt. Valerie Sinason (1992) describes how a therapist can be 'made stupid' in the way that the client themselves is made stupid by the disability itself and its labelling effects.

It is vital for these feelings and experiences to be aired in supervision, not only for the efficacy of art therapy, but also so that the individual concerned does not become a 'failed client', a label which is dangerously self-perpetuating. Some time ago, I took up a referral of a young woman with learning difficulties who had already 'failed' at all support which had previously offered to her, including a recent period of counselling. Although she was referred by her health visitor for art therapy, no-one who knew her seemed to hold out much hope that she would be able to benefit, not least herself.

Fortunately, I was receiving sound, supportive supervision at the time, and was able to make it clear that I recognised what was going on and had no intention of colluding with it. The young woman in question was in fact able to make use of the sessions and showed the thoughtful, creative, eloquent and assertive aspects of her personality. This was in conjunction with the damaged and helpless facets in which she had previously become enmeshed and which had also ensnared others. Towards the end of our time together, she produced a clay figure of 'an ugly duckling turning into a swan' which seemed a very appropriate metaphor for her own personal journey.

I have encountered some clients, particularly where they have been exposed to highly abusive relationships, who appear to be in the eye of a storm. The individual in question may be viewed as passive, unassuming or even helpless, but have an uncanny knack of arousing powerful passions in those supporting them. The key emotion is often anger, and workers may feel the urge to become a champion of rights on behalf of that person. Almost certainly, power and its location requires careful consideration in the case of an art therapist who finds herself operating within such a scenario.

Perhaps one of the most powerful and disabling counter-transference phenomena which can arise in working with people who have learning difficulties is what starts as a vague sense of ennui but may develop into an all-consuming boredom within the sessions. Such feelings are often far greater and all-encompassing than the feelings of inadequacy mentioned earlier. This tedium is a thick blanket which is thrown over the therapist preventing her from engaging with the client but also, at a more fundamental level, robbing her of her vitality and life force. On the one hand, we could speculate that this could be a mechanism which disarms the therapist and prevents the progress of useful but potentially painful therapeutic work. However, my hunch is that its source is much deeper and more profound. From my own experience of this phenomenon, I would equate it with a feeling of suffocation or drowning – in short, of dying. I wonder whether what I and other colleagues have experienced are powerful nihilistic forces which express the client's experience either of feeling dead or of wishing themselves dead. This of course could be true for other types of client. However, in people with learning difficulties such emotions may be exacerbated by subliminal messages that they should never have been born and would be better dead. Even the right to exist cannot be assumed when you have a learning difficulty. Art therapists encountering this dynamic will undoubtedly require the support of good-quality supervision in order to create a metaphorical survival space for therapy to live, grow and thrive.

CONCLUSION

As art therapists, it would probably be beneficial for us to be clearer or more explicit about our key supervision needs and the manner in which these may be fulfilled. On the other side of the coin, we already have an array of skills connected with our understanding of non-verbal communication, which could greatly enrich the process of supervision both within and beyond the profession. Art therapists who work with people who have learning difficulties may find that there are common or reoccurring themes which emerge during the course of their supervision. It would be interesting to make a study of such experiences and to compare these with the understandings of art therapists working within other client contexts.

BIBLIOGRAPHY

Bordin, E.S. (1983) 'A Working, Clinical-based Model of Supervision', *The Counselling Psychologist*, 2(1).

British Association of Art Therapists (1985) *Principles of Professional Practice for Art Therapists.*

British Association of Art Therapists (1992) *Suggested Scheme for the Compilation of Lists of BAAT Approved Supervisors.*

British Association of Art Therapists (1997) *Register of Art Therapists.*

British Association for Counselling (BAC) (1996) *Code of Ethics and Practice for Supervisors of Counsellors.*

Carroll, M. (1988) 'Counselling Supervision: The British Context', *Counselling Psychology Quarterly*, 1: 387–96.

Carroll, M. (1996) *Counselling Supervision – Theory, Skills and Practice.* Cassell, London.

Case, C. and Dalley, T. (1992) *A Handbook of Art Therapy.* Routledge, London.

Dearnley, B. (1985) 'A Plain Man's Guide to Supervision – or New Clothes for the Emperor?', *Journal of Social Work Practice*, Nov. 53–65.

Dryden, W. E. and Thorne, B. (1991) *Training and Supervision for Counselling in Action.* Sage Publications, London.

Edwards, D. (1993) 'Learning about Feelings: The Role of Supervision in Art Therapy Training', *The Arts in Psychotherapy*, 20: 213–22.

Erdman, P. (1994), 'Supervisor's Development: How it Effects Supervisees', *Counselling*, Nov. 275–9.

Hawkins, P. and Shohet, R. (1989) *Supervision in the Helping Professions.* Open University Press, Milton Keynes.

Holloway, E. L. (1994) 'A Bridge of Knowing: The Scholar-practitioner of Supervision', *Counselling Psychology Quarterly*, 7 (1): 3–15.

Houston, G. (1990) *Supervision and Counselling.* The Rochester Foundation, London.

Hughes, R. (1988) 'Transitional Phenomena and the Potential Space in Art Therapy with Mentally Handicapped People', *Inscape*, Summer: 4–8.

Klein, M. (1946) 'Notes on Some Schizoid Mechanisms', *International Journal of Psychoanalysis*, 31: 81–4.

Page, S. and Woskett, V. (1994) *Supervising the Counsellor.* Routledge, London.

Proctor, B. (1994) 'Supervision – Competence, Confidence and Accountability', *British Journal of Guidance and Counselling*, 22 (3): 3009–318.

Rees, M. (1996), 'The Supervision of Art Therapists', unpublished MSc Thesis, University of Bristol.

Schneider, S. (1992) 'Transference, Counter-transference, Projective Identification and Role Responsiveness in the Supervising Process', *The Clinical Supervisor*, 10 (2).

Shohet, R. and Wilmot, J. (1991) 'Key Issues in the Supervision of Counsellors: The Supervisory Relationship', in Dryden, W. and Thorne, B. (eds) *Training and Supervision for Counselling in Action.* Sage Publications, London.

Sinason, V. (1992) *Mental Handicap and the Human Condition. New Approaches from the Tavistock.* Free Association, London.

Thomas, D. (1976) *Selected Works.* Book Club Associates, London.

Wilson, L., Riley, S. and Wadeson, H. (1984) *Art Therapy*, October.

Winnicott, D.W. (1979) *Playing and Reality*. Penguin, Harmondsworth.

Wolfensberger, W. (1972) *Normalisation: the Principle of Normalisation in Human Services*. National Institute on Mental Retardation, Toronto.

Index